ROUTLEDGE LIBRARY EDITIONS:
SUDAN

Volume 1



# GORDON

# GORDON

## The Sudan and Slavery

PIERRE CRABITÈS

1877-1943 U.S.

Routledge
Taylor & Francis Group
LONDON AND NEW YORK

First published in 1933 by George Routledge and Sons, Ltd.

This edition first published in 2017
by Routledge
2 Park Square, Milton Park, Abingdon, Oxon OX14 4RN

and by Routledge
711 Third Avenue, New York, NY 10017

*Routledge is an imprint of the Taylor & Francis Group, an informa business*



*British Library Cataloguing in Publication Data*
A catalogue record for this book is available from the British Library

ISBN: 978-1-138-20168-2 (Set)
ISBN: 978-1-315-43940-2 (Set) (ebk)
ISBN: 978-1-138-21648-8 (Volume 1) (hbk)
ISBN: 978-1-138-21655-6 (Volume 1) (pbk)
ISBN: 978-1-315-44220-4 (Volume 1) (ebk)

**Publisher's Note**
The publisher has gone to great lengths to ensure the quality of this reprint but points out that some imperfections in the original copies may be apparent.

**Disclaimer**
The publisher has made every effort to trace copyright holders and would welcome correspondence from those they have been unable to trace.

# GORDON

## THE SUDAN AND SLAVERY


By

PIERRE CRABITÈS


*With an engraved portrait of General Gordon*


LONDON:

GEORGE ROUTLEDGE AND SONS, LTD.,

BROADWAY HOUSE, 68–74 CARTER LANE, E.C.

1933

PRINTED IN GREAT BRITAIN BY
STEPHEN AUSTIN AND SONS, LTD., HERTFORD

TO MY WIFE

WHO HAS PLAYED AN ACTIVE AND IMPORTANT

PART IN THE WRITING OF THIS BOOK

# CONTENTS

# PREFACE AND ACKNOWLEDGMENT

THE critics of Charles George Gordon accuse him of vacillation and of instability of character. While admitting his sincerity, they say that he blew hot one day and cold the next. His partizans refuse to admit that he was inconstant. They take the position that it was the Gladstone Cabinet which manifested a spirit of indecision that was fraught with terrible consequences.

General Gordon was a prolific letter-writer. He also kept a journal which covers the fateful weeks when his life hung in the balance. Many official notes and dispatches deal with his final mission to Khartoum. Lord Cromer has written at some length upon his relations with Gordon during this period.

It has struck me that the best possible way to get at the truth in regard to Gordon's proper place in history is to let these letters, this journal, these notes and despatches, and also the comments of contemporaries high in authority, like Lord Cromer, tell their own story.

I have, it is true, drawn my own deductions from this mass of evidence. I have not waited to sum up until all this proof had been put into my pages. I have, on the contrary, punctuated it, as it were, with my own views. I feel, however, that quotation marks make it easy for my reader to distinguish between the testimony and exhibits which are presented, and the remarks and the arguments which deal with them. I trust that my observations may help to bring out the truth. This is all that really interests me. The case upon which Gordon must be judged depends, nevertheless, not upon what I may have had to say or may desire to establish, but upon the record as composed by himself, by Downing Street, and by Lord Cromer.

I feel deeply indebted to all of those who have permitted me to make up this transcript. First and foremost, my thanks are due to King Fuad of Egypt for having given me unrestrained access to the Royal archives of Abdine Palace, Cairo. His Majesty's kindness to me is but another evidence of that love for historical truth which is so characteristic of him.

I desire also to express my appreciation of the courtesy shown me by Messrs. Blackie and Son, Ltd., Chatto and Windus, Thomas de la Rue and Co., Ltd., Hutchinson and Co., Ltd., and Macmillan and Co., Ltd., in permitting me to quote from published works which are their copyright, as indicated in the footnotes to this book.

PIERRE CRABITÈS.

CAIRO, EGYPT.
*October, 1932.*

# GORDON, THE SUDAN AND SLAVERY

## Chapter I

## INTRODUCTORY

When the nineteenth century dawned the Sudan was closed to Egypt. The Ptolemies had been dead for nearly two thousand years. Their successors had long since lost control of the Black Country. But when, after the wars of Napoleon, Europe readjusted her maps, Africa found in Muhammad Aly a born leader of men. He took in his own hand the sceptre of the Land of the Pharaohs. He lost no time in widening the frontiers which he had taken over from the Mamelukes.

He believed in law and order. He had his own idea of law and his individual conception of order; but they were sufficiently orthodox to fit into their Levantine setting. He had a sharp sword, a ready wit, a stout son, Ibrahim Pasha, and a doughty son-in-law, the Defterdar. These helped him to carry out his policy of expansion and his theories of statecraft. This Muslim trinity created Modern Egypt. Muhammad Aly was its overshadowing genius. He delegated none of his authority. His rule was personal. His children were efficient instruments wielded by a master mind.

He made his power felt while he was still under the tutelage of Turkey. If Europe had not interfered he would in all probability have occupied Constantinople, and possibly have made Stamboul tributary to Cairo. But at that time the maintenance of the integrity of the Ottoman Empire was deemed essential to the welfare of the Occident. The Powers, therefore, decreed that the militant vassal should remain under the suzerainty of the effete Sultan.

Before the astute Albanian meditated defiance of his liege lord he made sure that his own Egyptian bailiwick was in order. The inland commerce of Egypt had, during the earlier years of his overlordship, suffered great interruptions from the confusion and discord to which the lands south of the first cataract were a prey. The chiefs of certain zones in that vast expanse had formed themselves into what has been described as "a singular aristocracy of brigands".[1] They pillaged all the provinces and caravans within their reach, without mercy and without restraint. Civil wars rent asunder the once powerful country of Sennaar. Anarchy prevailed in the Sudan.

Muhammad Aly resolved to put an end to this intolerable condition of affairs. He was no reformer who sought to constrain his neighbours to conform to his tenets. He was a practical statesman, determined to abate a nuisance in a territory which abutted upon his demesnes because he considered that the disorder there prevailing interfered with the commercial expansion of his subjects. Two other motives likewise impelled him to act.

The officers of the Sudan Government responsible for the official publication known as *The Anglo-Egyptian Sudan* say that "gold was doubtless his main object, for he had heard rumours of mines of vast wealth; but we must also give him credit for an honest intention to introduce commerce and civilization into the midst of Negro tribes".[2]

Dr. Sabry, an Egyptian who recently published an

[1] *A Narrative of the Expedition to Dongola and the Sennaar under the Command of His Excellency Ismail Pasha undertaken by Order of His Highness Mehemmed Ali Pasha, Viceroy of Egypt*, by an American in the service of the Viceroy; London, John Murray, 1822, p. ix.

[2] *The Anglo-Egyptian Sudan*, a compendium prepared by Officers of the Sudan Government, edited by Lieut.-Colonel Count Gleichen; London, printed for His Majesty's Stationery Office by Harrison & Sons, 1905, vol. i, p. 231.

authoritative history of the reign of Muhammad Aly, is not quite so complimentary to the founder of the Forty-fifth Egyptian Dynasty. He writes that Muhammad Aly undertook the conquest of the Sudan in order to find " in that vast country of slaves the man-power necessary for the formation of his new armies ".[1] Colonel Elgood, in his *Transit of Egypt*, takes the same point of view as the Egyptian writer. This author sums up the situation most happily by saying that : " Early in the course of his reign he (Muhammad Aly) perceived the necessity of raising a national army. His Albanian militia was costly to recruit, their loyalty to his person doubtful. He went methodically to work. From France he imported a number of officers, from the Mameluke families he enlisted cadets, and from the Sudan he recruited rank and file." [2]

The meaning of all this is that whether the quest for gold and " an honest intention to introduce commerce and civilization into the midst of Negro tribes " played a part in turning Muhammad Aly's eyes towards the Sudan or not, a desire to tap the slave preserves of the Black Country was at least one of the great incentives which led his armies into those parts. He needed recruits for his wars. The population of Egypt at that time numbered less than three million souls.[3] His ambition knew no bounds. Without *kanonenfudder* he was powerless. With blacks to stop enemy bullets the key to success was within his grasp.

It thus came about that the slavery question dominated Egypt's relations with the Sudan from the day when Muhammad Aly sent his sons to chastise the recalcitrant tribes of the southern stretches of the

[1] *L'Empire Egyptien sous Mohammed-Ali et la question d'Orient* (1811–1849). Paris, Librairie Orientaliste Paul Geuthner, p. 68 ; see also pp. 70 and 72.

[2] *The Transit of Egypt*, by Lieut.-Colonel P. G. Elgood ; London, Edward Arnold, 1928, p. 50.

[3] Ibid., p. 51.

Nile. That problem never once ceased to be in the ascendant during the whole time that the Sudan was Egyptian territory. It was the rock upon which Gordon perished. England did not understand the problem with which her heroic son had to deal.

And to accentuate, as it were, the strange fatality which hovered over Egypt's attempt to harness the Sudan to her chariot, Muhammad Aly soon found that the black troops of Central Africa could not endure the Egyptian climate.[1] He therefore deemed it useless to count upon them as the military backbone of the Viceregal armies. If the negroes, as a whole, were unable to resist the mild temperature of the Nile Delta, it was obvious that they could not survive the hardships of the regions towards which the Pasha's ambition called him. He did not, therefore, scour the Black Country in search of slaves for any great length of time. As soon as the earlier supplies had been tested and found inefficient, his agents were no longer urged to impress men of fighting age and drive them to Cairo.

It is quite likely, however, that Muhammad Aly's agents in the Sudan, most probably acting largely on their own account, found that it paid to import into Egypt negro boys, girls, and young women. During the earlier days of the last century both Europe and America looked upon slavery as a more or less beneficent institution. Islam did likewise. There was, therefore, an admirable general market in Egypt for imported black human flesh. But as long as the creator of Modern Egypt was alive, the exportation of slaves from the Sudan was kept within reasonable limits. The practice was perhaps allowed to continue, but it was not encouraged by those in authority in Cairo. On the other hand, they fostered what may be called legitimate trade, more particularly the shipment of ivory.

[1] Ibid., p. 51.

When Muhammad Aly passed away in 1849 his successor, Abbas, inherited neither his brain nor his energy. "My grandfather," he was accustomed to say, "thought himself an autocrat. He was one to his subjects and to his children: but to the consuls of Europe he was no more than a shoe. If I, too, must submit to someone, let me be then the servant of the Khalif, and not of the Christians whom I hate."[1] The grandson, who thus sought to emancipate himself from the traditions of the past decades, found himself not only the puppet of the Sultan, but soft clay in the hands of commercial adventurers. They saw the opportunity of making money by importing not white but black ivory.

During the years when old age weakened Muhammad Aly's hold upon affairs Khartoum had become a central market for a huge slave trade. When Abbas came into power his satellites were not satisfied with handling the slave business that flowed into that metropolis. They organized armed bands which went out to capture slaves. They led *razzias*, as these marauding expeditions against surrounding tribes were called. They introduced system into slave-driving. They took the local government men into partnership with them. They ran things with a high hand, and made slave-raiding pay. They became rich and respected, and their corrupt official friends wealthy and esteemed.

Abbas had but a short reign. His brother, Muhammad Said, succeeded him in 1854. The new Viceroy posed as a constitutional ruler "deferring publicly to the counsel of his advisers, when their opinion did not conflict with his own".[1] He was one of those well-meaning men who sow good intentions and reap disappointments because they are carried away by the glamour of the word "reform". He forbade the slave trade, but had not the energy to

[1] Ibid., p. 55.

translate his decrees into results. Had not death called him in 1863 he might possibly have ceased anathematizing and got down to action. But it is useless to theorize. All that can be recorded is that, when Ismail became Viceroy of Egypt, he found the slave-traders enthroned in Khartoum, the civil service of the Sudan thoroughly corrupt, and the slave aristocrats so powerful in Cairo that their fiat made mock of the law. The new ruler also discovered that Egypt was heavily indebted to Europe, his predecessor having borrowed extravagantly in 1858, 1861, and 1862.[1]

Ibid., p. 56.

## Chapter II

# ISMAIL, KHEDIVE OF EGYPT

Though Ismail had faded from the political scene before Gordon returned to Egypt on his fateful mission, he played so large a part in the Scotsman's life that it may not be amiss to seek to understand what kind of a man he really was. So many fables revolve around his memory that we cannot always separate truth from legend. What is certain is that when he abdicated in 1879 Egypt was insolvent. This bankruptcy, and the disorder born of it, brought England to Egypt. But the fact that the imperious laws of economics required that Ismail should go does not necessarily mean that Gordon gave his friendship to a megalomaniac. To be brief, in order to understand the working of Gordon's mind we should endeavour to visualize the first Khedive in his proper perspective.

Ismail was not an Adonis. When Gordon came into touch with him he had long since lost his waist-line. He had a peculiar roll in his walk, which developed into a waddle. So great was his dignity, however, that after a few seconds the dominant impression made by him was not that of a fat man but one of strikingly gentlemanly bearing. His left eye drooped more than the other, and when he was listening seemed closed, while the right wandered all over his *vis-à-vis* as if looking for weak points. When he began to speak his head was jerked aside, the right eye half closed, while the left gleamed with intelligence. People said that he heard with one eye and spoke with the other. Moberly Bell, for many years the Cairo correspondent of *The Times*, from whom this description has been borrowed, once repeated this to Ismail. "Yes," said the Khedive, "and I think with both." [1]

This ready repartee shows that Ismail had a quick wit, a sense of humour, and enough confidence in himself to permit his visitors to speak their minds to him frankly. He was an excellent judge of human nature. To one man he would be all suavity and mannerism. One would praise him for his polished manners and his tact; another because he was business-like and went straight to the point.

When he was carrying out his plans for the establishment of sugar refineries in Egypt he had to deal with two different groups of negotiators, one French, the other English. With the former the business took days. They were charmed with his complete knowledge of details and the care with which he had examined the minutest particulars of their proposals. With the latter all was arranged in a few hours. The Manchester men went away saying that he was the sharpest business man to be found away from the banks of the Irwell. When this story was told to the Khedive, his speaking eye lit up with a keen smile. "One man rides a horse," he said, "another a donkey, another a camel. Each of these animals has a different stride. The best rider is he who can ride all three equally well." [2]

Another time, when he was talking of dispatching a special mission to Europe, he lamented that he had no one to send to Paris. "Nubar would do for Constantinople, because he can *tell stories*; Cherif for England, for he likes shooting; but neither would do down in France. We want lighter material for Paris wear."

Ismail's most extraordinary gift was his power of fascination. No man was ever known to resist him

[1] *Khedives and Pashas*, Sketches of Contemporary Egyptian Rulers and Statesmen by One who Knows them Well; London, Sampson Low, Marston, Searle, and Rivington, 1884, p. 7.

[2] Ibid., p. 10.

when in his presence. All sorts and conditions of visitors, from Ministers downwards, were repeatedly seen to enter his reception-room bursting with indignation at some real or supposed insult or injury only to come out within a few minutes cooing reconciliation and purring contentment.

Speaking once to Moberly Bell of an amiable but rather weak Consul-General, the Khedive remarked : " I cannot understand that diplomat. He comes here, agrees with all I say, and then goes away and abuses me to his Government. Why should he say one thing to my face and another behind my back ? " " Has Your Highness ever asked him ? " inquired *The Times* correspondent. Ismail laughed. " *Mon Dieu*, twenty times ! But he said that he was wrong in his dispatch, and that he will explain it in the next. Then he makes it worse again. What can I do ? I can't sit over the man while he writes his dispatches." And at this he half closed his eyes, as he did whenever he said anything that pleased him.[1]

Need we say that the reports and accounts which have pilloried Ismail before the bar of history were written away from his presence, and generally by men who either did not know him at all or had but a superficial acquaintance with him ? This is not the moment to analyse the evidence upon which these indictments have been drawn up. Suffice it to say, for the present, that such damning charges have been levelled against a man of winning personality, alert intelligence, and resourceful mind. But such attributes, decorative and endearing though they may be, have nought to do with the tragic fate of Charles George Gordon. The personality of the greatest of the Khedives dovetails into that of the heroic Scotsman because Ismail's first important encounter with European thumb-screws was brought about by his stout opposition to slavery. Napoleon III caught

[1] Ibid., p. 8.

him in his toils because Ismail abolished the Egyptian *corvée* or unpaid labour. The staggering blow given the Khedive at that time played no small part in his eventual ruin.

Those who are acquainted with the history of the building of the Suez Canal will recall that Muhammad Said Pasha permitted his childhood friend, Ferdinand de Lesseps, to dictate the terms of the Viceregal decree under which the latter carried out one of the greatest engineering triumphs of the nineteenth century. The provisions of the grant contemplated that Egypt should furnish a certain sum in cash and *corvée* labour. Translated into practical economics, this meant that it was "nominated in the bond" that slave labour should be furnished by the Viceroy to the Company.

When, in January, 1863, Ismail succeeded the indulgent Muhammad Said, President Lincoln's proclamation had but recently decreed the abolition of slavery in the United States. The ports of the States of the Southern Confederacy were then blockaded. Cotton was worth its weight in gold in the international markets. Egypt had in those days the world's best and perhaps largest available supply of that commodity. The Khedive was in 1863 by far the greatest cotton planter known to history. He thus became fabulously wealthy at the very time when the public conscience of mankind was aroused by the burning words of the American statesman. Rolling in money though he was, Ismail caught the significance of Lincoln's message and ordered the abolition of the *corvée*.

This resolute stand for freedom was met by the century-old cry of vested rights. The Suez Canal Company in time brought diplomatic pressure to bear upon the Khedive to force him to sacrifice his people upon the altar of wax and parchment. He was obdurate. He would not yield. Arbitration was proposed. The French Emperor undertook the task.

He dared not fly in the face of the aroused conscience of mankind and ordain the continuance of slave labour. But he gave a decision which amply safeguarded what were then predominantly French interests. He ruled on 6th July, 1864, that the *corvée* should remain abolished, but that Ismail should pay the Suez Canal Company damages amounting to 84,000,000 French francs, or, in round figures, £3,400,000.[1]

While Ismail was "long" on cotton in those "bullish" days, he did not have the ready cash wherewith to disburse this sum. Doubtless the Imperial arbitrator knew this. He perhaps preferred that the award should not be settled at once. The Viceroy's credit was such that, had he so decided, he could have raised the cash and paid off the amount of the award then and there. At all events, Napoleon III stipulated that the liquidated damages should be wiped out in annual instalments. Ismail did not meet these payments as they matured.

In 1869, when the great waterway was opened, the Khedive was heavily in debt to the Compagnie Universelle. An agreement was entered into between Ismail and the Canal authorities by which the former ceded to the latter any and all dividends that might be earned by his stock for the next twenty-five years. This implied that while his portfolio held 177,642 shares out of the total of 400,000 issued by the Company, his holdings were destined to bring him in no cash for the rest of his life expectancy. This disposed him to get rid of such a non-productive asset. Disraeli was alive to the opportunity thus presented. It was therefore decreed by *Kismet* that England should profit by a condition brought about largely by France, but primarily due to the Khedive's war on the *corvée*.

[1] *Ferdinand de Lesseps, Sa Vie, Son Œuvre*, by Alph. Bertrand et Emile Ferrier; Paris, Charpentier, 1887, p. 257.

The moral courage shown by Ismail in refusing to countenance forced labour in the construction of the Suez waterway is emphasized by his attitude in regard to slavery in the Sudan. It has already been said that, on his accession, he found the slave-traders ensconced in power. They ruled Khartoum with a rod of iron. Their influence in Cairo was so all-pervading that the Viceroy recognized that heroic measures were necessary if these pariahs were to be dominated. He felt that he needed an Englishman's sense of duty, fearlessness, and driving force to cleanse the Augean stable, and at the same time to extend Egypt's frontiers to the Equator. Luckily, the then Prince of Wales, who afterwards won lasting fame as Edward VII, was able to put the Egyptian ruler in touch with the right man. He suggested that this double task be entrusted to Sir Samuel Baker, a well-known traveller and sportsman, the discoverer of one of the sources of the Nile.[1] The Khedive did not hesitate. He engaged the Briton at a salary of £10,000 a year, and conferred upon him plenary authority.

At the time that Sir Samuel Baker returned from his tour of exploration, and therefore before there was any suggestion of his taking over his new billet, Ismail had already made known his dual intention of extending his territories and of suppressing the slave trade. Not only had he issued orders to this joint effect, but he had begun their execution by establishing an Egyptian camp of 1,000 men at Fashoda in the Shilluk country, where Marchand and Kitchener crossed paths some three decades later.[2] It was because the Khedive soon saw that his efforts to act through Egyptian agencies were thwarted by subterranean methods that he welcomed the opportunity

[1] *Gordon and the Sudan*, by Bernard M. Allen; London, Macmillan & Co., 1931, p. 1.

[2] *The War in Egypt and the Sudan*, by Thomas Archer; London, Blackie & Son, 1886, vol. i, p. 121.

of retaining the services of a man whose ability, resourcefulness and character were above reproach. Accordingly a decree was issued in April, 1869, giving the explorer absolute power over all the country south of Gondokoro,[1] so that he might extend the annexations as far as the equator and completely suppress slave-hunting and the slave traffic in this, its very centre.[2]

The detailed story of Baker's achievements, his battles with native tribes in league with the slave-hunters, his explorations, his sporting and hunting adventures by which he provided his followers with the meat of elephants, hippopotamuses, antelopes, crocodiles, and all kinds of birds, beasts, and fishes, have nothing to do with this narrative. Baker enters into the story for one reason alone ; namely that the mandate given him by Ismail brings out that monarch's opposition to slavery, and thus throws light upon Gordon's attitude towards the sovereign who called him to Egypt.

Sir Samuel Baker caught the true significance of Ismail's conduct. He thus summed up the situation, when he was still under the spell of the Khedive's magnetic personality.

"The employment of an European to overthrow the slave-trade, in deference to the opinion of the civilized world, was a direct challenge and attack upon the assumed rights and necessities of his own subjects. The magnificence of the operation could not be understood by the general public in Europe. Every household in Upper Egypt and in the Delta was dependent upon slave service ; the fields in the Sudan were cultivated by slaves ; the women in the harems of both rich and middle class were attended by slaves ;

[1] Gondokoro is on the Nile at 5 degrees N.

[2] *Ismailia, a Narrative of the Expedition to Central Africa for the Suppression of the Slave Trade organized by Ismail, Khedive of Egypt*, by Sir Samuel Baker, *Pacha* ; London, Macmillan & Co., 1874, vol. i, p. 7.

in fact, Egyptian society without slaves would be like a carriage devoid of wheels—it could not proceed." [1]

Two letters written by Sir Samuel Baker, long after he had left the Khedivial service, are even more emphatic. Their dates show that Ismail was then an exile and Gordon hemmed in at Khartoum. The first, dated 19th August, 1884, reads as follows :—

" I am glad that I was not present at the Jubilee, as I should have felt the want of warmth which the speeches exhibited, and I am quite sure that General Gordon will share my views that the ex-Khedive Ismail would be much hurt by the absence of all allusion to his name as the first Oriental Ruler who ever dared to lift a finger towards the forcible suppression of slave-hunting. Unless we make some acknowledgment of the great sacrifice which such a ruler makes in the endeavours to meet our wishes upon such an important question we cannot expect Orientals to exhibit an interest in the work.

" When you consider that our cruisers obtain head-money £2 for every slave captured we can hardly term our action disinterested, and it compares unfavourably with the liberation of the White Nile Slaves, where the Khedive's troops received neither bonus nor regular pay, although they were suppressing slavery in its own nest.

" Neither Gordon nor myself ever received the slightest recognition from the English Government nor were even cold thanks conveyed to the Khedive Ismail. The reward for him was deposition and the great slave-hunting field has been restored to the slave-hunters of the Soudan." [2]

The second letter, written on 20th August, 1884, makes it clear that it was no passing irritation that had dictated the former one. It said :—

" I regret also that in the Report of the various

[1] Archer, op. cit., vol. i, p. 123.
[2] Royal Egyptian Archives, Abdine Palace, Cairo.

endeavours to suppress the slave trade there is no mention whatever of His Highness Ismail Pacha the ex-Khedive. He was the first Oriental ruler who ever struck a decisive blow, and it should be remembered that although I led the first expedition, both General Gordon and myself were the Khedive's officers, and the credit of our work was due entirely to the Khedive.

"I hope you will include this note in the Anti-Slavery Reports in justice to the Khedive, His Highness Ismail." [1]

Baker returned to Cairo in August, 1874. He had, technically speaking, achieved as far as possible the objects for which the expedition had been organized. He had closed the Nile waterway to the slave-traders, and had thus made their calling more expensive and more hazardous. In the last analysis, however, all that he did was to cause the slave-hunters to trek, with their black ivory, across the burning sands of the desert, instead of taking advantage of the less trying river route. Such practically negative results meant nothing to Ismail's sense of the realities of life. The slave menace in 1874 was, to all intents and purposes, as great as in 1869. The Khedive was faced with a condition and not with a theory. He did not lose heart. He determined to find another Englishman to complete the unfinished task.

Now a new difficulty crossed his path. His creditors were up in arms at the money expended in fighting the slave trade. Baker's expedition had been carried out on an extensive scale. It took money, in those days, to penetrate into the unknown recesses of Darkest Africa. Everything had to be organized, immense distances traversed, and means of communication located, established, and maintained at incalculable cost. The bill brokers resolutely opposed an outlay which had no revenue-producing value. Coupons, not humanity,

[1] Royal Egyptian Archives, Abdine Palace, Cairo.

interested them. They issued their veto against the grant of any further large credits to Baker's successor.[1] All this shows us that Europe had made Ismail's task doubly difficult when he transferred to Colonel Gordon of the Royal Engineers the mandate which Sir Samuel Baker surrendered.

[1] Archer, op. cit., vol. i, p. 135.

## Chapter III

# GORDON CALLED TO CENTRAL AFRICA

Ismail and Baker were " Prohibitionists ". They were committed to the task of stamping out the slave trade. It was their policy to strike at the base of supply and to prevent the importation of slaves. Baker appears to have recognized, as early as September, 1872, that the unwillingness of the bondholders to permit the Khedive to spend money on " Prohibition " enforcement was bound to result in the failure of this programme. He therefore let Cairo know, some time about that date, that he did not care to remain in his impossible position after the expiration of his four-year contract.

The Khedive accepted the inevitable with a good grace. He was not discouraged. He determined to attack the evil from another angle. He made up his mind to face realities and to do all that he could within the limits imposed upon him by his importunate creditors. But his primary need was not to work out a feasible plan. His crying necessity was to find a man who possessed Baker's courage, driving power, and personality. He wanted an Englishman, not only because such a choice was a guarantee against the possibility of corruption, but also because the terms of the expiring agreement stipulated that Baker's successor should be a Briton.[1]

The delicate mission of finding this dynamic personality was entrusted to Nubar Pasha, to whom, as Moberly Bell put it, " is due the execution of nearly

[1] *Gordon and the Sudan*, by Bernard M. Allen ; London, Macmillan & Co., Ltd., 1931, p. 1.

every good project that emanated either from the fertile brain of Ismail or from his own."[1] That statesman had gone to Constantinople with his sovereign in order to secure from the Sultan a firman giving Egypt a large measure of financial independence. The Khedive, having obtained his coveted charter, went back to Cairo. His Minister remained on the Bosphorus in order to adjust certain details and to take up with the British Embassy the question of the choice of Baker's successor.

Lieutenant-Colonel Charles George Gordon, R.E., was passing at this time through Constantinople. The contrast between this officer's reputation for romantic bravery and his unmilitary appearance was so great that the Egyptian was taken aback when a short, unprepossessing, timid-looking man was introduced to him as the Commanding-General of "the Ever-Victorious Army". The hesitation, however, was but momentary. There was something in Gordon's winsome, laughing, sympathetic eyes, "which sparkled like blue diamonds," that told Nubar Pasha that he was in the presence of an idealist of dauntless courage to whom impossibility was but an incentive. It took the Christian Minister of a Muslim Sovereign but an instant, therefore, to know that he had found the very man who would be able to work in double harness with Ismail, and whose appointment would be accepted by Europe as a pledge of the sincerity of the Khedive's new anti-slavery campaign.

The holders of Egyptian bonds had tabooed Baker's "Prohibition" enforcement policy. The Khedive, therefore, needed not only a soldier and an administrator, but a leader of Christian thought to carry out his programme of "Regulation" as opposed to "Prohibition". It was this happy combination of an international reputation, a stout sword and evangelistic

[1] *Khedives and Pashas by One who Knows them Well*, p. 149.

zeal that made Gordon the one man in all the world whose connection with slavery "Regulation", in contradiction to "Prohibition", would be a guarantee that Ismail intended to fight slavery with all the means that the money-brokers of Europe and Egyptian public opinion would permit him to employ.

We do not, of course, suggest that Nubar was such a superman that he read all these facts in Gordon's features. The interview at the British Embassy in Constantinople took place in September, 1872. It was not until October, 1873, that Gordon received a telegram offering him the appointment.[1] It is reasonable to assume that during these thirteen months the Egyptian Foreign Office took the trouble to obtain a full report upon the officer whose reputation had called him to Nubar's notice and whose personality had impressed itself upon that reader of men.

Information thus obtainable disclosed that Charles George Gordon was the fourth son of a family of eleven children. He was born at 1 Kemp Terrace, Woolwich Common, on 28th January, 1833. His father was of Highland and military descent, and was himself a Lieutenant-General. His mother came of a family of merchants, distinguished for their sea voyages into remote regions of the globe. As a boy Charlie, as his intimates called him, was remarkable for his high spirits, pluck, and love of mischief. Destined for the artillery, he was sent to the Academy at Woolwich, where some other characteristics made their appearance. On one occasion, when the cadets had been forbidden to leave the dining-room and the senior corporal stood with outstretched arms in the doorway to prevent their exit, young Gordon put his head down and, butting the petty officer in the pit of the stomach, projected him down a flight of stairs and through a glass door at the bottom. For

[1] Allen, op. cit., p. 9.

this act of insubordination the high-spirited youth was nearly dismissed.[1]

But though originally destined for the Royal Artillery, Gordon entered the Royal Engineers. When he obtained his commission he was sent to Pembroke to work at the erection of fortifications. It was there that religion gripped his soul. His sister, Augusta, and " a very religious Captain of the name of Drew ", led him into this path. He began to reflect upon his sins, to look up texts and to pray with the ardour of a neophyte. Though he was not confirmed—he was never confirmed—he received the Sacrament every Sunday. Books of piety were the dominant element in his reading. He became, in a word, a religious zealot.

He was in this frame of mind when the Crimean War called him to Balaclava. He was then twenty-one years of age. During the siege of Sebastopol he conducted himself with conspicuous gallantry. Not long after his return home in 1860 England declared war on China. Captain Gordon was despatched to the scene of operations. The fighting was over before he arrived. He nevertheless remained in China for four years, and there absorbed that knowledge of local conditions and formed those contacts which were destined to lay the foundations of his unusually brilliant career. He drew his sword on behalf of the maintenance of law and order in China. An article which appeared in *The Times* upon his return to England in 1864 thus summarizes his work :—

" Never did soldier of fortune deport himself with a nicer sense of military honour, with more gallantry against the resisting, and with more mercy towards the vanquished, with more disinterested neglect of opportunities of personal advantage, or with more entire devotion to the objects and desires of his own government than this officer, who, after all his victories,

[1] *Eminent Victorians*—" The End of General Gordon," by Lytton Strachey ; London, Chatto & Windus, p. 210.

has just laid down his sword. A history of operations among cities of uncouth names, and in provinces the geography of which is unknown except to special students, would be tedious and uninstructive. The result of Colonel Gordon's operations, however, is this : he found the richest and most fertile districts in China in the hands of the most savage brigands. The silk districts were the scenes of their cruelty and riot, and the great historical cities of Hang Chow and Soochow were rapidly following the fate of Nan King, and were becoming desolate ruins in their possession. Gordon has cut the rebellion in half, has recovered the great cities, has isolated and utterly discouraged the fragments of brigand power, and has left the marauders nothing but a few tracts of a devastated country and their stronghold of Nan King. All this he has effected first by the power of his arms, and afterwards still more rapidly by the terror of his name." [1]

For these services as Commander of "the Ever-Victorious Army" the Chinese Government conferred on Gordon the yellow jacket and the peacock's feather. He thus became a mandarin of high rank. He likewise received the title of Ti Tu, the most distinguished grade in the Chinese Army. English public opinion affectionately nicknamed him "Chinese Gordon". His Queen made him a Lieutenant-Colonel of Royal Engineers and a Companion of the Bath. He was then barely 31 years of age ; and was thus a world-renowned figure when upon the threshold of the thirties.

On his return to England from China he was appointed to a command at Gravesend to superintend the erection of forts on the Thames. During the five years that he held this post his life was dominated by his religious fervour. He specialized in what would now be called "social work". His activity during that period is, perhaps, best described in *Events*

[1] Archer, op. cit., vol. i, p. 136.

*in the Life of Charles George Gordon*, by Henry William Gordon. There we read :—

"It has been fully represented how, during his stay at New Tavern Fort, he devoted his spare time in endeavouring to help and befriend the poor, young and old, how he attended the ragged schools, and how he put boys out in life, and sent lads to sea, and watched for their return ; for when the vessels returned that had his boys on board a boat would be sent off to show how the lads had prospered. Of course, there were disappointments, but if the boy was on board he was brought to Gordon's house, his friends were asked to meet him and an enjoyable evening was spent." [1]

So anxious was Gordon to do his "social work" to his own satisfaction that he was always on duty. His frugal meals were so arranged that no one was ever prevented from seeing him because he was at table. He had his food placed in a deep drawer which was opened and from which he ate. If anyone called it was closed, and the visitor told him his tale of woe without knowing that he had disturbed his benefactor.[2]

Such self-sacrificing altruism would not of itself have made "Chinese" Gordon the well-known champion of militant philanthropy that the Khedive needed as the protagonist of his policy to "regulate" slavery. The Scotsman's proselytizing zeal was, however, so well known that he stood out among his fellows as a lay evangelist clothed in the uniform of a soldier. He was looked upon as being a nineteenth century mystic. And such, indeed, he was, although he kept himself in intimate touch with the world, throwing himself into the midstream of humanity and seeking to make known to others the great truths he had discovered.

During his residence at Gravesend he drew up

[1] *Events in the Life of Charles George Gordon from its Beginning to its End*, by Henry William Gordon ; London, Kegan Paul, Trench & Co., 1886, p. 103.

[2] Ibid., p. 103.

a tract from his own pen. He went about distributing it. " What hundreds," he wrote to his sister in after years, " I did give away : how I used to run miles if I saw a ' scuttler ' watching crows in a field." [1]

His subalterns could not understand such practices. They would turn their telescopes on their commanding officer as he went on his missionary rounds. Their tongues wagged. They called him a fanatic. They thought that he had religion on the brain. They told tales that surrounded his proselytizing zeal with just the kind of gossip which was bound to drift into the Cairo Foreign Office when Nubar was collecting his data before Ismail definitely chose Sir Samuel Baker's successor.

When Gordon received the cablegram offering him the appointment he accepted, subject to the assent of the British War Office. A letter which he wrote to his sister on 9th November, while awaiting an answer from his superiors, shows that the question of slavery was then uppermost in his mind. It is not to be inferred from this that he then had any intimation of the change of policy which had been forced upon Ismail. No information upon this score appears to be available. All that we know is that in unbosoming himself to his beloved Augusta he wrote :—

" God has allowed slavery to go on for so many years ; born in the people, it needs more than an expedition to eradicate it ; open out the country, and it will fall of itself. I am averse to the loss of a single life and will endeavour to prevent any happening, *if I go*. I have a Bank, and on that I can draw ; He is richer than the Khedive, and knows more of the country than anyone ; I will trust Him to help me out of money or any other difficulties." [2]

[1] *Letters of General Gordon to his Sister, M. A. Gordon* ; London, Macmillan and Co., 1888, p. 271.

[2] Ibid., p. 90.

There is far more in this letter than appears upon the surface. It contains the key to a proper understanding of Gordon's somewhat complicated mentality. It shows him as an idealist who reasoned like a realist. It demonstrates that he had hit upon the true idea that slavery is primarily not a moral but an economic issue. He grasped the fundamental fact that slavery was bound to fall by the wayside when Central Africa was made accessible to civilization. He saw that expeditions to eradicate slavery were pin-pricks that irritate, not the surgeon's knife that cures. He was bent upon doing his practical work of evangelization by opening up the land and thus letting economics solve the problem.

The charge of instability of character has so often been made against Gordon that it may be well to quote a second letter which shows how convinced he was that the best way to fight slavery was to open up Darkest Africa. "I believe, if the Sudan was settled," he wrote to his sister a few days later, "the Khedive would prevent the slave trade ; but he does not see his way to do so till he can move about the country. My ideas are to open it out by getting the steamers on to the lakes, by which time I should know the promoters of the slave trade and could ask the Khedive to seize them."[1]

It was in this spirit that Gordon accepted the Khedive's call. Like St. Ignatius of Loyola and St. Teresa of Avila, two of the great constructive idealists of Roman Catholicism, this Protestant Crusader in Her Majesty's livery lifted up his soul to heaven with the ardour of a mystic, and at the same time kept his feet on earth with the practical common sense of a man of affairs. But the world appears to have failed to grasp the far-sighted statesmanship which was transfused into this devotional exuberance.

[1] Ibid., p. 91.

It heard only of Gordon's citations of chapter and verse. It failed to comprehend that he was Adam Smith as well as William Wilberforce. And he himself in his public utterances so emphasized his abhorrence of slavery and its spiritual abomination that it is not surprising that England saw in him only the idealist and forgot that he was also a realist.

## CHAPTER IV

# ANTI-SLAVERY "PROHIBITION" AND "REGULATION"

THE War Office gave its consent to Gordon's acceptance of the post offered him. He arrived in Cairo on 6th February, 1874. Ismail made a favourable impression upon him. "The Khedive is an honest fellow," he observed in a letter to a friend, "and I like him very much, but I will not give it to the others." [1] He threw a bomb into the midst of "the others" by fixing his salary at £2,000 a year, and refusing to accept the £10,000 *per annum* which his predecessor had received.

No sudden impulse prompted this refusal. It was counselled by mature deliberation. Few men are more consistent than Gordon in adhering to a line of conduct he had once traced. The world has refused to see this, and has always insisted that he was continually being swept off of his feet by a passing whim. However, as early as 17th November, 1873, he wrote to his sister :—

"My object is to show the Khedive and his people that gold and silver are not worshipped by all the world. They are very powerful gods, but not as powerful as our God ; so, if I refuse a large sum, you—and I am responsible to you alone—will not be angry at my doing so. From whom does the money come ? From poor miserable creatures who are ground down to produce it. Of course, these ideas are outrageous. 'Pillage the Egyptians' is still the cry." [2]

[1] Letter to the Rev. Horace Waller, 14th February, 1874, quoted in *Gordon and the Sudan*, by Bernard M. Allen, p. 15.

[2] *Letters of General C. G. Gordon to his Sister*, p. 91.

By this deliberate act, born of careful thought and constantly adhered to, he at once established his position in Egypt as an exceptional man to whom the ordinary rules of conduct were not applicable. But the Khedive was one of the few persons who understood Gordon's disinterestedness in its proper light. A reciprocal confidence thus sprang up between them from this very first audience. There was therefore no disposition on the part of the Khedive to lay down hard and fast rules for the new Governor-General of the Egyptian equatorial provinces. The title given him emphasizes the elasticity of his mandate. He was designated as "His Excellency General Colonel Gordon, the Governor-General of the Equator".[1] No attempt was made to define the boundaries of "the Equator", or, more accurately, the Equatorial Provinces of Egypt. Everything was purposely left delightfully vague. Ismail went so far as to tell Gordon that he could give him no detailed instructions, and would be bound to leave much to his agent's discretion, but that he desired that Gordon should correspond with him direct and regard himself as independent of the Governor of Khartoum.[2]

Yet when the two men were together they threshed out matters as thoroughly as possible. They spoke French. Ismail had been educated in France, and used the language of that country with idiomatic ease. The numerous letters and reports in Gordon's own handwriting now filed in the archives of the Abdine Palace, Cairo, show that he had a facile knowledge of French. The Sovereign and his Governor-General thus had no need of an interpreter when conversing with one another, and were able to talk confidentially with no third party present to insulate the one from the other.

But while they trusted one another implicitly, it

[1] *Colonel Gordon in Central Africa, 1874–9, from Original Letters and Documents*, edited by George Birkbeck Hill; London, Thos. de la Rue, 1881, p. 6.

[2] Letter to the Rev. Horace Waller, quoted in Allen, op. cit., p. 13.

was deemed best that before Gordon left for the South a letter should be drawn up by the Khedive incorporating, as far as practicable, the broad outlines of their understanding. We find, therefore, that on 16th February, 1874, the eve of Gordon's departure for Central Africa, the Khedive submitted to him a memorandum in the shape of a letter putting their conception of policy in black and white. It reads as follows :—

"The province which Colonel Gordon has undertaken to organize and to govern is but little known. Up to the last few years it has been in the hands of adventurers who thought of nothing but their own lawless gains, and traded in ivory and slaves. They established factories and governed them with armed men. The neighbouring tribes were forced to traffic with them whether they liked it or not. The Egyptian Government, in the hope of putting an end to this inhuman trade, has taken the factories into its own hands, paying the owners an indemnity. Some of these men, nevertheless, have been still allowed to carry on trade in the district, under a promise that they would not deal in slaves. They have been placed under the control of the Governor of the Sudan. His authority, however, has scarcely been able to make itself felt in these remote countries. The Khedive, therefore, has resolved to form them into a separate government, and to claim the whole of the trade with the outside world as a monopoly of the State. There is no other way of putting an end to the slave trade, which at present is carried on by force of arms in defiance of the law. When once brigandage has become a thing of the past, and a breach has been made in the lawless customs of long ages, then trade may be made free to all.

"If the men who have been in the pay of these adventurers are willing to enter the service of the Government, Colonel Gordon is to make all the use of them he can ; if, on the other hand, they attempt to follow their old way of life, whether openly or secretly, he is to put in force against them the utmost rigour of martial law. Such men as these must find from the new Governor neither indulgence nor mercy. The lesson must be clearly taught that, even in those remote parts, a mere difference of colour does not turn men into chattels and that life and liberty are sacred things.

" One great error into which others have fallen must be avoided. The armament must be so well supplied with provisions that there is no need, as heretofore, to take from the tribes their stores of corn. By proceedings such as this distrust has been sown where the Khedive hoped to establish a feeling of confidence. The lands must be tilled by the troops, and crops raised. If, as seems to be the case, Gondokoro is an ill-chosen position, situated as it is on a thankless soil, the seat of government must be moved to a more favoured spot. Among the natives rescued from the slave-dealers will be found many who have been carried away from countries so far off that it would be impossible to restore them to their homes. They can be employed about the stations in tilling the ground.

" Another object of the new Governor should be to establish a line of posts throughout all his provinces, so that from one end to the other they may be brought into direct communication with Khartoum. These posts should follow, as far as possible, the line of the Nile ; but for a distance of seventy miles the navigation of that river is hindered by rapids. He is to search out the best way of overcoming this hindrance, and to make a report thereon to the Khedive.

" In dealing with the chieftains of the tribes which dwell on the shores of the lakes, the Governor is above all to try to win their confidence. He must respect their territory, and conciliate them by presents. Whatever influence he gains over them he must use in an endeavour to persuade them to put an end to the wars which they so often make on each other in the hope of carrying off slaves. Much tact will be needed, for should he succeed in stopping the slave-trade while wars are still waged among the chiefs it may well come to pass that, for want of a market, the prisoners would be slaughtered. Should he find it needful to exercise actual control over any one of these tribes, it will be better to leave the direct government to the chieftains. Their obedience must be secured by making them dread his power." [1]

Both Ismail and Gordon thoroughly understood the essence of this memorandum. It meant that the latter was to use practical common sense in discharging his duties. They both knew that Anti-Slavery "Prohibition", as conceived by Sir Samuel Baker, had been a failure. It might possibly have succeeded had the money-brokers not applied pressure to the Khedive. But to have tested the feasibility of "Prohibition" would have impoverished the Vice-regal treasury, and that Europe would not countenance. The two parties therefore evolved a policy of "Regulation" which they both felt would eradicate the basic curse of slavery. In a word, pending the complete opening-up of the Equatorial provinces, they resolved to fight slave *razzias* and the slave trade and to permit domestic slavery to die a natural death.

A letter addressed by Gordon to his sister on 25th June, 1875, gives us an idea of his mental approach to this programme of "Regulation". He wrote: "Egypt cannot exist without slaves, and yet the slave is his master's master in Egypt. We, after the flesh, are the masters of our appetites, but they in reality rule us, for we cannot well control them. Other nations would have Egypt (the flesh) give up those

[1] Royal Egyptian Archives, Abdine Palace, Cairo, provisional file No. 8047.

who minister to her wants ; but she cannot do without them ; they are essential to her existence." [1]

And, looking at Egypt's problems from the angle of practical common sense, he again wrote to his sister :—

"When in 1834 His Majesty's Government abolished slavery, they had an irresistible force, with fleets, troops, etc., at their disposal ; also a machinery of magistrates to carry out the emancipation. In my case I have nothing of the sort. . . . I read the Parliamentary papers on the Gold Coast. They make me smile, for His Majesty gives a proclamation, and it is over. Needless to say, that is not the case in these lands ; the state of affairs is not parallel, and I think though *razzias* may cease, the holding of slaves will *never* under any government, let it be as strong and as incorruptible as you like. . . . I dare say also that when the stations are broken up, their inmates who have a lot of merchandise on hand will be sending down larger allotments than ever ; so let the Anti-Slavery Society get the types ready for '*Increase of Slave Trade*' and for 'atrocious', 'disgraceful,' and 'Colonel Gordon' . . . I do not wish to be hard on individuals, but on the class who are bigots, whether it be on the churchyard, or temperance, or any other question, who do not consider the other side. Men who travel much are seldom bigots (Paul was not ; he let that badly behaved Corinthian off very easily)." [2]

But while Gordon thus wrote in perfect frankness to his sister and ridiculed the Anti-Slavery Society in this confidential manner, the realist in him knew that he could not proclaim any such principles from the house-tops. The rank and file of the militant anti-slavery groups would not have recognized any such concessions to the exigencies of the hour. We

[1] *Letters of Gordon to his Sister*, p. 110.
[2] Ibid., p. 148 et seq.

have no difficulty, therefore, in understanding why Europe failed to grasp the cardinal fact that it was Gordon the man of action, and not Gordon the dreamer, who dominated the situation.

The West assumed that the zealot who had distributed tracts in Gravesend was an intransigent slavery " Prohibitionist ". No one brought out the fact that because he was the most irreconcilable of anti-slavery champions he committed himself to slavery " Regulation " as a rational means to a laudable end. And it is because of this mastery of the realist over the idealist, or, to be more accurate, because of the sanity of the idealist in Gordon, that it is so difficult to gauge in their proper perspective the manifold phases in the life of this truly Christian gentleman who is destined perhaps never to be understood.

Gordon spent a fortnight in Cairo discussing his plans and getting his staff together. Two American officers were his chief military aides. These were Lieutenant-Colonel Charles Chaillé-Long and Major William Campbell. The former, a native of Maryland, had served in the Union Army during the Civil War in the States. The latter, a Tennesseean, had fought in the Confederate Navy. Both of them had enlisted in the Khedivial forces, and were in Egypt when Gordon arrived. They were seconded to the Equatorial expedition.

The civilian members of the staff were headed by Romolo Gessi, an Italian, who had been connected with the British forces during the Crimean war. He subsequently went into business in Rumania, at Tulcha, near the mouth of the Danube. Gordon came across him there when acting as British representative on the International Danube Commission. Their friendship of Crimean days was renewed. When Gordon was offered the Equatorial appointment, he at once invited Gessi to go with him and take charge of organizing the supplies and of making the detailed arrangements for the expedition.

Two Englishmen—a nephew, Willy Anson, and Frederick J. Russell—were assigned to assist the Italian in his task. A Frenchman, Auguste Linant de Bellefonds, long a resident of Cairo, who spoke Arabic, was engaged as secretary and interpreter. A German botanist named Witt and two German naturalists, Josef Menges and Friedrich Bohndorff, were added to the contingent. There were thus nine foreigners all told, representing five different nationalities, in Gordon's original official family.[1] He appears to have desired in this way to emphasize the fact that the work on which he was engaged was undertaken in the general interest of civilization.

Gordon also remembered the black man. One was appointed his deputy on the western bank of the Nile, the other on the eastern. For the latter post he selected Abu Saoud, a man whom Sir Samuel Baker had denounced as a slave-trader and a traitor, and who was at this time in prison awaiting trial for his misdeeds. Gordon asked for the slaver's release, as he wished to have him as one of the chief members of his staff, and the Khedive complied with the request.

Sir Samuel Baker was dumbfounded when he heard that Abu Saoud " had been appointed assistant to his successor ". The manuscript of the explorer's book, *Ismailia, a Narrative of the Expedition to Central Africa for the Suppression of the Slave Trade*, was almost complete when knowledge of this choice reached London. Baker added an appendix in which he wrote that : " It is useless to shut the eyes to the support thus openly given to the greatest slave-hunter of the White Nile " ; and, growing sarcastic, the author continued : " It is not improbable that Abu Saoud may succeed Colonel Gordon in command of the

[1] Allen, op. cit., p. 15.

expedition to *suppress the slave trade*. The government may require black troops for the army. The new territory has added some millions of subjects to the Khedive. They will be liable to the law of conscription. Abu Saoud would be an excellent recruiting officer in Central Africa, as the kidnapping of slaves has been a useful apprenticeship."

Martin Hansal, the Austrian Consul at Khartoum, who knew the Sudan from end to end, looked at the matter from another angle. He applauded the new Governor-General's bold stroke. "He has a European head on an African foot," wrote Hansal. "Unlike Baker, he uses the slave-holders for his own purposes; a bold step and one that is inexplicable to those who do not appreciate his energy and resolution." [1]

It is all very well for the Austrian Consul to speak of Gordon having "a European head on an African foot" and to laud the Briton's energy and resolution. What the Governor-General really did, though Sir Samuel Baker failed to grasp it, was to adapt to the problem with which he had to deal the unflinching laws of economics. Like the American anti-saloon leaders of the twentieth century, who quote the Bible and play at practical politics, Gordon applied business methods to a commercial proposition.

He knew that Abu Saoud had become a slave-trader because he had found that it paid to defy the law. He determined to make it financially attractive to the prisoner to help the Government break up the "bootleg" slave trade. He acted as Porfirio Diaz did some twenty years later in Mexico when he formed his *Rurales* or Rural Constabulary of bandits by persuading the brigands that they could earn more money as policemen than as desperadoes. In a word, from the very first hours of his African mission the British idealist, like his American anti-saloon emulators of the present day, was a keen psychologist. He knew

[1] *Austrian Geographical Journal*, 1874, p. 380, quoted in Allen, op. cit., p. 16.

how to steer the ship of State while chanting a hymn. He was no more a hypocrite than they are. Men of this type know what they want, and know how to get it. Their sincerity enlarges their bump of economics.

But whether this theorizing is well founded or not, the fact stands out that the policy traced by Gordon, while he was still in Cairo, meant that he took into his service a man who knew every trick of the slave-running trade. One hesitates to say that, with bland and childlike eyes, he set a thief to catch a thief. It would perhaps be better to affirm that he retained an expert in order to thwart fellow experts.

Such tactics had as their logical consequence the beginning of an intelligent warfare on promiscuous slave-raiding and the inauguration of civilization's rational campaign of peaceful penetration. Gordon did not have a " poker face ", but he knew how to defeat the " bootleg " slave-runners at their own game. His countenance was that of the mystic who, through long hours spent in self-contemplation, learns not only to know himself but also how to impose his will upon others.

## CHAPTER V

# GORDON LEAVES FOR GONDOKORO

GORDON left Cairo for Suez on his way to his post on the morning of 21st February, 1874. With him were his Chief of Staff, Lieutenant-Colonel Chaillé-Long, and Lieutenant Hassan Wassif. Major Campbell, Gessi, the two Englishmen, and the others remained at the Egyptian capital in order to finish their task.[1] At Suez ship was taken for Suakin. From the latter harbour the little party started across the desert for Berber on the Nile. Two hundred and fifty miles of sand lay before Gordon. It was his first experience of camel riding, but he covered the distance in record time. A four-day river journey brought him from this point to Khartoum, the capital of the Sudan. He had then crossed more than a frontier. He had entered a land of which he said :—

" Egypt in her greatest days never seems to have extended permanently farther south than Wadi Halfa. There are certainly near Khartoum some ancient ruins of the time of the Pharaohs, and at Merowa there are some pyramids ; but the occupation of these large regions was only ephemeral. To what was due this apparent indifference to conquest on the part of Ancient Egypt ? The explanation is to be found in the difficulty of access to the Soudan—the Country of the Blacks, as the word means. From Wadi Halfa southwards to Hanneck—a distance of 180 miles—an utter desert extends, spreading also for miles and miles eastwards on both sides of the Nile. For the same length the river also is encumbered with ridges

[1] *My Life in Four Continents*, by Colonel Charles Chaillé-Long ; London, Hutchinson & Co., 1912, vol. i, p. 69.

of rock. Any invader who should have succeeded in passing the waste tract would have found deployed against him the warlike tribes of the Soudan. Ancient Egypt might certainly have penetrated from Suakin on the Red Sea to Berber on the Nile. But her forces coming by this route would have had to cross a desert of 280 miles, and would equally have had to face the enemy at the end of their wearisome march. It was therefore this boundary of the desert that kept the warlike and independent tribes of the Soudan quite apart from the inhabitants of Egypt proper, and has made the Soudanese and the Egyptians two distinct peoples, that have not the least sympathy one with the other." [1]

Khartoum was reached on 9th March, 1874, at daybreak. In a letter to his sister Gordon wrote :—

" The Governor-General met your brother in full uniform, and he landed amid a salute of artillery, and a battalion of troops with a band. It was a fine sight. The day before your brother had his trousers off, and was pulling the boat in the Nile in spite of crocodiles, who never touch you when you move. . . . The Governor had news the day before I arrived that the dense mass of vegetation—the sudd—in the Bahr Gazelle had been removed by the soldiers, so that Gondokoro is only three weeks from this." [2]

Another letter, dated 17th March, gives some interesting information about this " sudd ". " I have spoken of the opening of the sudd," he wrote. " You know that the Nile comes out of Albert Nyanza Lake. Below Gondokoro it spreads out into lakes ; on the edge of these lakes an aquatic plant, with roots extending five feet into the water, flourishes. The natives burn the top parts when dry ; the ashes form mould and fresh grasses grow, till it becomes like

[1] *Gordon in Central Africa*, 1874–9, George Birkbeck Hill, p. xxxv.

[2] Ibid., p. 5 ; all other citations in this chapter are taken from the same work unless otherwise stated.

*terra firma*. The Nile rises and floats out the masses ; they come down to a curve and there stop. More of these islands float down, and at last the river is blocked. Though under them the water flows, no communication can take place, for they bridge the river for several miles. Last year the Governor went up, and with three companies and two steamers he cut large blocks of the vegetation away. At last one night the water burst the remaining part and swept down on the vessels, dragged the steamers down some four miles, and cleared the passage. The Governor says the scene was terrible. The hippopotamuses were carried down, screaming and snorting ; crocodiles were whirled round and round, and the river was covered with dead and dying hippopotamuses, crocodiles, and fish who had been crushed by the mass. . . . You can scarcely imagine the advantage of this opening to me."

It thus looked as if the fates favoured Gordon's expedition. If they did the storks of the neighbourhood did not voice their approval. On 26th March, when the Nile boat was carrying the party southward,

"We were going along slowly in the moonlight," he wrote, "and I was thinking of you all and Nubar, etc., when all of a sudden from a large bush came peals of laughter. I felt put out ; but it turned out to be birds, who laughed at us from the bushes for some time in a very rude way. They are a species of stork, and seemed in capital spirits and highly amused at anybody thinking of going up to Gondokoro with the hope of doing anything."

While the birds were thus poking fun at Gordon and warning him, in their own way, to turn back, "crocodiles were lying interlaced on the few rocks, with their mouths, garnished with teeth, wide open. Hippopotamuses were also active. Troops of monkeys were not far distant. They came down to drink, with very long tails stuck up straight like swords over their backs." And two days later he ran into "a huge troop of wild buffaloes, looking as black as coals. They are most ferocious animals, and by far the most dangerous to shoot of any wild animals ".

Gondokoro was finally reached on 16th April, "much to the surprise of the people who never expected one's arrival at all " and who did not even know of Gordon's nomination. He decided almost at once to return to Khartoum, but before doing so sent his American aide, Lieut.-Colonel Chaillé-Long, with presents to King M'tesa of Uganda.

Chaillé-Long's expedition was replete with hardships. After accomplishing his primary mission he discovered Lake Kioga, or, as he called it, Lake Ibrahim, which forms an important link in establishing the head waters of the Nile. This discovery was made by Chaillé-Long while he was under Gordon's orders, and is rightly credited to the Gordon expedition. The latter, however, with the chivalry of a gentleman to the manner born, always gave his American Chief of Staff full credit for this contribution to the clearing up of the mystery of the Nile. It is, therefore, most regrettable that upon Chaillé-Long's shoulders must largely be placed the blame for the idea prevalent in some minds that Gordon was a periodical and secret drinker.

It will be remembered that the late Lytton Strachey, after speaking of the consolation which Gordon found in religion, added :—

" But the Holy Bible was not his only solace. For now, under the parching African sun, we catch glimpses for the first time of Gordon's hand stretching out towards stimulants of a more material quality. For months together, we are told, he would drink nothing but pure water ; and then . . . water that was not so pure. In his fits of melancholy he would shut himself up in his tent for days at a time, with a hatchet and a flag placed at the door to indicate that he was not to be disturbed for any reason whatever ; until at last the cloud would lift, the signals would be removed, and the Governor would reappear, brisk and cheerful. During one of these retirements there was a grave danger of a native attack upon the camp. Colonel Long, the chief of staff, ventured, after some hesitation, to ignore the flag and hatchet, and to enter the forbidden tent. He found Gordon seated at a table, upon which were an open Bible and an open bottle of brandy. Long explained the circumstances, but could obtain no answer beyond the abrupt words 'You are commander of the camp', and was obliged to retire, nonplussed, to deal with the situation as best he could. On the following morning Gordon, cleanly shaven, and in the full dress uniform of the Royal Engineers, entered Long's hut with his usual tripping step, exclaiming : 'Old fellow, now don't be angry with me. I was very low last night. Let's have a good breakfast—a little b. and s. Do you feel up to it ?' And, with these veering moods and dangerous restoratives, there came an intensification of the queer and violent elements in the temper of the man." [1]

The sting in this word-picture lies in its opening sentences. It is concentrated in the charge that "for months together, we are told, he (Gordon) would drink nothing but pure water ; and then . . . water that was not so pure." Dr. Allen, in *Gordon and the Sudan*, says that "there are two writers from whom the material for Mr. Lytton Strachey's paragraph has been taken—Sir Richard Burton and Colonel Chaillé-Long ". [2]

It appears that the incomparable translator of the *Arabian Nights*, in a review of Gordon's Khartoum journals, attributes what he calls the curious changes of policy and conduct which perplexed the Governor-General's best friends to " constant reliance on direct

[1] Strachey, op. cit., p. 226. [2] Allen, op. cit., p. 83.

Divine guidance", in which he was "acting under a 'control' as peculiar as the dæmon of Socrates". The Burton article cites what its author takes to be instances of change of policy, and adds: "And so in minor matters, for months he would drink nothing but water, and then prefer, very decidedly, water with whisky".

Dr. Allen, after thus recording Burton's language, adds:—

"It has sometimes been supposed that Burton and Gordon were intimate friends and met frequently. But a scrutiny of the records of the lives of the two men shows that although they exchanged a good many letters, they cannot have met on more than two occasions, and in all probability only met on one occasion."[1] Gordon's great panegyrist thus very properly brushes aside Sir Richard Burton's evidence. He then proceeds to belabour Lieutenant-Colonel Chaillé-Long for various and sundry shortcomings. He even charges the American with a "tendency deliberately to distort facts to suit his own ends".[2]

When, however, we re-read Lytton Strachey's reference to Gordon's melancholy and to his hand "stretching out towards stimulants", and compare such word-painting with Chaillé-Long's narrative, we note that the American Chief of Staff says nothing about melancholy, and does not accuse his superior officer of inebriation. Here are his words:—

"A few days after my return to Lado the camp was attacked in force one night. I had great difficulty in repelling the savage hordes, who, with lighted torches, were endeavouring to drive me out. Gordon was in his hut and gave no sign of coming out. It was during one of the oft-recurring periods when he shut himself up and placed a hatchet and a flag at the door as a sign that he was not to be disturbed, a seclusion which sometimes lasted from three to

[1] Ibid., p. 84. [2] Ibid., p. 90.

five days. I sent an officer to warn him of our danger, but, receiving no reply, went myself. I entered abruptly and found him seated very calmly at a table, on which were an open Bible and a bottle of cognac and sherry. I told him of the situation, to which he made abrupt answer: 'You are commander of the camp.' Whereupon I hastily turned and left him, but not before I had posted an officer with a half dozen men specially charged with Gordon's safety. The savages were driven away by a vigorous sortie. The next day Gordon entered my hut in the full dress uniform of the Royal Engineers, and cleanly shaven. He came forward with a quick, tripping step, as was his habit, and said: 'Old fellow, now don't be angry with me. I was very low last night. Come and dine with me. We will have a glorious dinner.' This was a meat-offering of peace."[1]

It will be observed that Chaillé-Long makes the categorical statements: (1) that he found Gordon "seated very calmly at a table, on which were an open Bible and a bottle of cognac and sherry"; (2) that he said "You are Commander of the camp"; and (3) that the next day he was clean-shaven, walked with a quick, tripping step, and invited his junior officer to "have a glorious dinner".

Not only are we not told whether the bottle was empty, full, or half-full, or even opened, but it is clearly brought out that the Bible *was* open. The statement: "You are Commander of the camp," was consonant with the facts, for when Gordon and Chaillé-Long first met at Cairo on the night of 19th February, 1874, the former said to the latter: "The Khedive spoke to me about you to-day. You are to go with me as Chief of Staff. You will command the soldiery. I don't want the bother."[2]

It is perfectly obvious that an intensely religious man who had perfect confidence in his Chief of Staff

[1] Chaillé-Long, op. cit., vol. i, p. 122.

[2] Ibid., vol. i, p. 66.

would not permit his spiritual communion with his Maker to be interrupted by so mundane an affair as an attack by natives, and this all the more as Gordon appears to have believed in the doctrine of Predestination. Had he been imbibing freely for several days he would have shown ill effects on " the morning after ", and would have court-martialled anyone who spoke in his presence of " a glorious meal ". He would never have referred to food.

In another book, *The Three Prophets*, published as early as 1884, Colonel Chaillé-Long writes :—

" I had occasion to remark the singular habit which Gordon had of retiring to his hut, where he would remain for days at a time, engaged in the perusal and meditation of his ever present Bible and prayer book. When in this retirement his orders were that he should not be disturbed for any reason of service whatsoever ; a hatchet and a flag were placed at his door as a sign that he was unapproachable."

Nothing is said here about a bottle. The reference to Gordon's shutting himself up for days at a time, however, is repeated. Dr. Allen belittles the practice which Chaillé-Long thus imputed to his Chief. Yet the allegation bears all the internal evidence of veracity. It is just such seclusion that an emotionally religious man would be most likely to seek. The story rings true. It is not an indictment ; it is not a disparagement ; it is not even a criticism. It is praise, for it shows us the detachment of Gordon's mind, and enables us to visualize the intensity of his piety.

Even if Gordon felt the need of brandy, it should not be forgotten that he made no claim to be a teetotaler. He did not pose as an impeccable " dry ", like those superior beings who either implicitly criticize Christ for having changed water into wine at the wedding feast or blame Him for having tricked wine-drinking Jews by palming off on them unfermented grape juice for the beverage they supposed He was giving them. Baker's successor was, in a word, a Scottish gentleman who drank moderately and who did not hold the twentieth century American theory that adultery and alcohol are interchangeable words.

The " hatchet and flag at the door " incident, far from casting aspersions upon Gordon's sobriety, throws light upon an important phase of his mentality. The story brings out the unity of his mission. Sir Richard Burton's reference to " curious changes of policy and conduct which perplexed his (Gordon's) best friends " is explained by the fact that the great Orientalist failed to grasp the true inward character of the author of the Khartoum journals. No man was ever more consistent in adhering to the line he had marked out for himself. Gordon was convinced that by carrying the flame of civilization into Darkest Africa he would burn away the curse of slavery. He looked upon the native slave-traders as instruments to be used for a righteous end ; and he adhered unswervingly to this course largely because frequent spiritual contact with the Almighty, as exemplified by the " hatchet and flag at the door ", steeled his nerves against deviation from his self-appointed task. His safety meant nothing to him. The interruption of his meditations was gall to his emotionally sensitive nature.

## Chapter VI

# EVER ON THE TREK

"I staid six days at Gondokoro, and then finding I could do nothing till my baggage came, I have come back in eleven days to bring it up. I got here in the evening, and found that my baggage is at Berber." [1] Thus Gordon wrote at Khartoum on 4th May, 1874. He at once hurried north to Berber, "to whip up the end of his baggage," and was there met by those members of his staff who had not left Cairo with him. Indefatigable, he lost no time in returning to Khartoum.

Such restless energy completely nonplussed the Egyptian officials. Gordon's ubiquitousness flabbergasted them. They did not know what to make of it. While they were ruminating about the matter he hauled the Governor-General of Khartoum over the coals. "Your brother wrote to him and told him that he told *stories*. It was very undiplomatic of me, but it did the Governor-General good."

But Khartoum could not hold Gordon. His Equatorial Provinces called him. On his way south he established a station at the mouth of the Sobat River and "made great friends with the Shilluk natives, who came over in great numbers from the other side of the river. A man, his wife, and two children came over, the first colonists, and settled close to the station."

There was a reason why "the first colonist" was willing to lead the vanguard of civilization. "It

[1] *Colonel Gordon in Central Africa*, 1874–9, p. 15. Unless otherwise stated, all quotations used in this chapter are taken from this work.

appears that the man had some time ago stolen a cow from one of his neighbours, and had run away. The man from whom he had stolen the cow found him, and claimed the cow—which, however, had been eaten. I happened to go round," continued Gordon, "and passing the hut saw only one child. 'Where was the other?' I asked of the mother. 'Oh, it has been given to the man from whom the cow had been stolen.' This was said with a cheerful smile by the mother. 'But,' I said, 'are you not sorry?' 'Oh, no; we would rather have the cow.' 'But,' said I, 'you have eaten the cow, and the pleasure is over.' 'Oh, but all the same we would sooner have had the cow.' This is perfectly true. The other child of twelve years old, like her parents, did not care a bit. A lamb taken from a flock would bleat, while here you see not the slightest vestige of feeling. Is it not very odd? If the mother had expressed the slightest wish, I would have rescued the child again; but it was evidently a matter of rejoicing, and she did not care as much as if she had lost a handful of dhura."

This first contact with an African colonist undoubtedly impressed Gordon greatly. It taught him that he was absolutely right in holding that the solution of the slavery question was entirely dependent upon opening up Central Africa to civilization. What was the use of attacking such an institution as slavery when mothers themselves looked upon their children as being worth less than "a handful of d'hurra"? The thing to be done, as he had already worked out in London, was to bring the light of the Occident to the Dark Continent and not to concern oneself, except incidentally, with the necessary concomitants of an essentially perverted view of life.

As he revolved these facts in his mind, Gordon's calm, benevolent blue eyes flashed fire. His righteous indignation was aroused by such inhumanity. When he had sufficiently adjusted himself to personal contact with such heartlessness to put his ideas into black and white he wrote :—

"Sobat, 3rd August, 1874. In spite of what Livingstone says, I do not myself, about here, find that any affection exists between the parents and children ; there is mutual pleasure in parting from one another. I think that the slaver's wars, made for the purpose of taking slaves, are detestable ; but if a father or mother, of their own free will, and with the will of the child, sells that child, I do not see the objection to it. It was and is the wholesale depopulation of districts which makes slavery a curse, and the numbers killed or who perish in the collection of slaves. A fair and properly conducted emigration would be the best for these parts, and I think the blacks would gladly respond to such a scheme. It will be a very long time before much can be done to civilize them ; the climate is against it, and there can be no trade, for they have nothing to exchange for goods. Poor creatures. They would like to be left alone."

While Gordon was philosophizing in this strain he caught sight of "a wretched sister struggling up the road. She was such a wisp of bones that the wind threatened to overthrow her ; so she halted, preferring the rain to being cast down." The next day he wrote :

"I am bound to give you the sequel of the lady whom I helped yesterday in the gale of wind. I had told my man to see her into one of the huts, and thought he had done so. The night was stormy and rainy, and when I awoke I heard often a crying of a child near my hut within the enclosure. When I got up I went out to see what it was, and passing through the gateway I saw your and my sister lying dead in a pool of mud ; her black brothers had been passing and passing and had taken no notice of her. So I went and ordered her to be buried and went on. In the midst of the high grass was a baby about a year or so old left by its mother. Children are always a nuisance. The baby is taken care of by another family for a consideration of maize per diem."

Undeterred by such callousness on the part of those whom he was determined to protect, Gordon remained on guard at the mouth of the Sobat River. He knew that the slave-hunters would sooner or later attempt to pass that strategic point. At last they did so. On 20th August, 1874, he captured one hundred and five slaves "stowed away in wood". A day later, twenty-one fell into his hands. None of them expressed any desire to return home—they had no idea of home. All of them wanted to remain where they were, so the Governor-General, after confiscating them, gave them clothes and allowed them to join his agricultural colony. Assured that no more "black ivory" was then coming down the Sobat, he pushed on to Gondokoro, reaching his capital on 4th September, 1873.

He had been led into error. No sooner had he departed from his Sobat River station than two days later his *Mudir* [1] connived at the passing of a convoy of slaves, receiving £75 for doing so. The convoy went right into the lion's mouth: namely to Fashoda. There Rattaz and Kutchuk Ali were waiting for them. There were 1,600 slaves and 200 cows, and the whole lot were arrested. "Kutchuk Ali and Rattaz will get five years and be ruined. I told them," recorded Gordon, "that if they brought the slaves to me I would let them off. I told them that the *Mudir* of Fashoda would not dare to let the slaves pass, as I had written to the Khedive that they were *en route*. Yet they persisted in saying that there were none; so it is their own fault. I have sent for my *Mudir* and he will catch it."

While the unsophisticated-looking soldier showed that he understood human nature by not taking the

[1] *Mudir*, Arabic equivalent for Governor.

slave-traders' word that they had no caravans on the march, he was somewhat precipitate in saying that "Kutchuk Ali and Rattaz will get five years and be ruined". It took more than a psychologist to read the mind of an Egyptian official of the 'seventies. Besides, no one who knows the Near East ever indulges in prophecy. It is obvious, therefore, that Gordon went wrong when he recorded on 5th October what was going to happen to the slave-hunters. He was forced to write on 23rd November :—

"You know all about the slave convoy at Sobat, how they were intercepted by the *Mudir* of Fashoda. It appears that Kutchuk Ali and Rattaz were not arrested but went down free. The Khedive writes to me quite harshly to stop this slave-trade, and you see his *Mudirs* help it on. So I answer : 'I ask His Excellency, if under these circumstances (as above) His Highness would think me justified in hanging the little men I find in charge of slaves. I do not think he would.' I then go on to say that I am reasonable in my actions, but that I should take extreme measures when the real culprits are his local authorities and the Khartoum merchants who are entirely in his power is more than he can expect."

But these were not Gordon's only worries. His immediate subordinates gave him trouble. The ex-slave-trader, Abu Saoud, whom he had taken from prison and converted into a government official, became obstreperous. The brigand of yesterday could not stand prosperity. His head swelled to inordinate proportions. Gordon wrote to his sister :—

"I have had to turn Abu Saoud out, I am sorry to say ; he got so bumptious and bullying to everyone that I could not stand it. He was very presumptuous with your brother, coming into his cabin on the boat without 'with your leave' or 'by your leave', even after he had hints given him that he had better look out. He bullied a poor Mudir of mine, Isib Aga, nearly to death ; and usurped all my functions till the cup was full."

While this letter emphasizes Abu Saoud's bumptiousness, it was not his conceit and his bad manners which cost him his position. Gordon knew human nature too well not to understand that a black could not be transferred overnight from a prison cell to a government billet without megalomania playing its part. He was bent on opening up Central Africa and teaching the natives that honesty is the best policy. So he would have closed his eyes to Abu Saoud's indiscipline if the latter had not had an itching palm.

"Abu Saoud has been tricking your brother," he told his sister, "and taking elephant tusks from the *sheikhs* or chiefs of the tribes who come to see me. Unfortunately one chief brought me a tusk and I saw it, and afterwards it disappeared. This made me suspicious. Now, whenever a tusk is brought me, I put it into the Government lot of ivory."

Abu Saoud's appointment was accordingly cancelled and he was instructed to await further orders. But his chief's forgiving nature gained the upper hand and the Sudanese was given another chance. He repaid this kindness by instigating a *sheikh* to make an attempt upon Gordon's life. No trace of bitterness creeps into Gordon's account of this dastardly act. He writes of it with a calm detachment which throws further light upon his character. He almost ignores Abu Saoud's existence, and getting down to the attack itself, says :—

"Coming to Rageef[1] I met the hostile *sheikh* on the road. He asked me to come to his house ; but I declined, as it was dusk. The next day I had a visit from him. He had a large number of armed men with him, and after some friendly intercourse he left me for a time, but soon came back and began to surround my tent with about one hundred of his men.

[1] Gordon had moved his headquarters to that spot.

I watched his movements, and then got up, took up my two guns, and put them down ready. I then told him to walk off—which he did. I feel sure he meditated hitting me on the head with one of his knob sticks."

The utter unreliability of his Egyptian troops added to Gordon's trials and tribulations. He summed up his opinion of them by recording that the Khedive's "officers and men are so wretched that they are not a match for the natives. There is no discipline at all. One of the men slept at his post on the night of 25th–26th August; he was caught and then he beat both sergeant and corporal; yet he was not made a prisoner of".

The only chance Gordon had of facing with success a situation thus beset with recurring difficulties lay in placing his sole reliance upon his European and American military and civil staff. Of the gallant nine who had enlisted under his banner in Cairo one, Lieutenant-Colonel Chaillé-Long, had already departed on his mission to the Equatorial Lakes. The health statistics of the remaining eight, or nine if we include Gordon himself, made up as early as 11th September, 1874, tell their own story. They read:—

"Your brother: well, but a shadow.

"Kemp, Engineer: well (subsequently fell ill and invalided home).

"Gessi: well, has had a severe fever.

"Berndorff, German, my servant: ill.

"Mengines, German servant: sent back ill.

"Anson: dead.

"Russell: ill, cannot be moved, invalided.

"De Witt: dead.

"Campbell: ill (did not recover, died).

"Linant: very ill, cannot be moved (did not recover, died)."

Not only was death thus stalking about in the shape of fever, but scorpions, too, were doing their bit to make Gordon's life unsafe. He describes in this wise one of his earlier adventures with these poisonous insects :—

"Last night, after going to sleep, I awoke and felt a sharp burn on the calf of my leg ; I felt something coming upwards, and got another burn above my knee. Jumped up and shook myself and then got a light. You know I have sewn a waterproof sheet on the bottom of my mosquito-net, leaving a hole to go in, so anything that gets in certainly can't get out. Looking about I pulled at the sheet and got another bite on the finger. At last I had him, got a tumbler with some water and put him in. He floated : so I tapped his back and sank him—a scorpion about two inches long. The sting is an odd one ; it burns for some time, and seems to palpitate as if the scorpion was at it again."

While Gordon was kept too busy and had too many responsibilities to break under the strain, his fatalism helped to steel his nerves. "The intense comfort of no fear, no uneasiness about being ill is very great and more than half the cause of good health. No comfort is equal to that which he has who has God for his stay ; who believes not in words but in fact, that *all* things are ordained to happen and must happen."

These are the thoughts of a man who believes in Predestination. Other passages from Gordon's writings could be cited to show that he was, in this respect, a Presbyterian. But while his critics accuse him of being the victim of caprices and of half-baked ideas, there was something so eminently practical about him that he coupled his acceptance of the dogma of Predestination with the maintenance of a medicine-chest. He made use of it, and went so far as to say:—

"I have been studying medicine a good deal, and found out a great thing, i.e. that ½ gr. of ginger,

½ gr. of ipecacuanha, and 3 grs. of rhubarb make a splendid daily pill, and can be taken without hurt for a lifetime. They keep me in perfect health ; they are taken either at breakfast or dinner ; not to be taken fasting." And Chaillé-Long quotes Gordon as saying : " Now do take some cognac and don't forget quinine." [1]

Not only did he thus emphasize the fact that his theories, and even his principles, were attuned to a realization of the stern realities of life, but he also took the precaution of moving his headquarters from Gondokoro to a point further south, to Rageef, which he describes as " such a nice climate and country "—but where scorpions abound, and hippopotamuses, " their fat sides gleaming from the water they have come out of in the moonlight, make such a fat, grunting noise, as if they did like it so much." In this atmosphere, where the grunting of contented hippopotamuses lulled him to sleep, and scorpions menaced his slumbers, Gordon began his work of initiating the black man into the mysteries of civilization. The first thing that he taught was the use of money.

" I have had great work with the native chiefs in teaching them the use of money," he wrote. " Up to the present time the habit has been to give the chief of a tribe some beads or calico, and he makes his men bring wood, or do any work. Now I want to break through the feudal system of chiefs ; the only way to do this is to let their subjects see that they can stand on their own feet. Before I began the system which I hope to establish, the chief would keep the mass of the things given to him, and give only a few to his subjects. I began by paying each man who worked some beads. Next day I gave each man who worked half-a-piastre (one penny) in copper and offered to sell him beads to that amount. They soon saw it

[1] Chaillé-Long, op. cit., vol. i, p. 145.

and would not buy. They said : 'We will keep the money till we get more, and can buy more expensive things.' I have fixed certain prices for certain things, and made out little lots of beads and wire to sell for certain prices—in fact, made a regular shop, much to the discontent of all the old hands, who are dead against these new-fangled ideas, though I say they will eventually gain, for they will be able to keep shops."

Gordon was so pleased with this first step towards opening up Central Africa to civilization that he lets his pen tell more of the same pioneer work. He adds :—

"To-day I made a first-rate affair. A chief brought a tusk, and wanted two bells for cows to wear around their necks in exchange. I said 'No, I will give you two dollars for the tusk'. He said 'Yes', so I gave him two dollars. 'Now,' I said, 'I will give you two bells for a dollar each,' which he agreed to and bought them. This was a great step to make ; he has brought some more tusks since, for which I gave him money, and he has bought from me copper wire."

# Chapter VII

# DEPARTS FOR LAKE ALBERT

Though teaching the native chiefs the use of money may have been the first step towards initiating them into the mysteries of civilization, Gordon's intelligent and aggressive fight against slavery required that he should open up the country as well as the minds of its inhabitants. It has already been said that Lieutenant-Colonel Chaillé-Long had been sent on a mission to King M'tesa. That officer returned to headquarters on 18th October, 1874. His chief characterized his subordinate's discovery of the water-passage between Urundogani and Foweira as an accomplishment of great importance. Later, Gordon wrote :—

"Those who care to study the successive steps which built up the map of the course of the Nile will know that to Speke is due the discovery of one portion, to Baker that of another, and to Colonel Chaillé-Long that of another portion and of the lake referred to" (Lake Ibrahim).[1]

This important exploration filled in a link in what is known as the "Victoria Nile". Speke and Grant had discovered Lake Victoria and had correctly conjectured that the Victoria Nile, which flows out of that lake, joins up with the White Nile and thus forms one of the head-waters of the Nile. Gordon's Chief of Staff definitely demonstrated the accuracy of the Speke and Grant surmise. He showed that the missing link was, in large part, that body of water now known as Lake Kioga, but which he called Lake Ibrahim.

[1] Chaillé-Long, op. cit., vol. ii, p. 555.

All this was very interesting from the scientific point of view, but it did not get Gordon very far on the road to those practical results which the man whom the world took to be a visionary had always in view. His primary concern was not the making of maps or adding to scientific knowledge. What he had at the back of his mind was to open up water communication between Gondokoro and Albert Nyanza. Baker had discovered that lake, but had not followed the White Nile from the Nyanza at the point where it flows out of Lake Albert. No white man—most probably no man—had ever traversed that distance, although geographers at that time unhesitatingly agreed that one of the head-waters of the White Nile was Lake Albert.

Gordon realized that he could not hope to eradicate slavery until this Nile passageway had been explored, and not merely traced on maps. He felt that until this water-channel was opened he was groping in the dark. His practical mind called for bald facts, not deductions. He therefore resolved to have these intervening miles, however great their length, not as the crow flies but as the stream winds, not merely opened up but kept open. He committed the preliminary path-finding mission to two Englishmen, Lieutenants Watson and Chippendall.

These officers had barely started on their expedition when illness overtook them. Gordon wrote from Lado on 11th January, 1875 :—

"Received a letter from Chippendall and Watson to say both are ill. I have sent a steamer for them, and will make a hospital here for all the maimed and sick. Of course, I have to give up, for the moment, the Lake Expedition. The fact is that no man under thirty years of age, unless he is more or less acclimatized, ought to come out here. Age is a benefit, for it has brought more or less experience with it, and you do not get so dismally down as young men do."

Watson and Chippendall, however, with true British grit returned to the charge and followed the White Nile to Lake Albert. They did not navigate the stream, as cataracts made this impossible for the craft at their disposal. When Watson, on his way back to England, reported to Gordon, " his (Watson's) clothes hung on him like a pole." Chippendall, his constitution shattered, had also to be invalided home. Broken health was the price they paid for helping Gordon to fulfil his mission.

With Watson and Chippendall's report in hand, Gordon felt that it was incumbent upon him to devise ways and means for establishing communication by boat between Gondokoro and Lake Albert. He was determined to police the lower stretches of the White Nile so as to cut off the slave trade at its fountain head. He therefore assumed personal charge of the expedition which undertook to go by water from Gondokoro to Albert Nyanza.

Writing at Rageef on 7th April, 1875, Gordon thus describes how he began this important work undertaken in the interests of the suppression of the slave trade :—

" I have just come back from a short tour. You must know that the great difficulty I have to contend with is how to get the heavy portion of the steamers to the point where the Nile is navigable above the generally accepted cataracts—a distance of a hundred miles from Gondokoro. . . . I am bound in honour to get the steamer on the Lake, and I saw months and months of work before me. . . . Continued thinking made me first give up all idea of taking up the heavy portions of the steamer with me this trip ; I would put off that difficulty until November. Next I gave up all thoughts of taking up the two life-boats in sections ; next I gave up all idea of taking up the timber I had prepared, with which to construct *nuggers*[1] above the cataracts, and next I gave up all idea of taking up a cart to try the road. All this was pain and wormwood to me, for eventually these things must come up, and I was only, I thought, putting off the evil day. I therefore determined to go up and place a station on the Nile a day's march from here ; then to bring up the *impedimenta* there, and then to make another station a day's march further, and take the things up there, and so on to the head of the Falls."[2]

Gordon's official correspondence with Khairy Pasha, hidden away for years in the Royal Archives of the Abdine Palace, but now, through King Fuad's wise initiative, made accessible to students, teems with evidence of his burning desire to get these *nuggers* on the upper stretches of the Nile and on the Great Lakes. The postscript of Gordon's letter to Khairy Pasha, dated Foweira, 16th January, 1876, brings out what was in the back of his mind. He wrote in French. Here is a literal translation of his words :—

"Even if we should take possession of these lakes by raising the (Egyptian) flag and by establishing troops on their shores, I think that after some little time, if we made no use of our possession, our rights may lapse. It is for this reason that I so strongly press for the construction of the *nuggers*. We have all the nails that we need."[3]

The Nile hippopotamuses objected to Gordon's effort to navigate the waters which were their home. They "were in large numbers in the river, and the

[1] "The boats which are used upon the upper waters of the Nile are called *nuggers* ; their construction, I believe, is unlike what can be seen in any other country of the world. They are as strong as they are massive, being built so as to withstand the violent pushings of the hippopotamuses, as well as the collisions with the mussel-banks which are scattered in various directions." Schweinfurth, *Heart of Africa*, vol. i, p. 50.

[2] *Colonel Gordon in Central Africa 1874–9*, p. 74. All subsequent quotations in this chapter, unless otherwise stated, are from this work.

[3] Royal Egyptian Archives, Abdine Palace, Provisional File No. 8180.

way they rushed in herds through the water was astounding; they made quite a roar like that of a cataract. They look like such queer creatures when by chance they get cut off from deep water and stand like mountains in shoal water." The presence of the *nuggers* in their midst infuriated the water horses. "We hit several on the back," wrote Gordon, "which they resented by heaving up the boat, really sometimes making one quite afraid of them. I never heard such a noise, nor could I have believed there were so many in the river. . . . After seven p.m. we had a serious time, for we were in an open boat, and the hippopotamuses were in force. We were afraid every minute of being swamped by them. Sometimes they are very fierce, and bite the boats in two. Their jaws are immense, and go back to their ears. A son of Muhammad Ali was killed by the bite of one in 1843. Their strength is terrible."

But since he had said that "I am in honour bound to get the steamer on the Lake", the creation of a line of army posts, even were it extended right through to Albert Nyanza, did not satisfy him. He studied the Nile and became convinced that his steamer the *Khedive* could safely pass through the Nile cataracts when the river was at its height. He accordingly ordered that the *Khedive* and the *Ismailia* be sent to him.

They were then at Khartoum—at all events Gordon thought they were. He cherished the hope that they would reach him before the Nile subsided. But on 25th June he exclaimed: "No steamer as yet; very trying for the flesh as the river is so very high." On 29th June he wrote: "It is now 129 days since the steamers arrived at Khartoum; and through some mishap or mistake they appear to have stayed." 2nd July brought the pathetic note: "No steamers: You will be sick of these two words." How ominous they sound now when we recall how nine years later he scanned the horizon and called out with courageous resignation : " No steamers."

Time for a while hung heavily on Gordon's hands while waiting for the boats. But on 12th August the natives " meant mischief. They came down close to the camp, creeping along the grass, but long range rifles made them think differently." A few days later an attack was made on another camp by " the natives of three tribes who combined their forces ". The situation was becoming more and more tense, when on 20th August word reached Gordon that the *Khedive* was approaching.

Four days passed, and the steamer failed to arrive. Gordon became uneasy, He feared that the unfriendly tribes might have attacked the boat. That evening Linant, a brother of the interpreter who had died in Gordon's service, suggested that if his chief had no objection he should cross the river and burn the houses of the hostile natives. " As I feared they might attack the steamer, and that, if worried, they would let it alone, I assented," wrote Gordon, " and sent thirty-six soldiers, two officers, and three irregular soldiers, with two boxes of ammunition. Each man had thirty rounds in his pouch. About noon they were on the hills ; and I saw Linant, in a red shirt which I had given him, on the hill. The men and he seemed quite at home." In a few moments they disappeared. Only one man of the entire detachment lived to tell what had happened. Every other member of the expedition had been killed outright, including the gallant Linant.

But the attack saved the *Khedive*. By 13th September all was ready for the dash to the lake. Fate, however, interposed her veto. As the steamer was passing through the rapids two *nuggers* got adrift, and the current caught the *Khedive* and sent her broadside on two rocks. It took three days to float her. Finally Gordon was able to write :—

" Certainly it does not seem very long from

1st August to 23rd September to be engaged in taking the steamer from Rageef to Moogie, in establishing my posts, and in bringing up all the necessary stores ; but it was years in time to me and has worn me very much. I shall never be fit for anything again, and shall try to retire if I live to the end of the work. *Bananas* in the upper country may make me feel better, but I doubt it. I am not fastidious, but cockroach nests in your sugar, rice, etc., do not tempt one to eat. I can talk to no one, so I write a great deal."

On 9th October Gordon left for Duffli, and eight days later he recorded :—

"It is all over ! I started from Duffli this morning, and keeping on a higher level to avoid the wet edges of the river, came on it about five miles from here. I fancied for some time I heard a noise like thunder, which increased as we approached the river. At last we stood above it on a rock bank covered with vegetation, which descended abruptly to the stream, and there it was appalling to look at, far less to think of getting anything up or down except in splinters. It was more a rush down a slope of one-in-six than a fall. Above it the water was smooth, and 80 to 150 yards wide ; and here it was suddenly contracted to two passages of 15 to 20 yards wide—for a rock isle stood in the centre. . . . It was a difficult path enough to get there, and few eyes have seen these falls. They are generally known as Fola, but by us by the name of Makadé. Below is clear, so that we have two miles of bad country over which to carry all the things. Of course, the idea is all over of taking up the screw steamer or the *nuggers*, or, indeed, anything."

It must have been most distressing for Gordon to have had the certainty that his steamer could not reach Albert Nyanza driven home to him. Open communication with the head-waters of the Nile was what he wanted in order to attack the slave-traders at their base of supply. He was convinced that if he could have put boats on the Lake it would have been of incalculable benefit to him in that work of civilization upon which his heart was set. But, allowing no difficulties to thwart and no obstacles to discourage him, he kept on hammering at his goal until success crowned his efforts.

He was not able to accomplish this result in person. Several months were to elapse before his deputies, Romolo Gessi, the Italian, and Alexander McComb Mason, an American, acting under his orders, were in a position to do so. Gordon's attention was riveted upon other work when Gessi, in 1876, dismantled a boat specially built for the purpose, carried it by land along the banks of the cataracts of Duffli, and was the first man—at all events the first white man—to circumnavigate Albert Nyanza.[1] In August, 1877, Mason gave scientific accuracy to Gessi's explorations, and also discovered the Semliki River, which connects Lake Albert with Lake Albert Edward, thus bringing to light what are now known as the Albertine head-waters of the Nile.[2] But Gordon is entitled to full credit for having inspired these two explorations. They formed part of his campaign against slavery and were directed by him while he was attending to other equally important aspects of the same problem.

His official letter announcing Gessi's circumnavigation of Lake Albert was addressed to Khairy Pasha. It is dated Kerri, May, 1876, and says :—

"The Egyptian flag was raised on Albert Nyanza on 10th April, 1876, and henceforth the navigation of that lake is vested in the Government. As soon as

[1] *Bulletin de la Société Khédiviale de Géographie du Caire*, ii série, A 7, Juin, 1885, Le Caire, Imprimerie Nationale, 1885, p. 348.

[2] Ibid., A 5, Mai, 1877, et Février, 1878, p. 5.

I receive the proof that the flag has been raised on Lake Victoria I shall advise you." [1]

However keenly Gordon may have regretted the fact that he personally did not get through with his steamer to Albert Nyanza, his letters fail to reveal the slightest sense of irritation. He did not even adopt the safety-valve so often resorted to of blaming someone else for the shattering of his hopes. On the contrary, in the very letter, dated 17th October, 1875, which began with the words: "All is over," he wrote :—

"To undertake what I am doing, were I under our Government, I should surely have some good men, instead of these poor, helpless, ignorant black officers. . . . One feels inclined to be vexed with the Khedive for this state of affairs, but it would be unjust to do so, for he has given, and gives all I ask for. If I asked for twenty European officers he would give me them, but if I had twenty how would I feed them ; how carry their tremendous amount of baggage ; and how many would sicken and die, or else force me to devote my transport to their removal to Khartoum?"

Such self-control and fairness did Gordon show when the climate alone would have blunted an ordinary man's sense of justice. He wrote at this very time :—

"What a climate it is! The only thing (except God's keeping, which is all) to keep well is to keep employed at anything ; never be idle or you will mope and succumb." And while thus depending upon his own will-power to keep well, harassing letters further taxed, though they could not break down, his self-control. His Journal records on 10th November :—

"The post came in last night. Its principal contents are : letters from Latooka, which say it is half-blockaded by the hostile natives. It is evident that the Mudir has been doing something to irritate them or they would not have attacked him. I have sent orders

[1] Royal Egyptian Archives, Abdine Palace, Cairo, Provisional File No. 8196.

to Bohr Station to help him. Next, letters from two captains, one lieutenant, and a corporal, stating that the different stations they are quartered in do not suit them, and they wish to change. Answered that their likes and dislikes are a matter of supreme indifference to me. Next a cry out for more troops; 120 with Remingtons, three hours from another station with 90, are not enough; 60 at another station are not enough. It happens that the Mudir of this last unfortunately states in another letter that he issued out and separated two tribes who were fighting one another; so he got for reply: 'If you can meddle with the internecine wars of the natives, you have enough troops for your station'; and generally as an answer to the Major, 'if you and your officers and soldiers are afraid, tell me, and I will send you all down to Khartoum.'"

Yet Gordon could not give these officers more men, not because the Khedive would not have paid them, but because as he said in another letter:—

"I have garrisons small on purpose to make them keep awake; and it has its effect, for they are in a frightful fright along the line. I cannot help feeling somewhat of a malicious enjoyment at their sufferings. If I personally am at any station, even if there are thirty or forty men there, the sentries all go to sleep in comfort. Not so in my absence; everyone is awake, I expect. Having nothing to do—or, rather, not doing anything, though there is plenty to be done—they sit and talk over the terrors of their position, until they tremble again. I never in the course of my life saw such wretched creatures dignified by the name of soldiers." [1]

But even Gordon's sense of humour and force of character could not for ever resist both the climate and the trials that were his daily lot. He was forced to record on 14th November that he "got to this

[1] *Letters of General C. G. Gordon to his Sister*, p. 115.

place (Duffli) yesterday. Nearly dead with an attack of liver. The heat was terrible. I was obliged to go for I had given notice that I should come. The suffering human nature undergoes in these parts is terrible ".

A month later he wrote from Moogie : " I had to sit up all night with my sergeant who had the fever, and who died at 1.30 a.m., while I started at 4 p.m."

This death affected Gordon, for in another letter he said :—

" I am very low. I feel my servant's death. I did not know he was ill till twelve hours before he left this world ; not that it is not better for him, in all the miseries of this wretched land. God will make it up for him. I am so angry with the Cairo people : they have no idea of the difficulties up here. However, it is all God's will, and I hope I shall be able to bear it."

## CHAPTER VIII

# SURVEYS THE VICTORIA NILE

As 1875 disappeared beyond the horizon Gordon determined to press on to Victoria Nyanza. He had been unable to reach Lake Albert by steamer. He set his teeth and made up his mind that Lake Victoria should not escape him. He felt that until the country adjacent to it was properly recorded by map-makers, peaceful penetration, so essential to civilization's warfare on slavery, could not begin. He had but recently read a paper by Dr. Schweinfurth in which that eminent explorer had said : " It may be that Lake Albert belongs to the Nile basin ; but it is not a settled fact, for there are seventy miles between Foweira and Lake Albert that have never been explored, and we are not authorized in making the Nile leave Lake Albert. The question is very doubtful." This statement caused Gordon to write : " It was contended that the Nile did not flow out of Lake Victoria, and thence through Lake Albert, and so southward, but that one river flowed out of Lake Victoria and another out of Lake Albert ; that these two rivers united and formed the Nile. This statement could not be positively denied, inasmuch as no one had actually gone along the river from Foweira to Magungo."[1]

Gordon reached Fatiko on his trek to Foweira on 3rd January, 1876. He had marched forty-eight miles in three days. " I have great pains in the back," he wrote, " and though I can walk my fourteen miles it makes me feel much fatigued, and I feel sure I ought to get out of the country as soon as I can."

[1] *Colonel Gordon in Central Africa 1874–9*, p. 177. All statements of fact made in this chapter are based upon this work.

The best proof that Gordon was an extremely temperate man and no secret drinker is to be found in the way in which, day after day, he stood up against the ordeal both of the climate and of the monotony of his daily existence. His own pen describes, without a word of ill-humour, the hardships that were part of his life. Referring to his journey from Fatiko to Foweira he said :—

" A more dreary, weary, set of marches you cannot conceive. The country is quite uninhabited—a vast, undulating prairie of jungle grass and scrub-trees ; after the first day the water is from swamps, and resembles muddy beer ; it is strongly impregnated with iron, and, in fact, the whole country's soil is as red as blood. . . . The halting places were terribly infested with earwigs and ants. The river is 250 yards wide with no current. South bank very marshy. This is the programme (D.V.) : in three days to surprise Mrooli, which is thirty miles south on the river ; to establish a post there ; to march to Urundogani and place a post there, and another on Ripon Falls ; to come down to Foweira, and thence to go to Magungo, where I mean, if I can, to place a station ; then to go down from there to Duffli by steamer."

There were, of course, no roads which Gordon could follow. He was in rags from the thorn bushes, bruised by stumbling over trees uprooted by elephants and by falling into the pitfalls, quite a foot deep, made in the soft soil by their heavy feet. One day he picked a fig. " I asked the black if it was good," records Gordon; " he said ' Yes ', and I bit it and just tasted it. It had an astringent, disagreeable taste, so I spat it out. Soon after that came on a violent sore throat, which nearly prevented my breathing, and this continued all night. Everything in this land is bitter or astringent or thorny or prickly. The nice green waving grass has silicious delicate hairs on it like spun glass, and quite as sharp. Nice looking turf has a seed like a crow's foot in it. You walk along and think to pluck a tuft of grass, and you get your finger cut to the bone. Everything is tough and strong, and as for plucking a switch, you never can."

After enduring all these hardships Gordon reached Mrooli on 22nd January, only to find that what he had thought was a capital was in reality the name of a district, and that its chief, Kaba Rega, had fled, carrying his " magic stool " with him. It appears that this sovereign had ideas about his " magic stool " somewhat like those that King James II of England had in regard to his great seal. The emblem of authority, of which Gordon spoke with scant reverence, was a throne composed partly of copper and partly of wood. It was an exceedingly small and ancient piece of furniture that had been handed down from generation to generation, and was considered to be a *coojoor* or talisman. The legend ran that should the throne be lost or stolen the king's authority would disappear together with the talisman, and disorder would reign throughout the country until the precious object should be restored.

The " magic stool " meant nothing to Gordon. His primary object was not to conquer but to open up the country. Conquest would not, of itself, have meant the death-knell of slavery. He was convinced that a proper exploration of the land was an essential prerequisite to an attack on the economic support of slavery. He did not permit his thoughts to deviate from this central conception of his mission, and he tarried in the land of the Mrooli only long enough to remark that " a miserable country, full of mosquitoes, is the much vaunted Mrooli ". But it was cold in those parts, for the very next day, before leaving for Foweira by canoe, he noted that " it is very cold this morning, and it forced one to put on a great coat ". This drop in temperature was due to the altitude.

It is somewhat difficult to understand why Gordon turned back instead of carrying through his original plan. He had written as late as 8th January : " I want to push on to the lake (Victoria Nyanza) to hoist the flag and to enable the *Khedive* to claim its waters." The most plausible explanation is that his liver went to pieces, and that, notwithstanding the tenacity of purpose which was characteristic of him, he was but mortal and could not throw off the intellectual torpor and temperamental depression engendered by a sluggish liver.

Before we reject this theory and fall back upon the more convenient charge of inconstancy which has so often been made against Gordon, it may be well to read what he wrote to his sister but a few days earlier :—

" This is a horrid climate. I seldom, if ever, get a good sleep. It is a very great comfort to feel that God will rectify one's defects in this life, and make right all mistakes, also that He governs everything. Is it my present temperament, or is it truly the case that things go untowardly more in this land than anywhere else ? . . . Every, *every* thing seems to go wrong. It may be my liver which makes me think this. . . . Oh ! how I wish I had finished this work. I have yet two months of weariness ; shall I get through it ? Who knows ?"[1]

As soon as Gordon had returned to Duffli he again spoke of his liver. Here are his words :—

" You will understand my grief at not having surveyed the gaps in the Victoria Nile. Whether I shall do so or not I do not know. . . . If I were well I would do it, but I keep day by day feeling my liver more." He wrote in this strain on 10th February. Six days later he added : " Out of sorts again with bleeding from the nose (not plague) ; nearly suffocated last night with blood."

[1] *Letters of General Gordon to his Sister*, p. 119.

While still at Duffli Gordon wrote a letter to Khairy Pasha, which emphasizes the importance he attached to the navigation of Lake Victoria. It is written in French. Its opening paragraphs may well be translated in full. They read as follows :—

" There is one thing that Egypt should watch with a jealous eye : the navigation of Lake Victoria by boats of powers other than Egypt.

" I have already written to you that after the unfurling of the Egyptian flag (which will shortly be an accomplished fact) Egypt should maintain her possession of Lake Victoria and prevent that lake being navigated by boats not authorized so to do by Egypt." [1]

But, liver or no liver, Gordon had pulled himself together by the end of February. He left Duffli on 7th March. On the 8th he wended his way down to the Fola Falls in order to complete his survey. " Such a walk ! " he observed. " There were ravines and gullies in abundance, and the ground was covered with loose stones. I never was so tired, but I finished the map." Stimulated by this work, he was able to write a few days later :—

" Is it not odd that since I left Foweira, where I was so unwell, I have been quite well—in fact as well as I ever was ? Whether one gets acclimatized all of a sudden or not, I do not know, but in my case it has been so. The mosquitoes are terrible here just now—burning Keatings insect powder does them but for a time ; carbolic acid powder is quite useless. I sit in the evening under a mosquito-curtain, but it is very hot in it. Of one's existence the time between sunset and sunrise is the most trying."

In another letter to his sister Gordon describes how these mosquitoes carry on their campaign. " The proboscis is formed like a bayonet with a hinge at the bend ; they turn it down for perforation and press

[1] Royal Egyptian Archives, Abdine Palace, Cairo, Provisional File No. 8199.

on it with their head, muscles, and chest. I am very susceptible of their bite or dig ; the least touch of the ' bayonet ' makes a lump." [1]

After several inspection trips along the lower stretches of the Nile, Gordon reached Labore on 4th July. He had ordered, for service on Lake Victoria, a 108-ton steamer which he had named the *Khedive*. He was once again in excellent fettle, and was able to write : " All my worries, with the return of my health, have disappeared. I am now preparing for the taking to pieces, at Moogie, of the *Khedive* and the putting of her together on Victoria Lake. This might, if He wills it, be accomplished in April next, and would secure the lake to the Khedive."

He left Duffli on 20th July with the steamer and two life-boats, and found the river " horrible, full of endless papyrus isles ", with a fringe of papyrus for ten or twenty yards along the banks. Eight days later he arrived at the debouchment of the Victoria Nile into Lake Albert, " after a night spent in the lake, owing," to quote his words, " to my stupidity. The entrance is masked," he continued, " by a mass of papyrus isles. There is no current at all, and it is a most miserable looking place. The people are quiet and well disposed to us. I saw a herd of elephants to-day feeding quietly and looking so happy. They pitch grass into their mouths with their trunks, as you would chuck water from your mouth into a basin. What a wilderness this is up here—not a sound to be heard, and so lifeless, and apparently miserable. . . . I propose (and God disposes) to go up from here to Foweira and then map that part ; to go then to Mrooli, and thence to Urundogani and to Cossitza (Ripon Falls) ; hoist the Egyptian Flag there on Victoria Lake, and then map the River from Cossitza to Urundogani ; and thence to Mrooli. From

[1] *Letters of General C. G. Gordon to his Sister*, p. 120.

Cossitza to Urundogani is forty miles by land—the river not being navigable. From Urundogani to Mrooli it is navigable, and I have done that part between Mrooli and Foweira. Then the Nile will be completed." [1]

"Then the Nile will be completed." To accomplish this result, which meant so much for his warfare on slave-raiders, Gordon had to tax his powers of endurance almost to breaking-point. He wrote on 6th August :—

"I am nearly dead. To map the river for eight or ten miles I have had to walk, in pouring rain, through jungle some eighteen miles ; but it is done, at any rate, and I am quite sure no one will ever do it again. . . . It is terrible walking." And on 7th August he added :—

"We went a weary hot march of fifteen miles, the path being about three miles from the river which I have mapped in from the ravine in which it runs." The next day it was the same story, and he said :—

"We got over fifteen miles to-day—terrible work. Such a country of ravines and gullies. As we got in down came a deluge of rain, and we have all our things wet. Poor men, it is terrible work for them. No one knows the country. I have never had such fatigue. It has utterly prostrated me—a deadly coldness and emptiness at the stomach makes you feel inclined to drop. Fifteen drops of chlorodine, however, set me up. What misery ! and what for ?"

But the next day being bright he was again early on the trek and covered 15 miles, only to do 14½ the day after. He covered these latter 29½ miles by literally forcing his way through a pathless jungle. "It has been terrible work," are his own words, "for what with wild vines and convolvuli and other

[1] An unofficial letter to Khairy Pasha, 28th July, 1876, confirms Gordon's arrival at Magungo. Royal Egyptian Archives, Abdine Palace, Provisional File No. 8189.

creepers, you sometimes get bound hand and foot. I have had several severe falls, shaking my poor liver terribly."

Onward the Christian soldier marched, and on 13th September he recorded :—

"Got over twenty miles to-day. The mosquitoes in the morning were terrible on one's neck ; passing a tree a hornet flew out and struck me on the nape, and made me suffer in both shoulders. He had let the whole caravan—two hundred people—pass him, and selected me—the only white of the party. The heat is terrible ; however (D.V.), one-and-a-half day's march will complete my journey and then I turn northwards."

The next day he was able to write :—

"Got over seventeen miles ; the first six of which were through a dense jungle, with large creepers and fallen trees right across the path ; a complete entanglement with constant marshes and mosquitoes in myriads. I did not feel at all comfortable ; when we had gone four miles I heard a shout and a crash of loads thrown down, and then a volley about twenty yards in the rear of me. About ten or twelve of those irrepressible vermin had made an attack on the porters. They threw their *assegais* but only wounded one man. This sort of work is much more dangerous for me, humanly speaking, than regular war would be. These blacks can throw their lances fifty yards with a sure aim ; and, as the path is very narrow and the bush very dense, one is not comfortable. Besides which I have not overmuch confidence in the troops or officers with me. However (D.V.), it will be over to-morrow. I do not carry arms as I ought to do, for my whole attention is devoted to defending the nape of my neck from mosquitoes."

On 15th September Gordon turned back near Nyamyongo, having definitely settled the question raised by Dr. Schweinfurth's inquiry. No note of exultation crept into his letters. All that he did was to complete his survey by accurately recording where landing-places were to be found in that mass of papyrus and marsh which marks the bed of these stretches of the Victoria Nile. Having done this, he worked his way by steamer to Magungo, which lies at the point where the Victoria Nile joins Albert Nyanza, only to leave a day later for Chibero, one of the Lake ports. He recorded that :—

"The Lake was pretty calm, but the swell was perceptible ; in the evening we got rolled about a good deal, which showed me that it is not a very safe thing to be on this lake with inexperienced sailors, who do not know what rough weather is, and who may not moor the steamer well."

After having thus completed the exploration of the headwaters of the Nile :—

(1) By the discovery of Lake Ibrahim, through the untiring efforts of his American Chief of Staff, Lieutenant-Colonel Charles Chaillé-Long ;

(2) By the survey of that stretch of the White Nile lying between Duffli and Magungo, through the tenacity of his English *aides*, Chippendall and Watson ;

(3) By the circumnavigation of Lake Albert, carried through by his Italian right-hand man, Romolo Gessi ; and

(4) By his own tracing of the Victoria Nile from Magungo to Foweira, Gordon felt that the time had come for him to return to Cairo. He was worn out and needed rest. He had accomplished the impossible. No man who was not the very embodiment of perseverance, tenacity, and constancy could have inspired such zeal in others and have done so much himself.

As Gordon's steamer pushed its way through the White Nile the natives gave him a parting shower-bath of arrows. Two of the darts fell in the steamer, but nobody was hurt. By 29th October he had reached Khartoum. He was delighted to see English sparrows there. But the letter in which this is mentioned added :—

"I have been terribly attacked here by cavalry (sand flies), infantry (tortoises), and artillery (opal-coloured insects), and have suffered a good deal especially from the artillery whose attacks are something fearful. You feel the wounds for days ; and yet there are not many in action, but ill-naturedly they attack much ground. I feel sure if you were wounded by an 'opal' you would feel it for a week at least." [1]

On the day that Gordon thus wrote to his sister of his insect bites in such warlike tones, he said in another letter :—

"I have telegraphed to Cairo to say that I hope to come down for a time ; but I have not said anything about coming home yet. I want to see my way clear first. Comfort-of-Body—a very strong gentleman—says 'you are well ; you have done enough ; go home ; go home and be quiet and risk no more'. Mr. Reason says, 'What is the use of opening up more country to such a Government ? There is more now under their power than they will ever manage. . . .' But Mr. Something (I do not know what) says, 'Shut your eyes to what may happen in the future, leave that to God, and do what you think will open the country thoroughly to both Lakes. Do this, not for H.H., or for his Government, but do it blindly and in faith.' An oracle also says, 'Let your decision rest on the way H.H. is disposed ; if he desires you to stay, then stay ; but if he seems indifferent, then do not hesitate, but go away for good.'"

"Comfort-of-body," "Mr. Reason," "Mr. Something," and "the oracle" appear to have held a conference shortly before Gordon reached Luxor on his way north. The cause of the discussion was the lesson

[1] *Letters of General C. G. Gordon to his Sister*, p. 135.

taught by the fate of Ismail Pasha Sadik. Gordon's own pen can best tell what brought these four heads together. "When I was in Cairo in February, 1874," run the minutes of this meeting, "I was delayed in my departure by the fêtes given by H.H. in honour of his daughter's marriage with the son of the Finance Minister, Ismail Pasha Sadik, who was one of his four great Pashas or *Muchirs*, the others being Chérif Pasha, Tewfik Pasha (his son), and Khairi Pasha, the keeper of his seal. . . . When, a few days ago, I got to Korosko, I heard this: 'a dahabeyah, with the windows nailed up, had passed up with soldiers all around it and at the door of the cabin. Two colonels were on board, and twenty-five soldiers. It went on to Wady Halfa, where camels were waiting for the inmates of the dahabeyah.' Who do you think was in it but my friend Ismail Pasha Sadik? According to what I picked up, it appears that the Khedive himself drove down with him to the Cairo arsenal about 11th November; went over a steamer which had her steam up; went with him into the cabin, and, leaving the cabin, said to him '*Restez ici*'. Ismail Pasha Sadik tried to follow him but was prevented. The Khedive got into his carriage, and Ismail Pasha Sadik steamed off without a single thing or servant, up to Asswan, where he was put on board the dahabeyah and the windows nailed up. At Siout a single box of clothes, sent from Cairo, was put on board, and then the poor man was, with no servant or food, going on a journey which in all my strength and health I find a terrible one. He tried, by setting fire to the cushions of the dahabeyah, to smother himself; but the fire was smelt and put out, and since then eight soldiers watch him day and night. He is allowed no light or cigarette; he eats very little, has only bread and dates, and is ill. I do not vouch for the mode of his arrest, but this is what I heard."

After having thus described what happened to the Viceroy's famous *Mufattish* Gordon added :—

" How God works ! When I was going up to the Sudan he was all-powerful ; when I am coming down few would envy his lot. Poor man ! Poor man ! He was a Turk, had charge of the stables of Abbas Pasha and Said Pasha (the predecessors of the present Khedive), and was made Minister of Finance by the latter. He is believed to have made millions out of the loans. What an affair ! Everyone speaks in bated breath of it. I have (D.V.) made up my mind to serve H.H. no more."

Three days later Gordon wrote from Cairo :—

" I arrived here to-day at seven in the morning, twenty days from Khartoum. I called on Cherif Pasha, who is Minister for Foreign Affairs, and he was very civil ; but I do not think he relished telling the Khedive I would not stay in his service. It appears H.H. was quite right in exiling Ismail Sadik Pasha."

Gordon arrived in London on 24th December, 1876. He had oysters for lunch that day—such, at least, is the treat he had promised himself when he was still in Central Africa.

## Chapter IX

# RETURNS TO THE SUDAN

Gordon's Christmas holidays had barely ended when he received a telegram from the Khedive in French. It said :—

" My dear Gordon Pasha :

" Mr. Vivian has shown me the dispatch in which you directed him to inform me that circumstances do not permit you to return to Egypt. I was greatly surprised to hear this after our conversation at Abdine during which I flatter myself that I made you see the necessity of your continuing the work which we began together and asked you to take up your post in Egypt again. As we parted you said : '*Au revoir*.'

" I, therefore, can but attribute your telegram to that first impression of most natural satisfaction which you felt on finding yourself once again at home. I refuse to believe that a gentleman like Gordon desires for any reason whatsoever to retract the promise which he has given me. Therefore, my dear Gordon, I cannot consider your telegram and I shall expect you according to your promise.

" Your affectionate

" Ismail." [1]

This telegram is impregnated with the very personality of the Khedive. The most charming of men, he cast his spell over Gordon and based his appeal to him upon an argument which was unanswerable. He addressed himself to a gentleman's sense of honour. And in doing so Ismail gave indisputable proof of the sincerity of his campaign

[1] *Letters from General C. G. Gordon to his Sister*, p. 136.

against the slave trade. Had his devotion to the cause of slavery "Regulation" weakened in the very slightest, he had in Gordon's retirement an ideal opportunity to rid himself of an embarassing idealist. He knew in January, 1877, where his officer stood, and that he could be depended upon to wage a persistent, relentless, and sane warfare on slave *razzias*. He understood perfectly the objective envisaged by the soldier whom he trusted. It was because he was willing to adhere to the campaign destined, by the operation of economic laws, eventually to stamp out domestic slavery, that he insisted that Gordon should return to the Sudan.

On receipt of the Khedive's telegram Gordon put himself in the hands of the Commander-in-Chief of the British Army, His Royal Highness the Duke of Cambridge, who told him that it was his duty to yield to the Viceroy's insistence. He therefore telegraphed that he would go back to the Black Country on condition that he was made Governor-General of the entire Sudan. He had been so much thwarted in the best part of his work by Ismail Pasha Yacoub, the Governor-General of the Sudan, that he was reluctant to assume his old duties as long as the Khartoum officials, led by their chief, could continue to make his task supremely difficult. It was because he knew that if he asked for Ismail Pasha Yacoub's decapitation he would be placing the Khedive in a most embarassing position that Gordon preferred to tender his resignation.

Gordon, to quote his own words, "had successfully checked slave-driving in his own province, but he could do nothing to stop it in the extensive Sudan district where Khartoum is the headquarters of the system." [1] The mapping of the sources of the Nile was an important step in opening up Africa to civilization. Gordon was not blind to the importance

[1] Op cit., p. 203. All quotations in this chapter are from this volume.

of that contribution to the warfare upon slavery, but that bolt had been shot, and it was from Khartoum alone that its practical effects could be controlled. It was a great deal to ask of Ismail that he should oust an Egyptian from a post which was coveted by Egyptians. It meant calling upon the Khedive to affront the bureaucracy of his own country, and this in order to facilitate an attack on an institution which was part of the traditions of Islam. It was because Gordon was genuinely fond of the Khedive that he was reluctant to put his friend in a most invidious position.

As soon as Ismail caught the significance of Gordon's proposal he did not hesitate an instant. He took his decision with his eyes wide open, after having thus had a second golden opportunity to get rid of the anti-slavery champion. He did so, moreover, knowing that his stand would cost him the implacable hatred of the slave-trading aristocracy of his capital, the subtle hostility of the civil servants of his realm, and the latent animosity of the radical section of Islamic thought which looked upon Gordon's anti-slavery activities as an impingement upon a bulwark of Muslim life.

This was not all. Not only was Ismail Pasha Yacoub's head thrown into the basket, but Gordon's authority as Governor-General of the Sudan was enlarged and his territorial jurisdiction expanded. Following the lead given in 1874 when the Briton first came to Egypt, the monarch and he thrashed out matters together, and their understanding was put into the shape of a letter addressed by the Khedive to his officer. It bore date 17th February, 1877, and read :—

" Setting a just value on your honourable character, on your zeal, and on the great services that you have already done me, I have resolved to constitute the Sudan, Darfur, and the provinces of the Equator into one great province, and to place it under you as

Governor-General. As the country which you are thus to govern is so vast,[1] you must have beneath you three *wekils* (or deputy governors) : the first for the Sudan properly so called, the second for Darfur, and the third for the shores of the Red Sea and the Eastern Sudan. . . . There are two matters to which I would draw your attention : the first, the suppression of slavery, the second, the improvement of the means of communication.

"As Abyssinia, for a great distance, lies along the borders of the Sudan, I beg you when you are on the spot to look carefully into the state of affairs there ; and I give you power, should you think well, to enter into negotiations with the authorities of that Kingdom, to the end that a settlement of the matters in dispute between us and them may be arrived at."

It will be observed that the Khedive stressed "the suppression of slavery" and "the improvement of the means of communication". The latter, of course, was but a phase of the economic strangulation of slavery. But Gordon preferred to devote his attention, first of all, to straightening out Egypt's relations with Abyssinia. It was all very well to carry on an active fight against slavery, but internal reforms could not safely be attempted while frontiers were menaced. The relations between Abyssinia and Egypt were more than strained. In the interests of the accomplishment of his mission, Gordon accordingly hurried to Massawah in order to smooth out the Egypto-Abyssinian controversy.

He reached the town on 26th February. His observant eye soon discovered that the war had

[1] The length of the province was 1,640 miles, the breadth irregular but averaging about 660 miles. This territory is larger than the British Isles, Portugal, Spain, France, Belgium, Holland, and pre-War Germany and Austria all combined. At the present moment the flag of Egypt does not wave in undisputed sovereignty over an inch of this vast area. Its place is taken by the Anglo-Egyptian condominium, and by the banners of Italy, Belgium, Abyssinia, and England.

pressed very heavily on the Abyssinian frontier peasantry. The Ethiopian army was made up of savage and undisciplined troops, who, having no regular commissariat, had pillaged right and left, friend as well as foe. As this had gone on for nearly eighteen months the Abyssinian rural districts were nearly ruined and their inhabitants were anxious for peace. To make Gordon's work easier the Khedive made him a *Muchir* or Marshal. "So," observed the Governor-General, "I and the Duke of Cambridge are equals. He has sent me the uniform; the coat is worth £150, covered with gold lace."

Gordon failed to tell us whether the costly garment fitted him. He hastened, on the other hand, to describe his journey from Massawah to Keren. His route lay over an undulating desert country, skirting the Abyssinian mountains. On the night of 18th March he wrote :—

"There was a herd of dog-faced baboons sitting on the edge of the gorge watching us; they have a regular mane, and look as if they were tippetted. They grunt and bark in an extraordinary manner. The little ones have no tippets. As among us, constant quarrels go on among them, in which we hear the little ones yelp. Now that I am launched again into these solitudes, and with these extraordinary animals (the camels), I think over my position. I have sent to offer Johannis [1] four conditions and I hope to see Aloula, his great general, near Senheit. If I succeed there I go on to Khartoum, and thence, after a short stay, to Darfur, which is, they say, in revolt; but I do not believe it. Nothing could exceed the kindness of all the Khedive's dispatches. He has put Zeila, Berberah, and Harrar under me. 'Ask of me and I will give thee to the half of my kingdom.'" And elaborating this theme of the Khedive's confidence in him, Gordon added :—

[1] Johannes, King of Abyssinia.

"I feel as if I had naught to do with the Government. God must undertake the work, and I am for the moment used as His instrument. I am not one jot, or I suppose I must say, only very, very slightly elated by the honours and power given me ; and this elation arises from a feeling of satisfaction that H.H. has confidence in me. I think how many would be weighed down by this immense charge ; how they would shrink from accepting it without some help, for fear of their reputation. But for me I must give the question a thought. I feel sure of success ; for I do not lean on my own understanding, and He directs my path. The events of the future are all written, and are mapped out in all their detail for each of us. The Negro, the Arab, and the Bedwin's course—their meeting with me, etc.—is decreed. How can man claim praise for anything that he does ?"

When Gordon reached Keren, he was met by a large body of Abyssinian troops in the pay of Egypt. Four of their officers were jet black Sudanese who had served under Bazaine in Mexico. Among those who came forward to meet him was "a man with a very white face, dressed as the Abyssinians are, viz. in a sheet wrapped around him." Gordon could not make him out, and addressed him in French, receiving to his surprise, in the Queen's English, the reply : "I am an Irishman. My name is Macilvrey. I came out here with Consul Cameron." But neither black officers nor Irish Abyssinian subjects could help Gordon to any appreciable extent in his solution of the Egypto-Ethiopian muddle. The best thing that he could do was to mark time and keep matters from coming to a head. His new and vast province demanded his attention. He could not tarry in Abyssinia longer than was absolutely necessary to secure his frontiers from immediate attack.

As Gordon hurried across country to Khartoum he stopped for the day at a place called Katarif. "There was a great fête," according to his notes, " as we came into this settlement, and I noticed a very odd thing. There were a number of men in regular chain-shirts of links, with a gorget ; they reached to their feet. They had helmets of iron, with a nose-piece and fringe of chain-armour. They rode on horses which had a head and cheek defence, and were covered with a sort of quilt of different colours that reached down to their feet. It reminded me of the fêtes at Charlton, where they used to represent the ancient tournaments. All their swords were like the ancient Crusaders'—straight, two-handed, and cross-hilted. Evidently these people have not changed since the Crusades."

A letter written by Gordon while his mind was still dominated by this atmosphere of bygone days shows how strongly he was committed to slavery " Regulation " as opposed to " Prohibition ". He spoke of stopping slave-raids, but said nothing about suppressing domestic slavery. Here are his exact words. They bear the date of 22nd April, 1877 :—

" With terrific exertion, in two or three years' time, I may, with God's administration, make a good province, with a good army, and a fair revenue, and peace and an increased trade, and also have suppressed slave-raids ; and then I will come home and go to bed, and never get up again till noon every day and never walk more than a mile."

But while it was thus Gordon's ambition not to walk more than a mile a day, the very next morning he set out on a camel trek which averaged 45 miles a day, during which biting beetles in myriads made his life hideous. On the last night of this portion of the journey there were at least eighty large beetles on his night-shirt—pyjamas were unknown to his generation—when he lighted his candle.

As soon as Gordon reached Khartoum he began to elaborate his plans for slavery " Regulation ". His words deserve careful attention. They are a permanent memorial to his abiding common sense and the sanity of his idealism. Had the world at large grasped how Gordon felt upon these crucial subjects either British public opinion would not have forced the Gladstone Ministry to send him to the Sudan after the death of General Hicks or the English nation, having insisted upon his nomination, with full knowledge of his attitude towards slavery, would have compelled Her Majesty's Government to nominate Zobeir and thus, perhaps, have saved Gordon's life. Fate willed, however, that what he wrote on 4th May, 1877, should be known to but a small circle. The Anti-Slavery Society does not appear to have caught the significance of his words. Yet they were perfectly clear, and were published to the world in 1881. There is nothing open to misconstruction about such language as this :

" I have no easy task before me, but (D.V.) I have solved the difficulty. My scheme is not yet matured or approved. You have little idea of the great difficulty, and the many questions involved in it, viz. in domestic slavery. First, I have to disband some 6,000 Turks and *Bashi-Bazouks*, who are the frontier guards, and who must be replaced, for they let the caravans pass. You might as well order the sea to stop the caravans as these men. Now, think of disbanding suddenly 6,000 men. You must do it neatly : you must see to replace them with trustworthy men. Let me ask, who that had not the Almighty with him could do that ? I have the Almighty with me and I will do it. Second, consider the effect of harsh measures among an essentially Musulman population carried out brusquely by a Nazarene—measures which touch the pocket of everyone. Who that had not the Almighty with him would dare to do that ? I will do it. . . . As Solomon asked, I ask wisdom to govern this great people ; and not only will He give me it but all else besides. And why ? Because I value not the 'all besides'."

Having thus unbosomed himself, Gordon went on to say that :—

" I am quite as averse to slavery and even more so than most people. I show it by sacrificing myself in these lands, which are no Paradise. I have naught to gain in name or riches. I do not care what man may say. I do what I think is pleasing to my God, and, as far as man goes, I need nothing from anyone."

Gordon having thus planted his feet firmly upon the ground, thought of the Khedive and of the criticisms which had been directed against that Monarch. He wrote that :—

" The Khedive never had directly gained any revenue from slaves. I now hold his place here ; and I, who am on the spot with unlimited power, am able to judge how impotent he, at Cairo, is to stop the slave-trade. I can do it with God's help and I have the conviction He had destined me to do it ; for it was much against my will that I came here again."

After thus insisting that he had been chosen by the Almighty to stop the slave trade and after saying nothing about domestic slavery, Gordon continued :—

" It is only my firm conviction that I am only an instrument put in use for a time that enables me to bear up ; and in my present state during my long, long, weary rides I think my thoughts better and clearer than I should with a companion. Any European would be a disadvantage at present. They are not always wise, are apt to be too energetic, and would thus get me into scrapes. I have upset so many vested interests, that the only people I can count on are the *Ulema*, to whom I gave back all their ancient privileges, which had been taken away from them by Ismail Pasha Yacoub."

After having thus given proof of his keen psychological insight by making it to the interest of the intellectual and religious aristocracy of the capital to support his administration, Gordon gave further evidence of the practical trend of his mind by working out a scheme of slavery control which had nothing intolerant about it, but was, in reality, as well conceived a device for suffocating slavery and depriving it of vitality as the brain of man could have evolved. It was Machiavellian in its subtleness, simple in its mechanism, and innocuous in its form. It was just the type of life-extinguisher than an idealist who was primarily a realist was best fitted to invent. Here is what is said of a measure which reveals him as a statesman with the deftness of touch of a master legislator :—

" I hope I have solved the slave question, by recommending to H.M. Consul-General, Mr. Vivian, the following scheme : 1st, By enforcing the law which compels runaway slaves to return to their masters, except when cruelly treated. 2nd, By requiring masters to register their slaves prior to 1st January, 1878. 3rd, By not enforcing law No. 1 if not so registered. 4th, By stopping all registration of slaves after 1st January, 1878."

Gordon's own words show the idea which he had at the back of his mind when he proposed these rules. He said :—

" By this I prevent, after 1st January, 1878, any new slaves being considered as property, which they are rightly considered to be until either the masters are compensated or a term of years has elapsed—we here being in the same state now as the West Indian colonies were at the passing of the Abolition of Slavery Act."

It was, nevertheless, in dealing with foreign slave-owners that Gordon gave the outstanding example not only of his clearness of vision but of a shrewdness which amounts to canniness. He spoke of " the European holders of slaves in these parts ". But his worldly-wise sixth sense visualized more particularly those Christians and Jews—and, perhaps, a few

Muslims—not only of Egyptian birth but of Egyptian ancestry, who, established in Egypt for generations, managed then—and still manage—by some hocus-pocus to acquire foreign protection. These men, who to all outward appearance were Egyptians, who lived as Egyptians, and who had no stake in any land other than Egypt, nevertheless had foreign passports, and were, technically speaking, what the French call *ressortissants* of foreign nations. Blended into the local landscape, they were not amenable to local laws, and grew rich by fattening upon the special privileges which their position made available to them. Such a manifest anomaly filled Gordon with disgust, and he went in search of these parasites. His first Khartoum letter thus deals with them :—

"I also meditate an attack upon the European holders of slaves in these parts. If they declare that they are foreign subjects I mean to liberate their slaves ; if they say they are Egyptian subjects I shall tax them heavily. Europeans come here, hold slaves, cultivate the ground and pay no taxes. I won't have this." Then, with that quickness of perception which always distinguished him from his fellows, he foresaw that the Anti-Slavery Society interests would probably criticize him for not taking even more severe measures. He therefore showed that he was prepared to brave such attacks, fully conscious of their driving force, for he added :—

"You will think I might do more. I cannot. Slaves are, to all intents and purposes, property until their owners are compensated, or till a certain number of years has elapsed. We cannot compensate, but we can decree their liberation after a certain number of years."

Gordon, after having thus defended himself, consolidated his position by insisting once more upon his fetish. It was that "Slave-hunting must be put down". Just as Cato of old kept ever repeating "*Carthago delenda est*", so did the Scotsman always insist that "slave-hunting must be put down. But," he continued in this memorable letter, "when men see that they have no more hold over slaves acquired after 1st January, 1878, they will not buy them. At any rate, slaves acquired after that date can run away, and the Government will not force them to go back. I consider this will succeed."

Gordon had been greatly impressed by Ismail's trust in him. Knowing that the procedure outlined in this letter meant the eventual death-knell of domestic slavery in Egypt, he thought that it was but fair to the Khedive to add :—

"I feel that I have been most unjust to the Khedive, knowing, as I now do, the great difficulties in abolishing slavery. That the question of domestic slavery is no easy one, the debates on the abolition of slavery in our colonies will show. There it was a question of colonies only ; here it is a question of home interests. You are no doubt better versed than I am in the history of our Abolition of Slavery. Men possessed slaves ; to liberate them without compensation was ruin to the owners, and our people, feeling that to do so would be robbery, did compensate them. Now in our case England dealt only with a colony. The question did not affect us directly ; but still she gave compensation. How different is this case ! Here slavery abolition touches everyone. How can you deal with it so as to avoid a servile war or a rising of the people ? You must either pay compensation or you must allow a term of years in order that slavery may die out."

It was a statesman who wrote these lines. Broadness of vision, boldness of conception, and deftness of touch are their predominant characteristics. But modesty and self-effacement—Christianity in its purest sense—were the touchstones of Gordon's very nature. His pen, accordingly, glided easily from such expressions of statecraft to the words of a man of God. He wrote :—

" I have an enormous province to look after, but it is a great blessing to me to know that God has undertaken the administration of it and it is His work, not mine. If I fail, it is His will ; if I succeed it is His work. Certainly, He has given me the joy of not regarding the honours of this world, and to value my union with Him above all things. May I be humbled to the dust and fail, so that He may glorify Himself. The greatness of my position only depresses me, and I cannot help wishing that the time had come when He will lay me aside and use some other worm to do His work. You have reached your happy eventide. I would that the head of my life-day was over, but He will aid me, and not suffer me again to put down anchors in this world."

# Chapter X

# INSPECTS DARFUR

After he had fixed the broad outlines of his anti-slavery campaign, Gordon looked round for a moment in order to get his domestic bearings. He found that he was " guarded like an ingot of gold ", and that the etiquette of the Palace was most irksome. " If I get up," he wrote, " everyone does the same. It is a misery, and I now feel what work princes must go through. I take advantage of their ignorance to say to the *sheikhs* ' Now, old bird, it is time for you to go ' ; they are delighted."

While Gordon was endeavouring to learn the ropes of Egyptian etiquette, the sister of Ismail Pasha Yacoub, his predecessor, brought home to him the plain fact that Oriental women are powers in the land—or, at all events, in the household. It seems that the Pasha took his removal with fairly good grace, but that when his sister heard the news " she broke all of the windows of the Palace—some hundred and thirty—and cut the divan in pieces out of spite." [1]

Gordon does not tell us what he did to get this belligerent lady out of the Sudan. He says nothing of having had the windows put in order. If he did it certainly took him months to do so, as it is very improbable that there were then 130 panes of glass in the entire Sudan. He passed straight on to more important problems, and records that he did away with flogging and arranged that anyone who had a grievance could drop a petition in a kind of lion's mouth rigged up at the entrance to his palace. He

[1] Hill, op. cit., p. 230. Unless otherwise indicated, all statements of fact in this chapter are based upon this work.

also made immediate arrangements to leave for his inspection of the province of Darfur.

Gordon drew up for himself a schedule of ninety-seven days of camel-riding. He felt that the exercise would do him good, for, as he expressed it :—

" I am a sufferer from the courash of Baker, a kind of eczema. It is very trying, just as if you were being bitten by mosquitoes all night. Baker says that it comes from the water. It attacks the extremities—the itching is intolerable at night. Truly this country is no Paradise ! Suffer as people may in England, it is one comfort that those who are well do not suffer. Here, whether you are well or ill, you have enough physical sufferings to make you realize your feebleness."

Gordon had barely started on his long journey when he felt it his duty to record that " the Khedive is exceedingly kind to me in every way, and I will use my very life to aid him ". And after having thus renewed his expressions of esteem for his chief, the Governor-General brought out the fact that he had been mistaken in assuming, when on his way to Khartoum, that Darfur was not in revolt. His more recent information was that not only was the province up in arms but that the garrisons of Fascher, Dara, and Kolkol were besieged. Some two years later Gordon thus laconically described the situation :—

" You know all about the Darfur affair, when Hassan Pasha had some 16,000 men and *I relieved him* with 300."

But if his presence played a preponderating part in putting down the revolt in Darfur, he had his hands full when wrestling with the slavery problem as there presented. He thus summed up the situation :—

" The immense difficulty there is in causing this slave traffic to cease has now come home to me. I wish one of the Anti-Slavery Society, capable of understanding the question, would come here and give me a solution of it. I have complete power—civil as well as military. No one would say a word if I put one or ten men to death ; and therefore I must be considered entirely responsible if the slave-trade goes on ; but here is my position. Darfur and Kordofan are peopled by huge Bedwin tribes under their own *sheikhs*, who are rather more than semi-independent. The country, for the most part, is a vast desert, with wells few and far between, some of which are only known to these tribes. Some of these tribes can put from 2,000 to 6,000 horse or camel-men into the field ; and a revolt, as I know to my cost, is no small thing in such a country. Now these tribes raid on the Negro tribes to the south, or else exchange cloth for slaves with the Bedwin tribes beyond even the pretended boundary of Egypt. The slaves thus enter the Egyptian territory four or five at a time. Nothing could prevent their coming in a hundred at a time, for we have no range of sentinels on our border like the Cossacks of Russia."

We have no difficulty in grasping what was running through Gordon's mind as he wrote this report. No better proof of the subordination of the idealist to the realist in him need be adduced than such language as has just been quoted. It is obvious that he recognized the practical difficulties with which he was confronted in fighting slavery in Darfur and Kordofan. Had he been an Abolitionist in the sense in which the equally high-minded Lloyd Garrison, the equally high-principled Wendell Philipps, or the equally high-spirited John Brown, were abolitionists, he would have refused to accept the realities of life, and, by attempting the impossible, would have paved the way for letting hundreds of slaves into Egypt in the vain hope of keeping out a paltry half-dozen. He had no great industrial "North" and no inexhaustible supplies of Irish and German immigrants whom he could turn into soldiers to fight for the cause of human liberty. He therefore looked the facts in the face and complacently accepted a leak in a pipe as something infinitely preferable to an avalanche.

After having emphasized the radical difference between " the slave caravans of a hundred at a time " and " little caravans of four or five at a time ", Gordon set his jaw as fire flashed from his soulful eyes, and wrote, with a ring of sincerity that carries conviction :

" I therefore say that the large caravans, with the *sheybas*,[1] will cease, and I consider have ceased ; but that it is impossible to prevent slaves passing down in small numbers with the petty merchants ; and I do not think it will ever be prevented until the frontier of Egypt extends up to the Negro frontier—if then."

A letter written by Gordon to his sister on 7th June, 1877, shows that in his heart of hearts he was convinced that by putting down the revolt in Darfur, he had really injected the virus of dissolution into the octopus of slavery. In fact, in his letter to his beloved Augusta, he spoke of " the deathblow I think slavery has received ", and he continued in a tone so typical of his spiritual exaltation that his words are almost a portrait of his soul :—

" It would be a long story to tell of this accomplishment, and you will know it more completely in a future life. Praying for the people whom I am about to visit gives me much strength, and it is wonderful *how something seems already to have passed between us* when I meet with a chief (for whom I have prayed) for the first time. . . . I have really no troops with me, but I have the Shekinah, and I do like trusting to Him and not to man. Remember, unless He gave me the confidence and encouraged me to trust Him, I could not feel it, so I consider in this confidence I have the earnest of success." [2]

[1] A *sheyba* was a heavy yoke that was fastened to the neck of slaves, writes Dr. Schweinfurth in *Darkest Africa*, vol. ii, p. 414.

[2] *Letters of General C. G. Gordon to his Sister*, p. 140.

Had Gordon been a sectarian, in the sense of adhering so uncompromisingly to a cult as to refuse to see good in any form of worship that was not his own, the intensity of his faith as portrayed in this letter might possibly have tended to warp his liberalism and to convert a zealot into a bigot. The line of demarcation between an intensely religious man and a blind partizan is sometimes—though far from always—shadowy. What made Gordon's spiritual uplift so all-compelling in its influence was not only the nobility of his outlook upon life but the ingrained fairness of the man. One incident will suffice to drive this point home. It shows that while Muslims looked upon him as being a militant Christian *marabout* they loved him for his religious convictions. It appears, writes Gordon, that :—

" When the Egyptians seized the country they took the mosque here (at Dara in the Darfur district) for a powder magazine. I had it cleaned out and restored for worship, and endowed the priests and the crier, and had a great ceremony at the opening of it. This is a great *coup*. They blessed me and cursed Zobeir Pasha who took the mosque from them."

There was practical politics in Gordon's act. This is obvious from his reference to his " great *coup* ". But the next lines of the same letter show that the political strategist had a heart which rose above mere tactical exigencies. It continues :—

" To me it appears that the Mussulman worships God as well as I do, and is as acceptable, if sincere, as any Christian. What caused the lot to fall on those who occupy the ' Hill ' to be born in Christian lands, while others are born in Mussulman lands ? "

It was such statements as these, and not considerations of expediency, that won for Gordon that secure place in the hearts of the Muslim blacks which enabled him, all alone in the Sudan, to hold his power for month after month in the face of the Mahdi.

And the mention of that *Sheikh*, who finally wore down the Scotsman's almost superhuman resistance, calls attention to the fact that his next letter begins with the ominous words : " Still waiting ! "

Such seems ever to have been his lot in the Sudan. Had he been superstitious, instead of being merely a believer in Predestination, this continuous, never-ending waiting would have driven home to him the lesson, that the gods were seeking to warn him that one day he would wait in vain and find a bloody grave because " too late " had already been inscribed in the ledger of his life. His exact words on 24th July, 1877, were :—

" Still waiting ! I expect the troops which went out on an expedition in two days' time. I have no news from Fascher or from Shaka, and am worn to a shadow with doing nothing for days and days."

Three days later Gordon heard of his expeditionary force. It had had a two days' battle. It had run into a flock of Gallabats or " petty merchants on donkeys. It is they that take the slaves from those who make the raids. They are the vultures."

Notwithstanding all that Gordon had said in June as to the days of large slave caravans being over, this expedition captured 210 slaves. The Governor-General was no doubt greatly surprised to have received this emphatic proof that he had been too optimistic. His notes fail to disclose how he felt. All he remarked was that :—

" These 210 are either slaves which were owned by the tribe, or else these are Furs, i.e. natives of Darfur. If they are Furs then they are Mussulmans and ought to be set free ; if they are slaves who have been possessed by the vanquished tribes then they need not be given back."

Gordon's practical mind was in a quandary. His heart was rent in twain. " It is a sad sight to see the poor little starved creatures looking so wistfully at one," he remarked, only to add "what can I do? I could only address the Arabs with me, and tell them that if they took Mussulmans as slaves they did it against the command of the Qurân; and I took sand and washed my hands in order that they might see I put on them the responsibility of the decision. What could I do? Poor souls, I cannot feed or look after them. I must leave it to God, who will arrange all in kindness. . . . I declare solemnly that I would give my life willingly to save the sufferings of these people; and if I would do this, how much more does He care for them than such imperfection as I am."

Gordon played his cards admirably. Notwithstanding his appearance of confiding innocence and of trustful simplicity, he was a reader of the hearts of men. He understood how to make the sons of the desert yield to his wishes without seeking vainly to impose his authority. When he imitated Pontius Pilate and washed his hands, his eyes were riveted upon those who surrounded him. He drove home the significance of his gesture in a way which carried, not a command from a Nazarene, but a message from Allah. He was therefore able to record later on the same day that:—

"I am glad to say my Arabs have decided on letting the captives go free. They went, 235 of them, arm-in-arm like a long string. They did this to prevent the vultures, the Gallabats, taking them as slaves, which they wanted to do. They were some poor little wretches, only stomachs and heads with *antennæ* for legs and arms. I wonder whether life is to them as precious as it is to us. The enormous stomachs are from grass feeding."

It would seem from what Gordon wrote at this time that word had drifted through to him that the Anti-Slavery Society was not enthusiastic about him. This caused him to say that he would like to receive the publications of that body and to comment that "people think you have only to say the word and slavery will cease".

"Of course, I must let time soften the ill effects of what is written against me in the papers, on account of my purchasing the slaves now in the possession of individuals in order to obtain the troops necessary to put down slavery," he wrote, "I need troops—how am I to get them but thus? If I do not buy these slaves, unless I liberate them at once, they still remain slaves, while when they are soldiers they are free from that reproach. I cannot liberate them from their owners without compensation, for fear of a general revolt. I cannot compensate the owners and then let the men go free, for they would only be a danger."

Had Gordon wanted to do so he could have added a still stronger argument in support of his point of view. He might have quoted an official letter written on 16th November, 1865, by Chérif Pasha, then Egyptian Minister of Foreign Affairs, to Charles Hale, Diplomatic Agent and Consul-General of the United States of America at Cairo. The Egyptian statesman said that:—

"In virtue of a principle made applicable as long ago as the reign of Muhammad Ali all slaves enrolled under the flag become free with rights of freedom."[1]

Gordon had, in all probability, never seen this particular letter, but he knew the principle enunciated in it. Yet he feared that his close friends would be annoyed by the attacks of the Anti-Slavery Society, for he said:—

"I want you to understand this, for I doubt not people will write and say: (1) 'Colonel Gordon buys slaves for the Government'; (2) 'Colonel Gordon lets the Gallabats take slaves.' To No. 1 I say: 'True, for I need the purchased slaves, to put down the slave-dealers, and to break up their semi-independent bands.' To No. 2 I say: 'True, for I dare not stop

[1] Records American Consulate, Alexandria, Egypt, No. 758, 1865.

it to any extent for fear of adding to my enemies, before I have broken up the nest of slave-dealers at Shaka.' I should be mad if I did. We should not, if at war with Russia, choose that moment to bring about any change affecting the social life of the Hindoos. The slaves I buy are already torn from their homes, and whether I buy them or not, they will, till twelve years have elapsed, remain slaves. After twelve years they will be free, according to the Treaty. It is not as if I encouraged raids for the purpose of getting slaves as soldiers. But people will, of course, say: 'By buying slaves you increase the demand and indirectly encourage raids.' I say: 'Yes, I should do so, if after buying them, I still allowed the raids to continue, which, of course, I shall not do."

We see from Gordon's language that, while he was intensely religious, he had the combative spirit of Saint Paul. There was nothing of the retiring Saint John in him. He had the energy, the fire, the militancy of a Crusader. But behind all his combativeness loomed ever the constructive genius which he had inherited from the race of hard-headed merchants who made up his maternal ancestry. He looked at every problem from the point of view of a practical man of affairs, however mystical may have been his religious reaction to it. So, while ever conscious of the ethical and economic aspects of the slavery question, he never ceased to accentuate the routine, humdrum, matter-of-fact phase of the issue. He was in the wilds of Africa. He was not seated in a comfortable armchair before a cosy fire studying an abstract problem. He was face to face with a living reality which translated into terms of flesh and blood, of men and women, the theories which read so well in print, sound so convincing in the pulpit, and make such admirable propaganda for home consumption. He accordingly wrote:—

"This slave question is most troublesome and difficult to manage. A number of the slaves who were taken in the last raid made near here on the sly by the Gallabats refuse to go back, for they find they are better fed with their new masters than they were with their old."

What was Gordon to do when faced with such a situation? The London Anti-Slavery Society had possibly never envisaged an issue of this kind. Yet to the man on the spot it represented a concrete, routine, pressing problem. His own words applied to a similar subject should be cited. They show that there was nothing impulsive, headstrong, or whimsical about Gordon. They demonstrate, on the contrary, that he carefully pondered all the many sides of his mission and that he took his decisions promptly not only because he was a soldier but also because the subject suddenly presented to him was, in many cases, one which he had earnestly considered for days and days. There was something of the Daniel Boone in Charles George Gordon. The Kentucky pioneer was always repeating "Be sure you're right, then go ahead". Such was invariably the line of conduct followed by the Scotsman. Not caprice or fleeting fancy, but deep thought and settled convictions were the spark that put his dynamic personality into action. The words that follow bring this out:—

"One thing troubles me. What am I to do with the three or four thousand slaves, women, and children, that are now at Shaka if we take it? I cannot take them back to their own country. I cannot feed them. Solve this problem for me. I must let them be taken by my auxiliaries, or by my soldiers or the merchants. There is no help for it. If I let them loose they will be picked up, in every direction, for an escaped slave is like an escaped sheep—the property of him who finds him or her. One must consider what is best for the individual himself, not what may seem best to the judgment of Europe." And after thus approaching the consideration of the impending problem from a point of view which probably had never struck an Abolitionist, Gordon went on to say : " It is the slave who suffers, not Europe."

It is clear, then, that the Governor-General's heart was in the right place. It was attuned, not to the tempo of a *solfeggio*, but to the gamut of the scale of humanity. His intellect caught the message of his love for mankind and inspired him to write : " There is not the slightest doubt but that if I let the slaves be taken by my soldiers, by the tribes, or by the Gallabat merchants, instead of there being a cessation of the slave caravans there will be a great increase of them for two or three months, and a corresponding outcry against me. But, at any rate, the slaves will go by frequented routes, and will not die on the road. I could let the matter solve itself, i.e. let the slaves stay as they are, and let the owners run the cordon as they best can ; but I should thus cause the slaves to undergo great suffering, and perhaps cause the death of one-half of them. Shall I be cowardly and do this, for fear of what ill-informed Europe may say ? "

Anyone who knows Gordon has no difficulty in divining his answer to this question. His reply has no apologetic note in it. It is that of a fighter, of a combatant who is angry but whose ire is that of righteous indignation, kept under control by a mind which rises above passion. Here are his words :—

" No, I will legitimize their transport and let them say what they will. There are the slaves ; around them the hungry vultures, and only one man to protect them, and that man has no means of feeding them or of sending them back to their friends. Had I a strong man to help me, who could stay at Shaka and see each slave personally, and ask him his wish, it would be better ; but that man is not forthcoming, and there is only one man who could do it, viz. Burton " (the African traveller).

Gordon then forgot he was the Governor-General,

and sought to place himself in Burton's shoes. We read :—

"Strange to say, these wretched slaves have their likes and their dislikes. Some would sooner go with the Gallabat merchants, some with the tribes, and some with the soldiers. They are of different minds. Even if they could, they would not go back to their desolate homes ; if they did, they would be attacked by more powerful tribes, and be made slaves to them. Their own country is probably a desert, their people dispersed, and the land run over with weeds. It would be a long time ere they could get their crops again."

And while thus considering what he should do when the responsibility of dealing with so many slaves should be thrust upon him, Gordon looked further into the horoscope of the future and observed :—

"It makes one wink to think how on earth the slaves of all of these Bedwin tribes are to be freed in twelve years! Who is to free them? Will Great Britain? When the trees hear my voice and obey me then will the tribes liberate their slaves. The only thing the Government can do is to prevent their getting new ones."

## CHAPTER XI

# FINISHES HIS INSPECTION

WHILE Gordon was thus meditating what he should do when in possession of Shaka, he had other problems of a nature which called for more immediate decision. His cavalry returned one afternoon bringing in some prisoners, among them a well-known chief, who, overcome by thirst, had surrendered. The Governor-General pardoned the rebel, and sent him to tell his tribesmen to give up their spears and come and drink.

The swearing of the forgiven leader to fealty was somewhat curious. A Qurân was sent for and a clean cloth. The holy book of Islam must not be touched by " unclean " hands, though it came out of the insect-infested breast-pocket of one of the True Believers. It was opened, and a passage read, which the penitent repeated. He then washed his hands in the sands of the desert, recited some other words, and the ceremony was finished.

The night which followed was very windy. The gale drove a number of scorpions into Gordon's tent. He managed to kill six of them, two of which were 5 inches long. It is obvious that his sleep was disturbed, between the wind whistling without and scorpions running about within. But the hemmed-in capital, Fascher, summoned him to hurry forward, and he lost no time getting under way. After an abominable march through 30 miles of quagmire, he reached his objective on 18th August as darkness fell. He had 150 men with him. He relieved 600, and two days later, after a most fatiguing ride, he arrived at Kario. This time a thunderstorm welcomed his coming. His camp was a veritable pigsty, and misery stalked around him. Political unrest had played its part in bringing about this poverty. Gordon hoped that by re-establishing the rule of law and order he could help to alleviate the lot of those who surrounded him.

Having done everything that could be done to that end, the Governor-General made his way to Dara. He covered the distance of about 85 miles in a day and a half. About 7 miles from that place, while still in the desert, the expedition ran into a swarm of flies which annoyed Gordon and his camel so much that he annihilated space and outran the others. " Upwards of 300 flies were on the camel's head," he wrote, " and I was covered with them. I suppose that the queen fly was among them. If I had no escort of men I had a large escort of these flies. I came on my people like a thunderbolt. As soon as they had recovered, the salute was fired. My poor escort ! Where is it ? Imagine to yourself a single, dirty, red-faced man on a camel ornamented with flies—arriving in the divan all of a sudden. The people could not believe their eyes." [1]

The Orient revels in pomp and solemnity. It is dangerous, in those parts, for a potentate to descend from his pedestal. But Gordon, of course, was above all ordinary rules. He was *sui generis* or, as the Arabs say, *foq el kanun*—above the law. But it is hazardous to press matters too far. The Scotsman was too good a psychologist to attempt to do so. Under the pressure of these flies he had brushed aside conventionality and had ridden pell-mell into Dara. His own pen can best describe how he followed up this unceremonious entry.

" No dinner after my long ride, but a quiet night, forgetting my miseries. At dawn I got up, and putting on the golden uniform the Khedive gave me, went out to see my troops, and then mounted my horse, and

[1] Hill, op. cit., p. 271. All other citations in this chapter, unless otherwise stated, are from this work.

with an escort of my robber *Bashi-Bazouks*, rode out to the camp of the other robbers three miles off. I was met by the son of Zobeir—a nice-looking lad of twenty-two years—and rode through the robber bands. There were about 3,000 of them—men and boys. I rode to the tent in the camp; the whole body of chiefs were dumbfounded at my coming among them. After a glass of water I went back, telling the son of Zobeir to come with his family to my divan."

It took sheer nerve on Gordon's part for him to beard this bandit chieftain in his den. The name of Zobeir will subsequently play a large part in our story, as we trace the tragic end of the Governor-General. For the moment, suffice it to say that that chief and his son were powers in the land, whereas Gordon was a lone white in a sea of blacks, and had nothing to fall back upon in the long run other than his strength of character and the prestige of his great name.

"But," as Gordon himself put it, "they all came, and sitting in a circle I gave them in choice Arabic my ideas: that they meditated revolt; that I knew it; and that they should now have my ultimatum, viz. that I would disarm them and break them up. They listened in silence and they went off to consider what I had said. They have just now sent me a letter stating their submission and I thank God for it. They have pillaged the country all around, and I cannot help it. I feel very sorry for the poor people, for they were my allies at Wadar, and through their absence with me their possessions were exposed to the attacks of these scoundrels. What misery! But the Higher than the Highest regardeth it and can help them. I cannot."

It appears, however, that Zobeir's son sought to break his plighted troth. And, to add to his deceit, he asked for robes to be given him, such as were generally bestowed as a mark of favour. Gordon flatly refused to comply, and told the young man some very plain truths. Those who were present were completely taken aback by such frankness. "The chiefs are disgusted with me for not using treachery," is the way Gordon summed up the situation, "but I will not do it *coûte que coûte*. Even putting aside moral considerations, *it never pays*."

Gordon thus held his own at a moment when he had not the least confidence in his officers or in his men. He feared that he would have to make his "Absalom", Zobeir's son, a prisoner, together with his three adherents, for "the little chap is very irate—in fact furious". But the youthful traitor preferred to decamp. Four chiefs and 1,400 men accompanied him to Shaka. Ten of his lieutenants and 1,500 of his soldiers refused to follow him and adhered to Gordon's colours. The net result was that the young rebel saw that he had over-reached himself. He accordingly wrote the Scotsman a letter which the latter thus summarizes :—

"He was my son (undutiful enough I thought) and I his father, etc., and would I give him a government? I have replied to him that I am glad to hear he gives in, but that until he either goes to Cairo to salute His Highness or else shows some other proof of his fidelity, I would never give him a place, even if refusing it costs me my life."

This summary refusal to trust a man who had broken his word brings out the fact that Gordon proclaimed :

"I want in each Governor three qualities : (1) Courage ; (2) Honesty ; and (3) Kindness. I find men with No. 1 who lack No. 2 and No. 3. I find men—few, it is true—with Nos. 2 and 3 who lack No. 1. I cannot find one man with the three qualities. No. 1 is never very prominent."

But if Zobeir's son failed to get the office, he was, nevertheless, forced to bite the dust. This caused Gordon, as he approached Shaka, to write :—

"There are some 6,000 more slave-dealers in the

interior, who will obey me now that they have heard that Zobeir's son and other chiefs have given in. You can imagine what a difficulty there is in dealing with all these armed men. . . . Would you shoot them? Have they no rights? Are they not to be considered? Had the planters no rights? Did not our Government allow slave-trading? Do you know that cargoes of slaves came into Bristol harbour in the time of our fathers?"

We have here but one more proof of how hard Gordon strove to understand the other man's point of view. All that he asked in return was that his attitude towards slavery might be grasped. It was, as he expressed it at this same date, 11th September, 1877:—

"I will do what I like and what God in His Mercy may direct me to do about domestic slavery; but I will break the neck of slave-raids even if it cost me my life."

With such sentiments inspiring him, Gordon entered "the slave-nest Shaka". "Only one foreigner—an American named Mason—had ever been there before." Gordon had already made up his mind regarding the treatment he would mete out to the slavers. He found the town "full of slaves" and left there saying: "I hope that the Shaka business is satisfactorily disposed of, but looking at the mass of slaves there it will be a long time ere that work is ended." And as he wended his way toward El Obeid, he could not help smiling as he wrote:—

"*Entre nous* I think I am conveying from Shaka to Obeid a caravan of slaves. I cannot help it. One man says that the seven women who are with him are his wives! I cannot disprove it. There are a a number of children—the men say that they are their offspring! When you have got the ink which has soaked into blotting-paper out of it, then slavery will cease in these lands."

The practical difficulty which confronted Gordon

in his fight against slavery is exemplified by an incident which happened to him the day after he ran into this man with seven wives. Here is his version of it :—

" This morning I came on a caravan of slaves, which is accompanying me—some sixty or eighty men, women, and children chained. What am I to do? If I release them who could care for them or feed them? Their homes were too far to send them to; so I decided to make the slave-merchant take off their chains as scandalous, and then to leave them with him. He, looking at them as valuable cows, will look well after them. Don Quixote would have liberated them, and made an attempt to send them back some forty days' march, through hostile tribes, to their homes—which they would never have reached. The slave-merchant had done no harm in buying them, for it is permissible in Egypt, and he had not taken them from their homes. The only remedy is to stop slave-raids on the frontier; and this will only be done when I have put the slave-traders' *seribas* under my own people. You must stop it at its source. Once the slaves have left the source it is useless to try. The frontier is the place on which to stop it."

The same letter which tells us that Gordon was not a Don Quixote but a strong-minded Briton gives us also an insight into certain of the hardships which became part of his life :—

" The water on the way consists of pools of rain. Caravan A comes and drinks and bathes in it; then Caravan B comes and does the same; then Caravan C, and so on. It is dreadful; but I have given up all ideas of this sort. I have no pleasure in eating or drinking and do both to keep myself alive; and, with these ideas, it makes little matter if the water is a solution of blacks or not." He drew a moral from all this. Only a born optimist could have written :—

" If I were fastidious, I should be as many weeks as I am now days on the road; I gain a great deal of *prestige* by these unheard-of marches. It makes the people fear me much more than if I were slow. I consider that the camel, though wonderful in endurance, has been overrated in this respect ; they cannot go ten days consecutively without being considerably distressed. Six days is the average for good camels."

Gordon was, perhaps, unfair to " the ships of the desert ". He was no ordinary man. The reputation of camels was and is based upon their adaptability to the use of ordinary mortals, not to the demands of such an exceptional person as the Governor-General. Yet on 23rd September this human machine with a heart of gold was forced to record :—

" I am tired out to-day—what with the camel riding, the troubles of the government and the incessant work. No Sundays ever come to me now ; it is every, every day the same thing—work from morning to night, either on camel or in my tent. I calculate that when I get to Obeid I shall have ridden on camels 2,300 miles since I left Massawah in March (that is to say in six months) ; and what a great many more I have to ride ere I finish this year." Such a feat of endurance performed under the most trying climatic and physical conditions once more brings out the fact that Lytton Strachey and Sir Richard Burton were absolutely mistaken in inferring that Gordon was a periodical and secret drinker. No man could have lived through what he did who was not temperate and abstemious. He was forty-three years of age when he gave such proofs of resistance, and he had already spent many years out of England.

Gordon appeared, however, to attach no importance to his exceptional stamina. He mentions the subject merely incidentally. He passes on to speak once again of slavery, remarking that :—

" There is no doubt I could stop the slave-gangs

in one way—viz. by telling the tribes to capture and keep all gangs that pass. They would soon do it, but would use no discrimination and would plunder everyone ; besides which I think the slaves would prefer servitude with the Arabs of the town to servitude with the Bedwins."

We see that Gordon kept continually harping on the same theme. He wanted to do the right thing by the slaves. He thought in terms of men and women, not of theories and institutions. Here is a story that he tells :—

" When I was in my hut at Edowa a big black woman crept in. I did not see her come in, but heard her sobs. She could not stay with the Bedwin she was with : so I sent for the man whose slave she was, gave her thirty dollars, and made her give them to him. She then chose another master and had her way. She was a huge woman and had a nice black face."

Another incident illustrates the same point. It is best told in Gordon's own words :—

" When nearing the end of our long weary march I noticed a very small black boy in the path who could not get out of it. As he looked quite a scrap to be left thus in the road, I immediately suspected something ; and on going on I came across a lad with a chain of slaves, and I noticed a number more chained together under some trees. My little friend, who had been put on the croup of my clerk's camel, denied belonging to the slave-party ; but it was evident that he did so, and that the slavers had pressed their march when they heard I was coming, and the little chap was left behind. . . . Well, I got the whole gang together and told them to go on to the watering place ; for, poor wretches, they would otherwise have been kept there in the sun out of my way. Now, what was I to do ? I could not with the three men undertake the convoy of them to Obeid ; and when there how much better off would they be ? The little chap, perched up behind my clerk, said to him :

'Give my master a piece of cloth for me. I should like to stay with you.' Poor little soul! He valued himself at a dollar, which is the price of the piece of cloth he named. He said this in quite a 'chirpy' way, as if he did not think anyone would give more for him. I shall pay for him."

We are not told how much was given for "the little chap". All that we know is that the deal was made. "The little boy is like a spider with legs like a fly," is Gordon's description of the child. "He is about seven years of age. He has just come up to return me a biscuit of which he does not approve; he wants some *dhoora*, which I have not got." The exigent boy then fades out of the picture, and Gordon, with merely a period to mark the change of subject, goes on to say:—

"I have not yet made up my mind what to do about the slaves and the slave-question; but I mean to stop, and that at once, the slave-markets at Katarif, Gallabat, and Shaka; next, I must prevent the raids on the black tribes near the Bahr Gazelle, for which I have given orders."

But while thus shaping his policy Gordon recognized the fact that it is public opinion even more than the strong arm of the law which enforces legislation. He was definitely committed to a programme of slavery "Regulation". He was alive to the outstanding difficulties of his task, for he wrote:—

"In all previous emancipations either there has been a strong government to enforce obedience, or a majority of the nation wished it. Here, in this country, there is not one who wishes it, or who would aid it even by advice. I know there are many who would willingly see the sufferings of the slave-gangs cease and also the raids on the Negro tribes; but there they would stop. Besides this, the tenure of slaves is the A B C of life here to rich and poor; *no one* is uninterested in the matter."

When Gordon spoke of " here " he referred to the Sudan and, more particularly to the Province of Darfur. He meant to, and did, bring out that the economic existence of the Black Country was tied to the chariot-wheels of slavery. This fact, thus emphasized by Gordon, should constantly be borne in mind. It explains the financial unrest which the Mahdi capitalized in 1881 and in the years which followed. It shows that the religious rising which drove Gordon to his grave was born of economic laws rather than of sectarian fanaticism. It demonstrates that, with that keen discernment so characteristic of him, he put his finger on the sore spot in the Sudan when he said that " the tenure of slaves is the A B C of life here to rich and poor."

On 3rd October Gordon reached El Obeid, that town of tragic memory so indissolubly associated with the sad fate of General Hicks. The Governor-General " had a warm reception from the people who were much surprised at the finale at Shaka. I have had to put my trust in God ", continues the writer, " much more than my flesh would have wished—things were so black that human help was evidently useless. Do you know that with a sedentary life people seldom realize the leaning on God, except in sickness or in trade losses—indeed, only when they see *man* cannot help them ? "

It was in this spirit of deeply religious fervour that Gordon returned to Khartoum on 15th October. " The six elephants which had come up from Cairo since I left salaamed me on my arrival," is all that he says of his entry into his capital.

While he had been away on his tour of inspection a Treaty had been entered into between England and Egypt which gave concrete expression to his policy of slavery " Regulation ". Article II of this pact read :—

" Any person engaged in the traffic of slaves,

either directly or indirectly, shall be considered guilty of stealing with murder."

A decree of His Highness the Khedive was couched in these terms :—

"Article I. The sale of slaves from family to family shall be prohibited. This prohibition will take effect in seven years in Cairo and in twelve years in the Sudan.

"Article II. After the lapse of this term of years any infraction of this prohibition will be punished by an imprisonment of from five months to five years." [1]

[1] H. W. Gordon, op. cit., p. 126.

## Chapter XII

# SUMMONED TO CAIRO

Gordon was a shadow when he reached Khartoum. But, however emaciated he may have been, within less than a week he was again on the move. This time his tour was planned to cover Berber, Dongola, Wadi Halfa, Asswan, thence across to Berenice on the Red Sea, from that point to Massawah, from there to Bogos, and, by way of Massawah, back to Khartoum.

He had a hard time of it at his capital before getting away. " I hung, at eighteen hours' notice, a noted murderer, which will tend to keep this town quiet for some months," wrote the mild-mannered man. " You can have little idea of the amount of work I have to do, and I never have a Sunday or a day of rest. . . . Were it not for the very great comfort I have in communion with God, and the knowledge that He is Governor-General, I could not get on at all." [1]

One of Gordon's besetting difficulties was that he could not go out without people running after him with petitions asking for their sons to be released from prison. He refused to allow them to be beaten away, as had formerly been the rule. " Your brother is much feared, and I think respected, but not overmuch liked," is how he analysed the situation. " His refusals are most definite, and very strongly couched. ' Never,' is the answer to many requests, shouted with a loud voice, and followed with : ' Do you understand ? ' and ' Have you finished ? ' The people of the Sudan tremble before your brother. Sometimes

[1] Hill, op. cit., p. 292. Unless otherwise indicated, all quotations in this chapter are from this work.

I take my watch and say, 'Now you may talk for an hour.' They do talk for a long time, then I say, 'Have you finished?' They begin again. At last, worn out (for I give them no answer till they say they have finished), I say, 'I will not hear of it.' Then they begin again, and when they own to having finished, I give them the same answer. They then give up and go away. I am a Job for patience in these matters."

It might have been thought that such longanimity would have made Gordon many friends, but he was, perhaps, correct when he said that he was respected but not "overmuch liked". The reason for this was the perennial slavery question. "The tenure of slaves" was, as he expressed it, "the A B C of life" in the Sudan. His reform measures, salutary and conservative though they were, struck at the pockets of the people of Khartoum. "The fêtes (which were called for by his arrival) were somewhat damped by the knowledge that" he "was hatching something about slaves". The proclamation carrying the Khedivial ukase into effect and giving force to the Anglo-Egyptian Anti-Slavery Treaty was scheduled for 3rd November. The people knew it. It touched their purses. It made them lukewarm in their welcome to their Governor-General.

But if this lack of sympathy with Gordon's anti-slavery policy damped the people's enthusiasm for him, it did not dull the sense of recognition of his all-pervading kindness. To them, Government signified paternalism. It meant even more than that. It implied that the chief of State was a patriarch and that their worries were his responsibilities. "The people are most unreasonable," wrote this most forbearing of men; "they expect me to do the Governor's work, and to investigate all squabbles. One man writes that he and his wife have quarrelled, that his neighbour has interfered, and that he wants me to investigate the case. Men telegraph to me, from hundreds of miles off, to say their slave has escaped ; will I see to it. Now they have a Governor on the spot, as good a one as I can get, and yet they will not go to him."

When Gordon was on his inspection tour of the Darfur district he said something about camels. Of these supercilious-looking beasts, as he was *en route* from Berber to Dongola, he wrote thus :—

"Only gentlemen camels travel ; the ladies stay at home looking after their families ; the boy camels travel with their fathers for a year or so, but carry nothing, so as to accustom them to their work." And after having expounded this bit of desert lore Gordon added :—

"I was very tired last night, and felt as if I should fall off of my camel ; you have but little idea how fatiguing it is. The quiet of the desert is something wonderful—you never hear a sound ; the camel's cushion foot makes no noise ; and the air is perfectly pure."

On 15th December Gordon reached Senheit or Keren and decided to set out for the camp of Walad el Michael, one of the Abyssinian leaders. "The road over two mountains was simply fearful," he wrote. "It was terrible work indeed to scale the last. The camp of Walad el Michael and his brigands is on a sort of plateau on an immense mountain. He has fully 7,000 men here all armed with muskets. They were all drawn up to receive me, and his son met me on the road. Michael was ill, or pretended to be ; I was met by a troop of priests with sacred pictures."

These Christians played a sorry part in the slavery trade. According to the report of the collector of the customs at Gallabat, the frontier Abyssinian town, King Johannes levied blackmail of nearly £20,000 a year upon the slave caravans which passed that strategic point.[1] Their Muhammadan neighbours hold these Oriental Christians in contempt. "Every

[1] *Egypt as it is*, by J. C. McCoan, London, Cassell, Petter & Co., 1877, p. 370.

one at Senheit," said Gordon, "was dead against my coming here, but they could not explain the grounds of their fears, and a sort of instinct kept me to my resolution to face the difficulty. *I do try to think and try to put in practice* that God is the supreme *power* in the world and that He is Almighty ; and though 'Use-your-judgment' people may say 'You tempt God, in putting yourself in positions like my present one,' yet I do not care. . . . If He wills me to fail, so be it."

After having thus found consolation in religion for whatever evils might befall him, Gordon sought in sleep repose for his tired limbs. But the filth of the Abyssinians caused him to be tormented all night with fleas. To make matters worse, a number of priests sang hymns near him, to exorcise him, as he said. But these were fastidious fleas. They like cold, bracing air, and do not descend from the summit of the mountains. They cannot stand hot weather.

Notwithstanding fleas and hymns, Gordon was at his post of duty at an early hour the next morning. He had a long conversation with Michael and urged the chieftain to make peace with King Johannes and beg that monarch's pardon. This latter condition, however, the bandit leader at once said was impossible. He asked, on the contrary, "for more districts to plunder, and Gordon compromised with him by agreeing to pay him £1,000 a month."

Two days later Gordon, that most mild-mannered of men and most Christian of soldiers, did not hesitate to write :—

"How I hate these Abyssinians, Walad el Michael, etc. Their Christianity is only in form, for they seem very little more civilized than the Equatorial tribes. I would care but little for Johannis were it not for the European Governments." And, thinking of the Muslims over whom he ruled, the Governor-General added :—

"*My Bedwin Arabs* of Darfur and hereabouts are fine handsome fellows and quite gentlemen. Some of the younger ones have a style and carriage which I envy. I never was dignified or grand, and could not be, but these young Ishmaels are every bit the Prince. They do not loll about, or spit about, or smell like these Abyssinians, though I expect neither wash at any time."

As Gordon was writing this severe indictment of a people whose nominal Christianity does not recommend them to any foreigner who knows them, the year 1877 was drawing to an end. Before its last sun had set the Governor-General had ridden on camels, during its twelve months, an aggregate of 3,840 miles.

Gordon decided not to go on to Bogos, but, on the contrary, to return to Khartoum by way of Massawah, Suakin, and Berber. While crossing the stretch of the desert which lies between the Red Sea and the Nile, the starlit nights in that vast sea of sand made him doubly conscious of the mystery of life. Gazing into the distance and awestruck by the absolute quiet which reigned about him, he wrote :—

"You ask me what my ideas are of a future life. I think that this life is only one of a series of lives which our incarnated part has lived. I have little doubt of our having pre-existed ; and that also in the time of our pre-existence we were actively employed. So, therefore, I believe in our active employment in a future life, and like the thought. We shall, I think, be far more perfect in a future life, and indeed go *towards* perfection but never attain it."

A few days after Gordon had thus expressed himself, and when he was nearing Khartoum, a telegram came to him from the Khedive Ismail asking if it were possible for him to come down to Cairo to arrange the ruler's financial affairs.

A memorandum drawn up by Gordon himself enables us to grasp under what circumstances he was summoned to return to Egypt. "In 1875," he wrote,

"Ismail Pasha began to find the interest upon the usurious loans he had entered into very onerous, and he applied to the British Government to send out a financier to examine into his financial position. Mr. Cave, Colonel Stokes, and Mr. Rivers Wilson were sent out, and they made certain recommendations, among which was that an arrangement should be made with the holders of the loans to consolidate them, and to pay a lower rate of interest. Accordingly, in 1876, Messrs. Goschen and Joubert, on the part of the bondholders, went to Egypt and went into the finances, accepting Ismail Pasha's figures as correct; they united the loans into one paying a less rate of interest than before, and four gentlemen were appointed—Commissioners of the *Dette*—to look after the interests of the creditors (bondholders), also one to look after the receipts and another to look after the expenditures. . . .

"In February, 1878, I received at Khartoum a telegram from His Highness, saying his creditors were trying to interfere with his sovereign prerogatives, and that His Highness knew no one who could assist him in the position he was placed, but me, and ordered me to come to Cairo. I arrived on the 7th of March, at 9.30 p.m." [1]

This summons was not addressed to Gordon the soldier and Governor-General; it was directed to Gordon the man and friend. The Khedive knew that Gordon, the soldier and Governor-General, made obedience the watchword of his life. Ismail also knew that in appealing to Gordon, the man and the friend, he was turning to a gentleman who would require full and complete information about his financial tangle before throwing himself into its meshes. It was because Ismail welcomed Gordon's fearless scrutiny, keen analysis, and outspoken speech that he sent for the Scotsman to come to Cairo.

[1] H. W. Gordon, op. cit., p. 109.

In the light of the legend that has been built up around Ismail's name it will strike most readers as having been somewhat foolhardy on the part of that monarch to summon to his aid so high-spirited and high-principled a man as Gordon. Lord Milner, Sir Auckland Colvin, and Lord Cromer, to cite but three names among a galaxy of great authorities, have devoted their high characters, outstanding reputations, and unquestioned ability to proving that the Khedive was unworthy of the Briton's support. The author of *England in Egypt* says that no "equally reckless prodigal ever possessed equally unlimited control of equally vast resources" [1] In Colvin's *The Making of Modern Egypt* we read that "the idea that the interests of his people could be a trust committed to him no more entered into Ismail Pasha's head than it had entered the heart of Sultan Abdul Hamid".[2] The decisive *Modern Egypt* is more specific. It proclaims that :—

"Roughly speaking, it may be said that Ismail Pasha added, on an average, about £7,000,000 a year for thirteen years to the debt of Egypt. For all practical purposes it may be said that the whole of the borrowed money, except £16,000,000 spent on the Suez Canal, was squandered." [3]

If these indictments be well founded, Gordon, as an English gentleman, would have done better had he refused to accept the Khedive's invitation. It did not behove the Governor-General to depart from his mandate as a soldier and as an executive officer and throw himself into the defence of a profligate who was squandering the wealth of Egypt. It was not consistent with Gordon's circumspection to embark upon an enterprise whose fundamental morality he did not

[1] *England in Egypt*, by Viscount Milner ; London, Edward Arnold, 1904, p. 176.

[2] *The Making of Modern Egypt*, by Sir Auckland Colvin ; London, Seeley & Co., Ltd., 1906, p. 8.

[3] *Modern Egypt*, by the Earl of Cromer ; New York, The Macmillan Company, vol. i, p. 11.

approve. It is necessary, then, for a proper understanding of Gordon's character to know something more about these Milner-Colvin-Cromer charges. That preferred by Lord Cromer is the most categorical, and it will now be analysed.

It appears on the very first page of the first chapter of *Modern Egypt*, immediately following the Introduction. It brings out, as it were, the *leit-motif* of this masterpiece. It is based, in large measure, upon allegations compressed into a note which reads as follows :—

" Mr. Cave, after making out a balance-sheet for the years 1864–1875, adds : 'Two striking features stand out in this balance-sheet, namely that the sum raised by revenue, £94,281,401, is little less than that spent on administration, tribute to the Porte, works of unquestionable utility, and certain expenses of questionable utility or policy, in all amounting to £97,240,966, and that for the large present amount of indebtedness there is absolutely nothing to show but the Suez Canal, the whole proceeds of the loans and floating debt having been absorbed in payment of interest and sinking funds, with the exception of the sum debited to that great work.' "

The Mr. Cave to whom Lord Cromer thus refers, and whose words furnish one of the main foundations upon which the great Proconsul bases his argument, was an English financial expert who in 1876 audited the books of the Khedivial government. His findings took the shape of a somewhat lengthy document submitted to the Earl of Derby on 23rd March, 1876. It is known to history as the " Cave Report ", and was issued as a White Paper under the general heading " Egypt No. 7 (1876) ". It is reproduced in full as Appendix G in *Egypt as it is* by J. C. McCoan.[1]

This historic instrument was known to Gordon at the time the Khedive's invitation reached him. He

[1] McCoan, op. cit., p. 384.

may not have read it in its entirety when he started on his journey to Cairo, but he no doubt understood its general tenor. If our knowledge of the contents of the Cave report were confined to Lord Cromer's excerpt from it, we should be forced to consider that the Governor-General was prepared to lend an unsullied reputation to a prince who was unworthy of such endorsement. Fairness to Gordon accordingly requires that the source-material thus appealed to by the author of *Modern Egypt* be scrutinized somewhat carefully.

The passage which has been cited appears on p. 8 of the White Paper, and on p. 395 of the McCoan reprint. We are tempted to check from these pages just how much of the £97,240,966 spent by the Khedive and charged up by Mr. Cave to the four headings : (1) " Administration," (2) " Tribute to the Porte," (3) " Works of unquestionable utility " and (4) " Expenses of questionable utility or policy " falls under each one of the different subdivisions. This seems to be but fair, for administrative charges, tribute to the Porte, and works of unquestionable utility strike one as being, in principle, above reproach. The one item open to criticism appears to be that characterized as " Expenses of questionable utility or policy ".

The Cave report shows on these same pages the following figures :—

| | |
|---|---|
| " Administration . . . . . | £48,868,491 |
| " Tribute to the Porte . . . . | £7,592,872 |
| " Works of Utility, etc. . . . . | £30,240,058 |
| " Extraordinary expenses—some of questionable utility and others under pressure of interested parties | £10,539,545." |

It would seem, therefore, as if the original figure, £97,240,966, when carefully dissected, simmers down to £10,539,545, plus whatever hidden irregularities may have been latent in the other £86,701,421.

And Mr. Cave's own report tends to make one somewhat lenient with the Khedive regarding the ten and a half million pounds expended on works of " questionable utility ". Here are the words of the expert :—

" Immense sums are expended on unproductive works after the manner of the East, and on productive works carried out in the wrong way or too soon. This fact is a fault which Egypt shares with other new countries (for she may be considered a new country in this respect), a fault which has seriously embarrassed both the United States and Canada ; but probably nothing in Egypt has ever approached the profligate expenditure which characterized the commencement of the railway system in England." [1]

If our sympathy for Ismail is aroused by such language—just as Gordon's was—we can have little difficulty in grasping how the Scotsman's friendship ripened into advocacy when we also read in this Cave report that :—

" The Khedive has evidently attempted to carry out with a limited revenue, in the course of a few years, works which ought to be spread over a far longer period, and which would tax the resources of much richer exchequers." [2]

Our appetite thus whetted to learn more about the man who has been pilloried as the world's greatest spendthrift, we discover that this same Cave report, which Lord Cromer used as a club with which to annihilate the Khedive, put Gordon in possession of the concrete fact that Ismail had private means which permitted him to entertain most elaborately without squandering the money of the public. Mr. Cave wrote :—

" The Daira Saniah, or private estate of the Khedive, consists of some 350,000 feddans or acres of good

[1] Ibid., p. 384. [2] Ibid., p. 385.

land chiefly in Upper Egypt, besides 100,000 feddans or acres of poor land not under cultivation. Of the former, he lets about half and keeps about half in hand. The net revenue of the whole is estimated at £422,000 in round figures." [1] A man who in 1876 had a private annual income of such an amount was sufficiently well off to be able to spend heavily without necessarily impinging upon the State's exchequer. Knowledge of this fact played its part in convincing Gordon that it was land Ismail had inherited and not taxes rung from the fellah which permitted the Viceroy to entertain more than lavishly.

But such factors alone would not have sufficed to move Gordon. What made their way to his heart were such items in the Cave report as these :—

(1) "The occupation of Darfur and expedition to the equatorial lakes are not, commercially speaking, successful. The Khedive has engaged to some extent in these enterprises for the sake of the suppression of the Slave Trade, and the Abyssinian war was almost forced upon him. . . . Extension of territory and of trade may have attractions for the Khedive, but he is not dazzled by the barren glory of war.[2]

(2) "Education has been carefully attended to, the number of schools established on a European model having increased from 185 in 1862 [3] to 4,817 in 1875. In the latter year there were 4,817 schools, 6,048 masters, and 140,977 pupils, being an augmentation on the previous year of 1,072 schools, 1,615 masters, and 25,722 pupils. The quality of the education given necessarily varies, but it has, on the whole, decidedly improved, and is, in some cases, of superior character" [4] ; and

(3) "These statistics show that the country has made great progress in every way under its present ruler ; but notwithstanding that progress, its present

[1] Ibid., p. 387.
[2] Ibid., p. 389.
[3] Ismail came to the throne in January, 1863.
[4] McCoan, op. cit., p. 392.

financial position is, for the reasons that have already been stated, very critical. Still the expenditure, though heavy, would not of itself have created the present crisis, which may be attributed almost entirely to the ruinous conditions of loans raised for pressing requirements, due in some cases to causes over which the Khedive had little control."[1]

Gordon had been advised by Ismail that the latter could not find the cash necessary to pay the interest on the money which Messrs. Goschen and Joubert had enabled him to raise in 1876.[2] Gordon's attention was thus centred upon the claims of bondholders. Therefore, during the thirty days taken up by the journey from Khartoum to Cairo, he paid particular consideration to everything in the Cave report which bore upon the claims of the holders of the Khedivial bonds. One of the first items which struck his eye in this connection was the categorical statement that—

"The immediate pressure arises from the Khedive's inability to take up the bonds of his unfunded floating debt, now falling due at short intervals and estimated by His Highness at £18,243,076 at least, after deducting the £4,000,000 which have been extinguished by the purchase of the Canal shares."[3]

This paragraph, had it stood alone, would not have made any very forceful impression upon Gordon, for it told him nothing that he did not already know. He wanted to get to the bottom of the relations between the Khedive and his bondholders. He was anxious to find out all that he could in regard to the moral claims of the capitalists who were putting pressure to bear upon Ismail. He knew that the salaries of petty government officials and of the soldiers were unpaid. As he envisaged the question it was his duty, in wrestling with the Viceroy's finances, to consider not only the claims of the bondholders but also those

[1] Ibid., p. 392.
[2] Henry William Gordon, op. cit., p. 109.
[3] McCoan, op. cit., p. 396.

of the inarticulate mass of Egyptians who needed their pay in order to buy their daily bread. Approaching his mission from this point of view, he read and reread those portions of the report which stated that—

"None of the Egyptian loans cost less than 12 per cent per annum, while some cost more than 13¼ per cent per annum, and the railways loan even 26·9 per cent per annum including sinking funds."[1]

And what riveted these figures into Gordon's brain was the fact that they were emphasized by the very last paragraph of the report, which reads:—

"We gather from all the information that we have been able to obtain that Egypt is well able to bear the charge of the whole of her present indebtedness at a reasonable rate of interest; but she cannot go on renewing floating debts at 25 per cent and raising fresh loans at 12 or 13 per cent interest to meet these additions to her debt, which do not bring in a single piastre to her exchequer."[2]

The result of his study of the Cave Report was that when Gordon stepped off the train at the Cairo station on that March night in 1878 the word "bondholder" was anathema to him, and the very mention of the name of the Commissioners of the Egyptian Public Debt a challenge. The personality of the Khedive had faded from the foreground and appeared only in perspective. Gordon's attention was centred upon the Egyptian peasant, the petty Egyptian employee, and the Egyptian soldier. He was determined to stand by the Viceroy, but he was resolved to die rather than cede another piastre to the moneylenders. He looked upon them as vampires preparing to drain the life-blood of the sovereign whom he admired and of the people whom he loved. And he hated the Commissioners of the Debt as the personification of these destructive forces.

[1] Ibid., p. 395.

[2] Ibid., p. 402.

## Chapter XIII

# THE DEBT INQUIRY

Ismail sent his equerry to meet Gordon at the railway station. A command was conveyed to him to dine that evening at the palace. It was then after nine o'clock. Dirty and tired as the traveller was after a train journey of 350 miles, he had to obey. He was also no doubt quite hungry, but—

"Before dinner," he wrote, "late as it was, His Highness took me aside, and asked me to be President of an Inquiry into the state of the finances of the country; but said that the Commissioners of the *Dette* had proven so hostile to him, that His Highness wished me to object to their being on the Commission of Inquiry, saying that they had written against him in the papers, etc. I said 'I would accept the Commission of Inquiry as President', and His Highness said 'You see Lesseps, who will act with you'. . . . I said 'Yes' and accepted the mission with the agreement that the Commissioners of the *Dette* were not to be on the Inquiry. I was angry with the Commissioners of the *Dette* because I thought that they had been too hard on His Highness."[1]

It is thus clear that while Gordon would probably have preferred to have had this conversation on a full stomach, the Khedive's views fitted in perfectly with his. When he asserted that he was angry with the Commissioners of the *Dette* he meant exactly what he said. There was nothing personal about his ire. It was of that impersonal, objective character that burns

[1] H. W. Gordon, op. cit., p. 112. All subsequent quotations in this chapter are from this work.

into a white flame and that nothing can quench. The Lesseps referred to by the Khedive was Ferdinand de Lesseps, the man whose diplomatic skill and fighting spirit had brought the Suez Canal into being. Gordon had therefore willingly accepted the suggestion that his coadjutor in the contest with the official champions of the bondholders should be this resourceful Frenchman.

"The next morning," to allow Gordon to tell his own story, "I saw Mr. Vivian, the English Consul-General, and he said, 'I wonder if you could accept the Presidency of the Commission of Inquiry without the Commissioners of the *Dette*.' I said, 'I was free to accept or refuse.'"

Vivian does not appear to have pressed the subject any further. The men separated. Each knew where the other stood. Gordon continues his narrative in this wise :—

"I then called on the German Consul-General, and, when there, the French and Austrian Consuls-General and also Vivian came in and attacked me for having accepted the post of President. I said I was free, and then they said 'I was risking His Highness his throne ; that he ran a very serious risk personally if he formed the Commission of Inquiry without the creditors' representatives, viz. the Commissioners of the *Dette*.' I said, 'Why do you not tell him so ?' They said : 'You ought to do so.' I said 'Well, will you commission me to do so from you, with any remarks I like to make as to the futility of your words ?' They all said 'Yes, we authorize you to do so—in our names.'"

The Consuls-General knew that Gordon would not fail to deliver their message and then hammer it to pieces. True to his promise, he saw the Khedive that very evening. He does not say whether after his experience of the day before he had dinner before going to the palace. All that we know is that this time it was he who spoke before soup was served. Here are his words :—

" Just before dinner at Abdine I told His Highness I wished to speak to him. I said : ' I have seen the four Consuls-General to-day, and they told me to tell Your Highness, from them, that you run a serious personal risk, if you have a Commission of Inquiry without the Commissioners of the *Dette* being upon it.' His Highness did not seem to care a bit, and said : ' He was only afraid of England, who he was sure would not move.' He said : ' You see Lesseps to-morrow, and arrange the *enquête* with him.' "

The next day de Lesseps called upon Gordon and said : " We must have the Commissioners of the *Dette* on the *enquête*." Gordon answered : " It is a *sine qua non* that they are not on it." De Lesseps replied : " They must be on it." Then in came Chérif Pàsha, Ismail's Foreign Minister, and observed : " Are you agreed ? " De Lesseps' response was " Yes ". But Gordon interposed a quick " I fear not ". Thereupon the Frenchman and the Egyptian put their heads together, and after a few moments' conference de Lesseps agreed to serve on the Commission without the Commissioners, but with the proviso that he would ask permission to do so from Paris.

The afternoon passed without de Lesseps getting off his cable to the *Quai d'Orsay*. On the morrow, when the Frenchman, a man of seventy-three, called upon Gordon, he was accompanied by his charming wife. This is how Gordon, the confirmed bachelor of forty-five, describes what took place :—

" Lesseps said, looking at his pretty young wife of twenty-two : ' I am off to Helwan [1] and shall not be back until night. I have telegraphed to my Government to ask permission to be on the *enquête* with you ;

[1] Helwan, a resort near Cairo.

here is a copy of the telegram, will you give it to His Highness ?' He gave it over to me to read. I read it ; it was thus : '*Son Altesse le Khédive m'a prié de me joindre avec Monsieur Gordon et les Commissionnaires de la Caisse pour faire une enquête sur les finances d'Egypte. Je demande permission.*' I said : 'Oh (my dear old fellow), de Lesseps, this will never do.' He said : 'Well, at any rate, it is off, and I am off to Helwan and shall not be back until to-night.'"

The attitude of de Lesseps aggravated Gordon. The Scotsman had an ingrained antipathy to diplomatists. His journals show that, as a class, they invariably rubbed him the wrong way. The cool indifference with which a man of over seventy preferred a day of jollification with a wife of twenty-two to the routine duties of life did not tend to make the creator of the Suez Canal stand out from a caste which Gordon cordially disliked. He was therefore in no amiable frame of mind when he reached the Abdine Palace. He thus describes what took place.

"Chérif and Riaz Pasha were in the Antechamber, drowsy and happily smoking ; as I went in I saw a bald-headed coot, the Consul-General of the *Pays Bas*, going in to His Highness." To have a diplomatist thus get in immediately ahead of him did not add to Gordon's equanimity. So he was in no sense expansive when the Egyptian Minister spoke to him. We read in his memorandum that—

"Chérif drowsily said : 'Any news ?' I said : 'No, only I have a telegram for His Highness from Lesseps.' So Riaz and Chérif chatted away in Turkish till I saw the 'coot' go out and Chérif called in. Suddenly Chérif came flying out, all drowsiness gone, and said : 'Where is the telegram ?' I gave it to him, and then in came flying 'Pharaoh'[1] with Chérif. Pharaoh threw himself on the sofa, and said : '*Je suis tout à fait bouleversé par ce télégramme de Lesseps.*

[1] Ismail.

*C'est tout à fait contre mes désirs. Barrat!* (calling his scribe by name) *venez ici : dites à quelqu'un d'aller à Helwan et de dire à Lesseps de ne pas télégraphier à Paris*"[1]; and then turning to me His Highness said: 'I put the whole affair into your hands.' Then calling Barrat he said: 'Telegraph to Goschen: "Gordon is charged with the whole affair, arrange with him."'"

Thus the Khedive, harassed on all sides by the bondholders, and disappointed at the attitude of Ferdinand de Lesseps, turned to Charles George Gordon as his one anchor of safety. The latter accepted the trust with the words of the Consuls-General of England, France, Germany, and Austria still ringing in his ears. He knew that he had a thorny path before him. Not only was he prepared to play a lone hand without either de Lesseps or the Commissioners of the *Dette*, but his mind had been made up from his study of the Cave report to fight the bondholders to the last ditch. Perhaps a personal aversion to Major Evelyn Baring, then English Commissioner of the *Dette*, strengthened this determination. At all events he wrote:—

"When downstairs in one of the many antechambers of the palace His Highness gave me (shall I ever lodge in palaces again? I hope not!) I found Baring. Now Baring is in the Royal Artillery, while I am in the Royal Engineers. Baring was in the nursery when I was in the Crimea. He has a pretentious, grand, patronizing way about him. We had a few words together. I said: 'I would do what His Highness asked me.' He said: 'It was unfair to the creditors'; and, in a few moments, all was over. When oil mixes with water we will mix together."

Gordon wrote these words on 14th October, 1878.

[1] "I am altogether upset by this telegram of Lesseps. It is entirely opposed to my wishes. Barrat, come here. Tell somebody to go at once to Helwan and tell Lesseps not to cable to Paris."

Little did he know that Major Baring, then Britain's Commissioner of the *Dette*, would subsequently become Sir Evelyn Baring, Her Majesty's Consul-General at Cairo, and as such play a leading part in the last phase of his, Gordon's, life. Still less did he foresee that after Baring, as a diplomatist, had done his utmost to make Gordon's final Sudan mission a success, Baring, as Lord Cromer, would become an historian and pillory him. But, even though the future were hidden from Gordon's ken when he and Baring first crossed swords, the one stood forth as the champion of Egypt's creditors and as the personification of the *Caisse de la Dette*, the other as the advocate of Egypt's fellaheen and the mouthpiece of the Khedive.

It thus came to pass that, convinced by his study of the Cave report and perhaps spurred on by the personal equation, born of dislike for Baring, Gordon's first act, when vested by the Viceroy with sole and plenary authority, was to advise the bondholders that he had recommended—

"His Highness to suspend the payment of the next coupon, in order to pay the employees and meet pressing claims." And at the same time Gordon, to repeat his own words, "wrote to His Highness and proposed he should suspend the payment of the coupon, and pay the employees and pressing claims, that he should do it by decree and quote me, throw all the blame upon me, saying: 'If he did not like to do this, I would myself telegraph to Lord Derby to say I had recommended His Highness to do so and so, that I did not ask Her Majesty's Government to give any acquiescence to it, but merely to tell them if the Khedive did this, it was my fault.'"

It is obvious that Gordon's fighting blood was stirred. He felt that he was leading a moral crusade against financial pariahs. He may have exaggerated the callousness of the bondholders. The idealist in him may here have fought the realist for mastery.

But it is his point of view that shaped his conduct. He looked upon the problem with which he was called upon to deal as one of fundamental fair play. He felt that the rights of the employees and of the holders of pressing claims took precedence of those of the capitalists, whose bonds, according to the Cave report, were surcharged with usurious interest. He may have allowed his convictions to have carried him too far. He may have permitted his unwillingness to sit round a green table with Major Baring to have warped his judgment. But he was a brave man who had reached a decision upon a question of right and wrong, and no power on earth could have budged him one iota.

The Khedive caught the significance of Gordon's words. He knew what they meant. His penetrating mind saw pictures of an ultimatum delivered the next day by the Consuls-General of England, France, Germany, and Austria. His ears heard the Concert of Europe attuned to the music of " Pay youı coupons or abdicate ", and, as Gordon put it :—

" The Khedive hesitated and did not answer me, and shut himself up in his harem for two days, and the game was lost."

Gordon gives interesting details regarding the way in which the diplomatic corps set to work while Ismail was in eclipse. It would carry us somewhat too far afield to go into these details. Suffice it to say that the personal equation does not appear to have facilitated Gordon's relations with the British Consul-General, Vivian, any more than it did his dealings with the British Commissioner of the *Dette*, Baring. At all events, we read in Gordon's description of what transpired that—

" Vivian (who was a pretty black-eyed boy, and was put by General Fox under my care at the Royal Military Academy, and whom Ruck Keene kicked on the ankle when he was removed from that rough school)" got into touch with the French Consul-General and did things that his old mentor considered not quite cricket. And we are almost driven to infer that if England's Cairo Diplomatic Agent in those days had been almost anybody other than this "pretty black-eyed boy", it would have been far easier for him to have talked with Gordon as man to man. But the Governor-General was a fatalist. He probably felt that *Kismet* had made Baring and Vivian cross his path in order to strengthen his determination to lead the fight of the Egyptian employees against the bondholders.

But even if Baring had been in the nursery when Gordon was in the Crimea, and even if General Fox had once put Vivian under the Governor-General's care, these two boys of yesterday were men of mark during these fateful days. They carried their point. Gordon knew what was going to happen when he saw that the Khedive had failed to authorize the dispatch of the decisive telegram to Lord Derby. But Ismail, he wrote—

"Never told me he had given in: but four days after, I heard of it, and on my seeing him he said (for it was no longer a secret that he had ceded): 'Have you any news?' I said: 'Yes, I hear Your Highness has agreed to the four Commissioners of the *Dette* being on the Inquiry.' He said: 'Yes,' and the subject dropped. Five days after I left Cairo, with no honours, by the ordinary train, paying my passage. The sun which rose with such splendour set in the deepest obscurity. I calculate my financial episode cost me £800. His Highness was bored with me after my failure and could not bear the sight of me, which his surroundings soon knew."

No lines better portray Gordon's innate modesty than do these words. He spoke of "my failure" and added:—

"I dare say I may have been imprudent in speech.

I have no doubt it is better as it is. His Highness and I would have fallen out about the composition of the Commission of Inquiry, for I feel sure it was meant to be packed, and that I was only to be a figure-head."

Gordon bore with such complacency "the slings and arrows of outrageous fortune" because he was then in a frame of mind which prompted him to write to his sister on 21st March that :—

"God never hides His face ; we raise up the veil and hide ourselves, when we feel our own vileness. I have my Koh-i-noor with me, i.e. the presence of God, and who can take that from me or make me fear ?"[1]

[1] *Letters of General C. G. Gordon to his Sister*, p. 179.

## Chapter XIV

# THE AFTERMATH OF THE INQUIRY

On 30th March Colonel Gordon left Cairo for Suez. Thence he went to Aden, and then crossed over to Berberah on the African coast. Zeila was his next stop.

"Zeila," he wrote, "used to belong to Turkey. His Highness got it in exchange for some £15,000 a year extra tribute. And then he annexed Harrar. I hope to leave for Harrar this afternoon, 17th April; it is eight days' journey. Raouf Pasha is there; the same man who was at the Equator with Baker and with me, and whom I deposed from that province exactly four years ago yesterday. I am going to turn him out again, for he seems to be a regular tyrant." [1]

After what he describes as "a really terrible journey", Gordon reached Harrar on 28th April. At the entrance to the walled town he came across the palpitating carcases of two cows, whose throats had been cut in his honour. Near the divan was another cow sobbing out her life, with streams of blood flowing over the threshold. The sight made him so sad that he almost forgot about Raouf Pasha, who came forward to meet him. But Gordon pulled himself together at once. He paid £5 for the three sacrificed cows, and summarily dismissed the delinquent officer from his presence and from the Government service.

This important detail attended to, Gordon headed for Khartoum. He reached his capital during the first days of June. He found that the finances of the Sudan were in bad shape, and set in motion important

[1] Hill, op. cit., p. 310. All quotations in this chapter are from this work.

economies to meet the difficulties of the situation. By 25th July he was able to get a proper idea of the sequence of events which had called him to Cairo. He recorded on that date :—

"I am stronger than ever in my belief that if His Highness had taken my advice, he would be in a better plight than he is now, and, at any rate, would have fallen with dignity. Now I see by the papers he is offering to abdicate, etc. This sort of thing cannot last, and I fear for him."

The concluding lines of this letter make it clear that if Gordon's heart had not been centred upon the suppression of the slave trade he would never have returned to the Sudan. He had been very much hurt by the Khedive's attitude towards him. But the Briton preferred to suffer injustice rather than desert the poor blacks. "As for myself," he said, "I am exceedingly weary, and wish, with a degree of bitterness, that it was all over. I am cooped up here now, and am much occupied with the finances, which are in a very low state. My life is burdensome and weary ; but I feel that it is better to be employed here than to be idle elsewhere. I am striking daily deadly blows against the slave trade, and am establishing a sort of Government of Terror about it. I have hanged a man for mutilating a little boy and would not ask leave to do so."

He captured twelve caravans of slaves during June and July. He felt so much encouraged by these results that he did not hesitate to write that he hoped to be able to curb "this work ere long ". A few weeks later a steamer coming up from Berber caught a caravan of slaves which had refused to obey the *Mudir* of Darfur. "The sight of those ninety slaves was terrible. . . . Fancy, they had come over 500 miles of deserts, and were a residue of four times their number. It is much for me," continued Gordon, "to keep myself from illegal acts towards the slave-dealers ;

yet I think that I must not forget that God suffers it, and that one must keep to the law. I have done the best I can, and he is the Governor-General."

What with his disappointment at the treatment he had received at Cairo, his chagrin at not being able to crush the slave trade once and for all, and his worry over the finances of the Sudan, Gordon's health gave way under the strain. He was alone and had nobody with whom he could share his burdens. He therefore held to his post, although he was forced to record :—

"There are not nine Europeans in the Sudan, and they vegetate and do not live. Can you conceive what it is never to have any desire to eat? That is my case. I *hate* the operation. My *angina pectoris* has not troubled me lately. According to medical books it is not known what occasions this. It is heart disease, and makes you think you are on the brink of death. A rush of blood takes place to the head and you think all is over. I may say I have died suddenly over a hundred times; but in these deaths I have never felt the least doubt of my salvation." And on another occasion he observed : "It is a very great comfort to me never to have the least fear of death when I am ill."

Gordon's love of animals probably enabled him to bear with the solitude which his isolation thrust upon him. Only a man genuinely fond of God's dumb creatures could write with such obvious satisfaction that :—

"The steamer has just brought four little hippopotamuses, which are in my yard, and which are very tame. They are like huge pigs, and are so plump and soft and cool-skinned. They have only little teeth. The little elephant smelt them but did not like them at all (a nasty fishy smell, no doubt he said). The hippopotamuses, however, would have been friendly with the elephant, but after a few overtures on their part he butted at them and when in the pond with them he flicked water at them with his trunk."

Gordon dealt with his pets as if they were human beings. He punished them when they were naughty and rewarded them when their conduct was exemplary. His treatment of his ostriches shows that he was a strict but just disciplinarian. "This morning," runs his story—it was 19th February, 1879—"without any apparent reason the two ostriches (kept in the palace grounds) with one accord rushed at a black slave in the garden, and striking at him with their toes nearly killed him. One stroke from their toes tore off the poor man's nose. The culprits I have ordered to be sold into slavery and annually plucked. The proceeds of their sale is to be devoted to purchasing the freedom of the wounded slave, and to giving him a good *backsheesh*. It will be a just retribution."

And with his mind full of his friends of the animal kingdom, Gordon went on to say that :—

"I have a gentleman and two lady sheep of extraordinary size. They are really enormous. They and the gazelle hate the tortoise. They settle down in a corner and up he comes and turns them out. To them he is a slow-moving stone, and they cannot make him out, moving on so slowly and so surely."

Drawing maps helped to bring some measure of distraction into Gordon's busy life. But he soon came to the end of his tether in that field. It thus became increasingly difficult for him to obtain that intellectual diversion which he needed in order to keep fit. He was placed, in this respect, in a most awkward position, for, as he expressed it, "You see, one lacks books, and I scarcely see anyone except on business, for I have no associates here."

He finally hit upon the expedient of taking clocks apart. He describes his activity in that domain in these words :—

" Pulled another clock to pieces and put it together again, which is more difficult. I am getting quite an adept. How I wish I had learnt some smattering of trades. I wonder women do not take to watch and clock-making. That is such a clean, nice trade, and it is just the sort of work that women would be neat at. I would guarantee that you could take the clocks in the house to pieces and put them together after three days' tuition. As for a watch, I confess it is beyond me ; but this is because I have never been shown the way by a watchmaker. What a deal of amusement I should have here, did I know the elements of watchmaking ! "

Anyone who has ever heard cuckoo-clocks announce the hour knows that they are insufferable bores—if an inanimate object can be called a bore. Gordon, who has written so happily of the pleasure he had derived from taking clocks to pieces, was forced to record, the very next day, that " a cuckoo-clock has beaten me to-day. I cannot make it go. The dullness is almost insupportable." Only such a stupid thing as a cuckoo-clock would have played such a mean trick upon so loveable a man as Gordon. But its perverseness really amounted to nothing, for the same letter that spoke of this piece of bad luck says :—

" I am rather cheerful about the revolted slave-dealers at Bahr Gazelle. I have entirely blockaded them, and in four or six months they will be hard up for anything like luxuries or essentials."

A great deal of the work necessary to bring about this result had to be performed by Gordon in person. One little incident recounted by him will illustrate this. One morning, just as the sun was rising, he met three *Bashi-Bazouks*. " They looked so very guilty," is the way he tells the tale, " that I looked among the trees and thought I saw some figures. I remarked to Berzati Bey, my secretary : ' I smell slaves ; look under those trees.' He said 'No'. So I went on, though I was still suspicious. I could see no more of the figures under the trees. When my caravan came up it appears they saw the same figures creeping along in the grass off the road. These figures sank down in the grass when they saw they were noticed. Then my people captured the lot, and brought them here. The first thing was to give away the camel, saddle, two donkeys, £15 in cash and clothes of the *Bashi-Bazouks*. Everyone took from them what they liked, till they were despoiled. They were then beaten and dismissed. There were fourteen slaves—four young men, seven young women, and three little girls. They are quite delighted and making such a noise. . . . There is only one bad thing about letting the *Bashi-Bazouks* go so easily, for it will be known that I only flogged and despoiled them; but I had no help for it. How could I have escorted them to Obeid? . . . It is only the want of power and legality which prevented them being now on their backs, looking at the skies; for I had every wish to shoot them."

A few days later Gordon evolved what he felt would be a means of killing off the slave trade even if he could not get the legislation that he desired. It would appear, however, that *Kismet*, in the form of a scorpion, opposed its veto to this programme. At least, this is the deduction which the superstitious would be tempted to draw from Gordon's words. Here is what he wrote :—

"We started last night at 6.30 and marched till 3.30 next morning, when I halted for two hours. During the long ride I was able to see my way to crush out the slave trade—it is thus: 'All persons residing in Darfur must have a *permis de séjour*; all persons travelling to and from Darfur must have passports for themselves and suite.'"

Fearing that the significance of these two

requirements might not be as clear as he would like, Gordon hastened to add :—

" Now I want you to read these two rules carefully. As Darfur surrounds the Sudan, and all slaves must pass through Darfur before coming to the Sudan, no one can reside in Darfur without an ostensible mode of livelihood, and no one can go to or from Darfur without Government permission for himself and his followers." And knowing that a law without an adequate sanction was nought but " love's labour lost ", Gordon went on to say that :—

" I have added to these rules : 'All infractions of these orders will be punished with imprisonment and by confiscation of property.' (If you lack wisdom, ask it of God, Who is liberal and upbraideth not.) So far for my night thoughts. At 3.30 a.m. I laid down and slept ; at 5.30 a.m. I started again, and after two hours I met some chiefs of the Arab tribes, who had come to meet me."

Gordon had been travelling so rapidly—in 1879 he rode 1,620 miles through the desert on camels, notwithstanding the months consumed in his trip to and from Cairo and his stay there—that Fate had not been able to keep up with him. When he slowed down his march as he neared the spot where he was to meet these *sheikhs*, *Kismet* caught up with him, and, as he expressed it :—

" As I halted my camel to salute them I felt a very sharp sting in my knee. I knew what it was ; but there was no chance of getting at it, so I adopted the only course, which was to crush him on my knee. A small scorpion had, when I was asleep, crawled up my trousers."

While Gordon was thus wrestling with destiny, Gessi, his faithful Italian aide, was fighting, in the name of the Khedive, and under the Scotsman's orders, civilization's battle against Zobeir. This war to the knife went on at a time when Europe was failing to give the Khedive aggressive support in his life-and-death struggle against slavery. This may, perhaps, be a misstatement. However, it crystallizes the Governor-General's point of view, as set forth in this form :—

" I heard at Khartoum from one who came from Cairo that some of the Consuls-General did not take the least interest in the suppression of the slave trade ; they only moved in it because their governments, fearful of public opinion, obliged them to do so."

Shortly after having thus expressed his ideas about the diplomatists stationed at Cairo, Gordon showed that his old affection for Ismail had been rekindled, for he wrote :—

" I admire the Khedive exceedingly ; he is the perfect type of his people, thoroughly consistent to all their principles—a splendid leopard ! Look at the numberless cages out of which he has broken his way when it seemed quite impossible for him to do so."

It was not only reciprocal sympathy but a Scotsman's inborn love of fair play that made Gordon " admire the Khedive exceedingly ". The Governor-General knew that the ruler had his faults. But he also knew that it was not because of his faults but his virtues that Ismail was being hard-pressed by Europe. Had the Powers sought to drive the Viceroy from his throne on account of his shortcomings, Gordon would, perhaps, have viewed the matter with complacency. But the Governor-General had read the Cave report. He had seen the proof in black and white that his friend had a net income from his lands of £422,000 per annum.

With a revenue of such dimensions a few necklaces or diamonds for this singer or that dancer did not spell bankruptcy. And Ismail's gifts were not always proof of admiration for the fair sex. We read in *Khedives and Pashas* that :—

"The Consul-General of a certain Power had once offended him, peace had been made by a common friend, and he had buried the hatchet by sending a very handsome bracelet to the Consul's wife, who had a somewhat demonstrative but appreciative way of eating macaroni. When the mediator asked him why he had made such costly amends, he replied: 'I had no choice between that and asking them to dinner. *Mon cher!* I prefer war to seeing that woman eat macaroni.'"[1]

It made Gordon's blood boil to know that the Khedive was being driven into a corner by importunate creditors when the words of the Cave report kept ringing in the Scotsman's ears that "the Khedive attempted to carry out with a limited revenue, in the course of a few years, works which ought to be spread over a far longer period". It distressed Gordon that the bondholders, whom the Cave report accused of fattening upon usurious rates of interest, should be given access to the chancelleries of Europe. It made Gordon red with rage to feel that the Mixed or International Tribunals, which Ismail's sense of justice had called into existence, were being used as the lever with which to pry the Egyptian monarch off his throne. Gordon may have been mistaken in looking at matters from this angle. In the solitude of his life in the Sudan he had, however, become more and more wedded to his habit of solving problems and of adhering to his solutions with a tenacity of purpose which nothing could shake.

Gordon had cherished the hope that as the Khedive was a leopard who had broken his way out of numberless cages he would be able to escape from the subtle bars which the decisions of the Mixed Courts were welding around him. He had been encouraged in this illusion by the fact that he felt that, as long as the four

[1] *Khedives and Pashas by One who Knows them Well*, p. 13.

Great Powers which controlled the *Caisse de la Dette*—England, France, Austria, and Germany—abstained from acting in accord, the Sovereign whom he exceedingly admired would not be forced to abdicate. Great was his disappointment to learn, when the summer equinox of 1879 was approaching, that the sun of his friend's reign was setting. Dicey thus describes the final phase of what Gordon considered a tragedy :—

"The blow came from the quarter whence it was least expected. Germany had never previously displayed any great interest in Egyptian affairs. The number of German subjects holding Egyptian securities was, at this period, extremely limited ; and the policy of the Empire under the rule of Emperor William I and of his great Chancellor had been one throughout of non-intervention in all foreign issues which did not directly affect the safety or interests of the Fatherland. Suddenly the world learnt with astonishment that Germany contemplated active intervention in Egypt. Certain German subjects, who were creditors of the Egyptian State, had obtained judgment in their favour before the International Courts. These judgments had remained unexecuted owing to the refusal of the Egyptian executive to carry them into execution. The Courts had been established in virtue of an international agreement, to which Germany was a party ; and she therefore claimed the right to demand the fulfilment of the agreement on the strength of which she had agreed to the suspension of her Consular jurisdiction in civil matters." [1]

When Gordon learned that Germany was brandishing the tomahawk of war he was nonplussed. Those were the days when Berlin, under Prince Bismarck, had the reputation of never threatening unless it was prepared to strike. Gordon could not

[1] *The Story of the Khediviate*, by Edward Dicey ; London, Rivington, 1902, p. 214.

understand what had induced the Iron Chancellor to go out of his way to take the lead in a discussion with which neither Germany nor her people had any close concern. Reared in the common law of England, he could not fathom by what process of law the Egyptian State could be condemned, like a common every-day mortal, to pay a sum of money and in default of settlement seized and sold out of house and home. He felt that it had never been the intention of the Khedive or of the Powers to confer such extraordinary authority upon the Mixed Tribunals. His mind stood aghast at what he considered the immorality of Bismarck's brutal act.

But Gordon was above all things a realist. He knew that when the German Junker rattled his sword both France and England would be constrained by the logic of events to demand of the Sultan of Constantinople the deposition of the Khedive for a debt due, not by him, but by the Egyptian State. It was, therefore no surprise to Gordon to receive on 1st July a telegram from Chérif Pasha announcing that the Sublime Porte had named Tewfik Pasha Khedive.

This official information possibly came to the Governor-General somewhat sooner than he had expected. While aware of what was going on in Cairo and of the orientation of events, information reached him by letter and by word of mouth. The fatal news arrived by telegram and was accordingly received before Gordon was prepared for it. He says that "it did not affect me in the least". Yet on 21st July he wrote :—

"I shall (D.V.) leave for Cairo in ten days. . . . I am a wreck, like the portion of the *Victory* towed into Gibraltar after Trafalgar ; but God enabled me, or rather used me, to do what I wished to do—that is, break down the slave trade. . . . It pains me what sufferings my poor Khedive Ismail has had to go through."

A month later Gordon added : " I arrived at Cairo on 23rd March, at 7.30 p.m., very cross at the dismissal of Ismail. I refused a special train Tewfik had ordered for me, for in all probability they would have charged me for it. The Prefect of Police met me and told me that the new H.H. had put the Palace at my disposal. I said : ' No, I am going to the Hotel.' "

## Chapter XV

# THE END OF GORDON'S FIRST MISSION TO THE SUDAN

Before they left the Cairo railway station Gordon consulted his "black imp", his trusted and outspoken secretary, Berzati. They both came to the conclusion that as Tewfik Pasha's invitation had been extended in good faith it should be accepted. So the soldier went to the Palace instead of to Shepheard's Hotel.

The new Khedive sent for Gordon shortly after his arrival. Their conversation lasted almost until midnight. It dealt, in the main, with the threatened attack of Abyssinian forces on the Bogos territory. The next day the Briton was again summoned into the monarch's presence. Gordon told Tewfik that he could not remain any longer in his service, but would cheerfully go to Massawah and settle with Johannes of Abyssinia before returning home.

Tewfik willingly accepted the proposal, not only because Gordon was not popular with the Egyptian bureaucracy, but also because of his offer to do his utmost to adjust matters with the Abyssinians. Having accepted this new mission, Gordon lost no time in preparing for its execution. He wrote :—

"I may say I was very active in the affair. I attacked in an official letter the Italian Consul-General, for it is an Italian who has put Johannis up to this, and I expect I made him ashamed. . . . I have told the Commissioners of the Debt (privately) I expect I shall need £333,333 12*s.* 6*d.* for the war which is impending."[1]

[1] Hill, op. cit., p. 400. The other passages cited in this chapter are from the same source.

Determined to do his best, but conscious that without the financial support of the Commissioners of the *Dette*, whom he still cordially disliked, he could accomplish nothing, Gordon hurried to Massawah and found the heat in the Red Sea terrible. Upon reaching the capital of the Egyptian Eastern District he ascertained that the Abyssinians were in virtual possession of Bogos, and that it was not " a question of ceding or not the country but of retaking it ". This reality had barely been impressed upon Gordon before a telegram was received by him from Tewfik Pasha, in which the Khedive said : " Cede nothing, but avoid war ! " When the cable was read he made no comment upon it. All he did was to record : " I am low to a degree, covered with the prickly heat." A few days later, as his march carried him into the interior, he wrote :—

" 13th September, 1879 : We started at 2 a.m. this morning. The road was simply terrible, and I got off my mule and walked in a diabolical temper, for I had that palpitation of the heart which reduces one to zero."

" 14th September : We have only three hours more march ere we reach the place of rendezvous. I am glad of it, for this prickly heat-rash has turned into boils, so that I am a perfect Job. I have sad misgivings whether I can do anything or not. I see no mean on which we can meet if Johannis is determined to have Bogos ; for only yesterday H.H. telegraphed for the second time : 'Give up nothing but do not fight.' "

With prickly heat turned into boils and with impossible instructions from Cairo, Gordon pressed forward, and after two days came to the tent of Aloula, Johannes' right-hand man. The Abyssinian and his entourage were bundled up in their long robes which they held closely against their " mouths as if something poisonous had arrived ". After some delay Aloula said once or twice, addressing his visitor : "You are English, and your nation are my brothers." The Governor-General did not like Abyssinians. He did not take fondly to the relationship thus thrust upon him. He said : "Here I could only be looked on as the Envoy of the Khedive, and as a Musulman for the time." This refusal to accept the proffered brotherhood more or less cut short the interview between the two men. All that was accomplished was that Gordon decided to continue his march and to discuss matters with the King of Abyssinia.

He reached Debra Tabor, where the Ethiopian ruler was then in residence, on 27th October. The monarch was not in a particularly happy frame of mind. He began by recounting, at tedious length, his complaints against Egypt, and finished by promising to write a letter to the Khedive. Gordon could get nothing more definite from him than this, and so departed. "An hour later, just as I was starting," wrote Gordon, "the interpreter brought me the letter, and also 1,000 dollars which I sent back. When I halted I opened the letter. I felt sure there was some trick. It was some twelve lines. I counted two for salutations at the beginning and two for salutations at the end, and I saw that the remaining eight lines would not be enough for the demands, so I had it translated. The king says : 'I have received the letters you sent me by *that man*. I will not make a secret peace with you. If you want peace, ask the Sultans of Europe."

Gordon caught the meaning of the insult ; but he was powerless. His steps were turned towards the Egyptian frontier. Several days later, just as he was nearing the end of his Abyssinian march, 120 soldiers, with three high officers of Ras Ayra, swept down upon him. They showed him a letter of which they would permit him to see nothing more than the King's seal, and ordered him to turn back. "We were considerably bothered by these troops all night," said Gordon, "and back we marched in the morning, knowing nothing of our fate, or what the reason of our recall was, until the 16th, when we reached Ras Ayra's village again."

We can estimate the degree of culture of this Christian chieftain from the following lines taken from Gordon's records :—

"Ras Ayra sent word to say he could not see me, for he had taken medicine. (Every Abyssinian takes 'kosso' at certain fixed epochs—say, every ten days—to kill the tapeworms engendered by eating raw meat ; but this was not the regular day for Ras Ayra to take 'kosso', so I knew he lied.)" Another passage from Gordon's writings also tells that the King—

"Cuts off the noses of those who take snuff, and the lips of those who smoke. The other day a man went to salute Ras Aloula. In saluting him his tobacco box dropped out. Ras Aloula struck him with his sword, and his people finished him. The King is hated more than Theodore was. Cruel to a degree, he does not, however, take life. He cuts off the hands and feet of people who offend him. He puts out their eyes by pouring hot tallow into their ears."

Here is a further description of this Christian King taken from Gordon's letters :—

"He is a man of forty-five years, a sour, ill-favoured looking being. He never looks you in the face, but when you look away he glares at you like a tiger. He never smiles ; his look, always changing, is one of thorough suspicion. Hated and hating all, I can imagine no more unhappy man. Avaricious above all his people, who do not lack this quality, his idea of a free port is that fleets of steamers will arrive from the Powers of Europe with presents for him, to which he will reply by sending a letter with the Lion seal, saying : 'You are my brother, my mother, etc.

How are you?' Johannis is delighted with Her Majesty, because she called him her son."

The sovereign whom Queen Victoria thus honoured claims descent from the union of King Solomon with the Queen of Sheba. His escutcheon is a lion holding a cross, with the motto: "*Vicit Leo de Tribu Juda.*" But notwithstanding his claims to such remote ancestry, King Johannes, according to Gordon, lived in a palace which consisted—

"Of two large round conical roofed thatched houses, one for a reception room, the other his dwelling room—no attempt at the simplest window or door. His horses were in it as well as himself, but this is partly due to tradition".

Gordon does not say whether the horses shared the king's room as a result of tradition or whether he permitted them to do so in order to respect tradition. The narrative goes on to say that:—

"The country is far less advanced than I had anticipated. There are no houses beyond the ordinary, round, single-roomed hut. These houses—even those of the *sheikhs*—were so terribly dirty that I preferred usually to camp in the open, although the rains had begun and we had much wet. In the place where I had my first interview with Ras Ayra I changed my clothes for the great man; but as I was in the open plain, and as it was pouring cats and dogs, you may imagine what an absurd business it was. Everything was wet through in the act of changing."

Gordon does not tells us where he remained during those hours when he was detained by Ras Arya while that chieftain was presumed to be taking a "kosso cure", necessitated by his eating raw meat. All that we know is that at dusk the Abyssinian sent for him and said that "he would, in spite of the King, *bien entendu* for a consideration, send any telegram to Gallabat" that his prisoner might care to dispatch.

A present of £70 procured the forwarding of Gordon's messages, and likewise his release. But just as the party was getting under headway Ras Arya came forward and said : " Have you a watch to spare ? " The Khedive's emissary had not, but he saw the menacing look in the eyes of the " kosso " addict and " therefore seized a splendid silver one of Ibrahim's and gave it to him. The countenance of that dragoman was a study ", continues Gordon's narrative. " I told him, however, to fix a price, which I paid him. Really, for a presentation watch to a Prime Minister the sum—twenty-two dollars—could not be considered excessive."

Having thus ensured his freedom, Gordon, after various hardships, finally reached Massawah on 8th December. His eye almost immediately fell upon a copy of a newspaper which said that the Khedive, Tewfik Pasha, was greatly distressed at the failure of the King of Abyssinia to listen to Gordon. This publication flabbergasted the Scotsman. It is true that he had forwarded a confidential message to the Viceroy on 11th November, pointing out how things stood in Abyssinia and asking that a battalion of infantry be ordered to Massawah, but he never expected that the Press would be advised of the contents of an official dispatch of such moment. His chagrin was intensified by the fact that not a man had been sent to Massawah. The town was in a ferment. Everything tended to show that if British vessels had not been there the place would have been attacked by the Abyssinians.

Face to face with the emergency thus presented, and convinced that King Johannes was determined not to apply for the arbitration of France or England and that those Powers would not aid the people of Massawah by declaring it a free and neutral port, Gordon, on 18th December, telegraphed to Tewfik as follows :—

"As neither the French nor the English Governments will help you, and as you have not sent troops to defend Massawah, and as the Italians have acquired Assali, would it not be better to make a treaty with Italy and cede Annesley Bay upon the following terms: 'Mutual good-will and help; no sale of arms to Abyssinia or to the tribes; same taxes to obtain at Massawah and Annesley Bay; junction of telegraph lines; interchange of consuls; Italy to pay £5,000?'"[1]

Here we have an example of Gordon the realist at work. He saw that Massawah was not going to be defended. He felt that its capture by Abyssinia was imminent. He sought to save something from the wreck. His telegram was sent in cypher. It was intended for the Government and not for public consumption. Yet the Egyptian papers of 24th December carried an item to the effect that "Gordon desires Egypt to cede to Italy a port in the Red Sea in order to produce complications in the relations between Italy and Abyssinia."

When the Governor-General read this news he betook himself to Cairo. He thus describes his audience with the Khedive:—

"On coming to Cairo I sought an audience with Tewfik. Riaz Pasha, who was in the room, bolted out as I entered. I reproached Tewfik with promulgating opinions that were of a very confidential nature and that were offered for the benefit of Egypt alone. He replied: 'I am a young man. It is not my fault. The people write against me.' I told him that the telegram that had appeared in the *Standard* must have emanated from him or from his ministry. He tried to excuse himself, when I left him and resigned."

Gordon's last letter before sailing for England was addressed to his sister. It was dated 8th January, 1880, and said:—

[1] H. W. Gordon, op. cit., p. 134.

"You will, D.V., see me as soon as this letter, so I need not write what I have to say, for I will tell you in the kitchen where I can smoke."[1]

Gordon did not explain why he had to betake himself to his sister's kitchen if he wanted to smoke in her home. But we learn from his letters to her that he was very fond of her. He did not, however, hurry on to England quite as quickly as his last lines to her seemed to indicate that he would. On 21st January he was in Rome, and while there "had an attack of 'doles' for three hours. What a dire disease it is". Shortly after his arrival in England *Wanderlust* called him to Switzerland. A letter from Lausanne, dated 18th March, tells the story that his health had begun to mend, for he wrote :—

"It is odd that *longing with a great desire for death*, I am now quite well and have lost the numbed feeling I had in my arm both in Egypt and Southampton."

Gordon's work in the Sudan brought him to the notice of the Governor of the Cape Colony, who offered him the post of Commandant of the Colonial Forces. The offer was declined. But in the beginning of May he accepted an appointment as private secretary to Lord Ripon, who was going out to India as Viceroy. At a subsequent date he thus wrote of that experience :—

"In a moment of weakness I took the appointment of private secretary to Lord Ripon, and repented that I had done so at once, but I did not say so. I went out, and saw at Bombay that in my irresponsible position I could not possibly hope to do anything really to the purpose, in the face of vested interests out there ; so seeing this was the case, and also believing that my views were diametrically opposed to those of the official class, I gave up."

Gordon resigned his private secretaryship—an impossible post for a man of his temperament—on the

[1] *Letters of General C. G. Gordon to his Sister*, p. 204.

night of 2nd June, 1880. His resignation was accepted the next morning. It was published in the London papers on the morning of the fourth. These dates are thus insisted upon because in a letter to his sister the Scotsman wrote :—

"On the night of the 4th and on the 6th I received telegrams from China asking me to go there. In all this God has helped me wonderfully. I should like it to be known that I resigned before I knew of the China telegram, for otherwise it would seem that I had left Lord Ripon for this affair, which is not the case ; when I resigned, I knew nothing of what I should do, and thought of Zanzibar. I consider the coincidence of Hart's [1] telegram with my resignation is wonderful."

Before leaving for Hong Kong, Gordon handed to the Press the following memorandum :—

"My fixed desire is to persuade the Chinese not to go to war with Russia, both in their own interests and for the sake of those of the world, especially those of England. In the event of war breaking out I cannot answer for the present ; but I should ardently desire a speedy peace." On arrival at Point de Galle, upon 16th June, a message reached Gordon from the London War Office granting him leave of absence on condition that he took no military service in China. He immediately replied : "I will take no military service in China ; I would never embarass the British Government."

As soon as Gordon reached Shanghai he left for Tientsin to join his old friend and comrade, Li Hung Chang. Matters were found to be in a most unsatisfactory state. The majority of the Chinese Government, headed by Prince Chun, were for war, while the peace party had as its sole supporters Prince King and Li Hung Chang. The hold which the latter had

[1] Sir Robert Hart, head of the Chinese Customs Service and a power for good in China.

upon Gordon's heart was so great that he almost immediately sent off the following telegram to his military superiors : " I have seen Li Hung Chang, and he wishes me to stay with him. I cannot desert China in her present crisis, and would be free to act as I think fit. I therefore beg to resign my commission in Her Majesty's service."

But great as was Gordon's affection for Li Hung Chang, his love for peace was still greater. It was not out of Quixotic friendship but from an earnest desire to prevent the Far East from being plunged into war that he had taken this decisive action. And, ever practical, he proceeded at once to Pekin in order to back up his advice at the headquarters of the war party. The hotheads asked him what he advised. He replied that if they would burn the suburbs of Pekin and remove the Emperor to a place of safety, he would stay and help them, but that there was no use thinking of fighting under existing conditions as Pekin was too easily accessible.

A long discussion took place. Gordon told them it was no use ; that they could not go to war. This conversation was carried on through the medium of an interpreter. That dignitary " got so frightened at the words used that he upset the cup of tea that was standing by him. At last, he declared he would not repeat such expressions as Colonel Gordon made use of, so he (Gordon) took the dictionary, looked out ' idiocy ', and pointed it out to them and said : ' Make peace,' and wrote out the terms." [1]

There were five articles in all. The only one at which they hesitated was the fifth. It spoke of indemnity. They said this was hard and unjust. Gordon's answer to them brings out his sober common sense and his ability to strike the nail on the head. Here are his own words :—

" I said that might be, but what is the use of talking

[1] H. W. Gordon, op. cit., p. 149.

about it? If a man demanded your money or your life, you have only three courses open: 'You must either fight, call for help, or give up your money.' Now as you cannot fight, it is useless to call for help, since neither England nor France would stir a finger to assist you. I believe these are the articles now under discussion at Saint Petersburg, and the only one on which there is any question is the fifth."

Gordon was such an excellent psychologist that as soon as he saw that he had driven home his point he broke up the conference. Two days later he left Pekin. During this interval one of the belligerent ministers begged him not to leave his card anywhere or to let it be known that he was still there. Gordon thrust back at him the retort: "What does it matter? Neither you nor I will, in all probability, live more than ten or twelve years more. What does it signify if we shorten that?"

But the Chinese statesman did not agree with Gordon. A long life and a happy one meant a great deal to the Celestial. He accordingly worked for peace. By the middle of August the war cloud had disappeared. And when the sky was blue a telegram came to Gordon from England, dated 14th August. It read: "Leave cancelled; resignation not accepted." He did not answer at once. He was then on his way to England, his mission of peace a triumphant success. When he had reached Aden he felt that the time had come to get off his reply to the War Office message. His answer was couched in these words:—

"You might have trusted me. My passage from China was taken days before the arrival of your telegram which states 'leave cancelled'; do you insist on rescinding same?" England then knew that the world owed peace in China to Gordon. London, accordingly, answered: "Leave granted until 28th February, 1881." He continued his homeward journey and reached England on 21st October.

The hero of the hour did not remain at home long. He had heard of the sufferings of his fellow-creatures in the south-west and west of Ireland. He determined to study the problem on the spot. He drew up quite a lengthy memorandum in which his views were expressed with great force and clearness. It has little to do with the Sudan and Slavery. It may not, however, be amiss to cite a single sentence which stresses that love of religious freedom which made it so easy for Gordon, the zealous Christian, to see eye to eye with his Muslim friends. He wrote in his Irish notes :—

" In these days, in common justice, if we endow a Protestant University, why should we not endow a Catholic University in a Catholic country ? "

Shortly after Gordon's return to England from Ireland the post of Officer Commanding the Royal Engineers at Mauritius became vacant. A quarter of a century earlier, that appointment had been looked upon as one of the most favoured stations. A good colonial allowance, first-class society, and delightful climate had made it most attractive. But in the early eighties the island presented a different picture. A terrible fever had decimated the population, and a depression in sugar had impoverished those who had survived. The result was that nobody wanted to be assigned to Mauritius. Officers accepted half-pay rather than go there. It came about that it fell to the lot of Sir Howard Elphinstone, a close friend of Gordon's, to take over the disagreeable assignment.

At this juncture an old Crimean War comrade put the case before the former Governor-General of the Sudan. He was then at Southampton preparing his kit and making preparations for a visit to the Holy Land, one of his fondest dreams. Gordon said that he would go to Mauritius on two conditions. The first was that he should receive no money. The second was that Sir Howard Elphinstone was to make the move and obtain the necessary permission for the exchange. All was arranged. On 4th May, 1881, Gordon left for his new post.

Mauritius was a Colonel's command. On 24th March, 1882, Gordon was made a Major-General. This necessitated his transfer. Just at this time the Cape Ministry telegraphed to him to ask if he would go to their colony to consult with the Government as regards settling affairs in Basutoland. He accepted. His first official step was to cut down his own salary. He said : " I will not accept more than £800 per annum ; but I must have a private secretary." To the latter he gave the remaining £400.

The Cape mission was a comparatively short one. After a few months Gordon was again in London. Being unemployed he decided to go to Palestine. He remained there a year, devoting his time to the study of Biblical history and of the antiquities of Jerusalem.

## CHAPTER XVI

# THE SUDAN ABANDONED

WHEN Gordon retired from the Khedivial service the Egyptian dominions extended from Wadi Halfa on the north to the Equator on the south, and from Massowah on the east to the western limits of Darfur on the west; an area twice as large as France and Germany together. But in August, 1881, after both Ismail and Gordon had disappeared from the scene, a native of the Province of Dongola named Muhammad Ahmad proclaimed himself the Mahdi or Messiah of Islam. The people flocked to his standard. A series of minor military successes made a hero of him. It soon became evident that the Egyptian Government had to deal with a formidable rebellion, the suppression of which would tax their military and financial resources to the utmost. The English occupation of Egypt thus began at a time when religious fanaticism was sweeping over the Sudan and threatening to destroy the Empire of which Ismail had dreamed, and which Gordon had helped to make a reality.

The British Government had been led, much against their will, into the occupation of Egypt. They were fearful that they might unconsciously drift into military intervention in the Sudan. Lord Granville, then Her Britannic Majesty's Foreign Secretary, was determined to guard against this danger. He refused to have anything to say about Sudanese matters. Several British officers, chief amongst whom was General Hicks, had, however, been appointed to the staff of the Egyptian Army in the spring of 1883. Shortly after his arrival at Khartoum in March of that year, this gallant soldier made an appeal to Cairo for help.[1]

El Obeid had fallen on 18th February. This Egyptian defeat filled General Hicks with grave concern. He knew that the loss of that strategic point menaced the safety of the entire Sudan. He therefore repeatedly urged the Egyptian Government to give him more men and more money. These insistent demands caused Sir Edward Malet, then British Diplomatic Agent and Consul-General at Cairo, to telegraph to Lord Granville on 5th June :—

"Your Lordship is aware that it is already impossible for the Egyptian Government to supply the funds demanded for the Sudan, and the proposed operations will run a considerable risk of failure unless they are conducted on a large scale, and unless the army is well supplied in every respect. Under these circumstances, a question arises as to whether General Hicks should be instructed to confine himself to maintain the present supremacy of the Khedive in the region between the Blue and White Niles."

Sir Edward Malet thus made extreme prudence his watchword. He went so far as to envisage the necessity of instructing General Hicks to confine his activity to a relatively narrow zone. But even such circumspection alarmed the British Foreign Office. Lord Granville was perturbed by the continuance of communication between the British Resident and General Hicks. Her Majesty's Foreign Secretary accordingly wrote to Sir Edward Malet on 8th August :—

"It appears that General Hicks continues to communicate with you respecting the financial difficulties which he meets with in the Sudan, under the impression that you will exert your influence with the Egyptian

[1] *Modern Egypt*, by the Earl of Cromer ; New York, the Macmillan Co., 1908, vol. i, p. 354. All statements of fact contained in this chapter are based upon this same authority.

Government to induce them to give favourable consideration to his wishes. I need not remind you that Her Majesty's Government assume no responsibility whatever in regard to the conduct of affairs in the Sudan, and it is desirable that General Hicks should understand that, although they are glad to receive information as to the progress of the campaign, it is their policy to abstain as much as possible from interfering with the action of the Egyptian Government in that quarter."

Sir Edward Malet communicated these instructions to General Hicks in a telegram dated 18th August, which reads, in part, as follows :—

"Although I am ready to transmit to the Egyptian Government telegrams that come from you, I am debarred by my instructions from giving advice with regard to action on them, the policy of Her Majesty's Government being to abstain as much as possible from interfering with the action of the Egyptian Government in the Sudan."

And yet, to borrow the words of Grover Cleveland, London was confronted with a condition and not with a theory. General Hicks marched at the head of an expedition to Kordofan, fell into an ambush, and perished with his entire command. English public opinion was shocked when it heard the news. It cared nought for diplomatic quibbles. It looked at the question from a broader angle. It argued that the responsibility of the British Government for the loss of British lives and "for the general conduct of affairs in Egypt did not depend on a few phrases thrown into a dispatch and subsequently published in a parliamentary paper". It held that this accountability, to quote Lord Cromer again, "was based on the facts that the British Government were in military occupation of the country, that the weakness and inefficiency of the native rulers were notorious, and that the civilized world fixed on England a responsibility which it was impossible to shake off as long as the occupation lasted."

Sir Evelyn Baring, best known to fame as Lord Cromer, succeeded Sir Edward Malet as British Diplomatic Agent and Consul-General at Cairo on 8th September, 1883, three days after General Hicks had started on his ill-starred expedition. Baring, therefore, had nothing to do with shaping the policy of diplomatic subterfuge which led to this unhappy result. But it was not until 5th November of that year that the British soldier met his death while advancing on Kasghil. It thus came to pass that the great Proconsul played an active part in the chapter of history opened by the holocaust of that tragic day in the autumn of 1883.

Baring records in *Modern Egypt* that :—

" The first step of any importance taken in connection with Sudan affairs after my arrival in Egypt was on 19th November, 1883, on which I sent the following telegram to Lord Granville : ' The position of affairs in the Sudan is becoming very serious. Nothing definite has been heard of Hicks since 27th September. He only had provisions for two months. The Egyptian Government are very anxious and evidently expect bad news. Giegler Pasha, who was with Gordon in the Sudan, and whom I saw to-day, says that if Hicks is beaten, Khartoum will probably fall. . . . From some observations which Chérif Pasha let drop to me this morning, I think it not at all improbable that before long he will ask for the assistance of English or Indian troops. He said to me : " I suppose that Her Majesty's Government would not like to see the Turks intervene in the Sudan ? " Shall I be right in telling him, if the occasion arises, that under no circumstances must he look for the assistance of British or Indian troops in the Sudan ? As regards Turkish assistance, I should be glad to receive instructions as to the attitude I am to adopt.

It is a question which course the Egyptian Government would dislike most—to call in the Turks or to abandon the Sudan. My own opinion is that, if Hicks be beaten, the wisest course for the Egyptian Government to adopt is to accept defeat and fall back on whatever point on the Nile they can hold with confidence, although the adoption of this course would certainly give a great impulse to the Slave Trade.' "

This telegram was more than a routine despatch sent by a diplomatic officer in the field to his Foreign Office. It was a message which shows the drift of the envoy's mind. It marks an attempt by him to shape the policy of his Government. And it will be noted that Baring made it clear that "if Hicks be beaten, the wisest course for the Egyptian Government to adopt is to accept defeat".

To this despatch Lord Granville replied on 20th November in the following words: "We cannot lend English or Indian troops. It would not be for the advantage of Egypt to invite Turkish troops into the Sudan. If consulted, recommend the abandonment of the Sudan within certain limits."

Baring smiled complacently when he received these instructions. He had stolen a march on Downing Street. He had forced the Foreign Office to commit itself. So pleased was he at this adroitness in getting Lord Granville to unbosom himself that the Regenerator of Egypt takes the world into his confidence and proclaims that:—

"The principal object which I had in sending my telegram of 19th November was to draw the British Government out of the passive attitude which they had hitherto adopted. A short residence in the country had been sufficient to convince me that it was neither possible nor desirable to leave the Egyptian Government to manage Sudan affairs without any advice or assistance. My object had been attained. It is true that I was instructed only to give advice ' if consulted ', but as I was sure to be consulted the reserve placed on my action did not practically hamper me."

And after having in this wise expatiated upon how the man on the spot had managed to circumvent the inertia of politicians and bureaucrats at home, Baring thus analysed the net results of his finesse :—

" I had obtained a definite expression of opinion as to the Sudan policy which commended itself to the British Government in the event of a disaster happening to General Hicks' army. They would not afford military aid to reconquer the Sudan ; they were also averse to the employment of Turkish troops. Under these circumstances the only possible course would be to abandon the Sudan within certain limits."

When news reached Cairo on 22nd November of the death of General Hicks and of the destruction of his army, the first decision at which the Egyptian Government arrived was " to try and hold Khartoum and to reopen the route between Suakin and Berber ". In reporting this project to London, Baring said that " according to several telegrams received from Khartoum, there appeared to be a general opinion on the spot that it would be impossible to hold the town, and that it would be necessary to fall back on Berber ".

By 3rd December the English Agent and Consul-General had obtained the views of the principal military authorities in Cairo in regard to the situation created by the defeat of General Hicks. Baring was thus able to send the following report to his Foreign Office :—

" The most important question for the moment is to know whether an Egyptian Government will be able to maintain themselves at Khartoum. I have had the advantage of fully discussing this question with General Stephenson, Sir Evelyn Wood, and

General Baker. All these high military authorities are of one opinion. They consider that, if the Mahdi advances, it will be impossible for the Egyptian Government to hold Khartoum, I mean, of course, with any forces of which they now dispose or are likely to dispose. . . . If Khartoum is abandoned they think that the whole Valley of the Nile down to Wadi Halfa or thereabouts will probably be lost to the Egyptian Government."

The report concluded :—

"I need hardly say that these views are, not unnaturally, very unpalatable to the Egyptian Government. I hardly think that Chérif Pasha believes that he will be able to hold Khartoum if the Mahdi advances, but neither he nor his colleagues can make up their minds to abandoning it."

While this despatch was on its way to London it became clearer to Baring every day that if the Egyptian Government were left to themselves they would never decide upon any definite and practicable policy. The man who by his telegram of 19th November, 1883, had drawn Downing Street out of the passive attitude which it had hitherto adopted in regard to things Egyptian, did not contemplate sitting still while Cairo statesmen counted their beads and did nothing. On the contrary, while they were ruminating, he sent to Lord Granville a personal cable which was pregnant with meaning. It read :—

"I have not telegraphed for fresh instructions as I thought it useless to do so until events had developed somewhat, and I had something definite to recommend. But it is quite clear to me that more definite instructions must shortly be sent as to the attitude of Her Majesty's Government and as to the advice to be given to the Egyptian Government. At present they are drifting on without any very definite or practical plan of action, and will continue to do so unless they are told what course to pursue."

This personal message was, no doubt, put into code. The Egyptian Ministers, therefore, probably remained in ignorance of its exact text. They appear, however, to have been allowed to learn of its substance, for two days later Baring was able to send an official dispatch apprising the Foreign Office that the Khedive had held a Council of Ministers and that they had resolved to place themselves absolutely in the hands of Her Majesty's Government.

While thus putting on record their willingness to act as Sir Evelyn Baring should tell them to do, the Egyptian Ministers thought that the best solution of the question was to invite the aid of the Sultan. They desired that the British Government should arrange the conditions on which Turkish help would be afforded. Chérif Pasha, the Prime Minister, pointed out that as the rebellion in the Sudan was a religious movement, it would probably gather strength if British or Indian troops were employed.

When these facts were communicated to Lord Granville, he replied :—

"Her Majesty's Government have no intention of employing British or Indian troops in the Sudan. Her Majesty's Government have no objections to offer to the employment of Turkish troops, provided they are paid by the Turkish Government and that such employment be restricted exclusively to the Sudan, with their base at Suakin. Excepting for securing the safe retreat of the garrisons still holding positions in the Sudan, Her Majesty's Government cannot agree to increasing the burden on the Egyptian revenues by expenditure for operations which, even if successful, and this is not probable, would be of doubtful advantage to Egypt."

Important as all of these pronouncements were, they fade into insignificance before the recommendations which Sir Evelyn Baring was instructed to communicate to the Khedivial authorities. The language used by Lord Granville on this important point was as follows :—

" Her Majesty's Government recommend to the Ministers of the Khedive to come to an early decision to abandon all territory South of Asswan, or, at least, of Wadi Halfa. They will be prepared to assist in maintaining order in Egypt proper, and in defending it, as well as the ports of the Red Sea."

There was nothing minatory about this language. It was conciliatory in form, conceived in a spirit of abiding good will and born of a matter-of-fact appreciation of the difficulties with which the Egyptian Government were beset. And yet Chérif Pasha and his colleagues, while placing themselves on 12th December " absolutely in the hands of Her Majesty's Government ", announced on 22nd December that " they cannot agree to the abandonment of territories whch they consider absolutely necessary for the security and even the existence of Egypt herself." The Egyptian Prime Minister, however, reiterated his proposal that Turkish troops be sent under conditions to be negotiated in concert with the Egyptian Government.

In forwarding to London the substance of Chérif Pasha's reply, Baring observed :—

" I believe that the policy recommended by Her Majesty's Government is, on the whole, the best of which the very difficult circumstances will admit. No amount of argument or persuasion will make the present Ministry adopt the policy of abandonment. The only way in which it can be carried out is for me to inform the Khedive that Her Majesty's Government insist on its adoption, and that if the present Ministers will not carry it out, he must name others who will do so. Further, I am not sure that any Egyptian Ministers can be found who will be willing to carry out the policy and capable of doing so. If, therefore, it is forced on the Egyptian Government, Her

Majesty's Government must be prepared to face the possibility of appointing English Ministers temporarily."

There were teeth in this wire. Downing Street saw the indentation. It did not answer overnight. The matter required the most mature deliberation. General Hicks was dead. Other British lives were menaced, it is true, but they were not in immediate danger. Lord Granville desired to consider the matter from all possible angles before taking a decision. It was not until 4th January, 1884, that he communicated his official decision to Cairo. It was to the effect that England had no objection to the Sultan being asked to send troops, provided that there was no increase in Egyptian expenditure and provided also that the decision taken by the Egyptian Government as regards their own movements be not retarded. These instructions added that "Her Majesty's Government do not believe it to be possible for Egypt to defend Khartoum, and whilst recommending the concentration of Egyptian troops, they desire that these forces be withdrawn from Khartoum, as well as from the interior of the Sudan." This official message closed with the words: "And you will so inform Chérif Pasha."

This wire, specific though it was, had no bite to it. The pincers came in the shape of a further confidential message sent to Sir Evelyn Baring "for use", as he expresses it, "should occasion require." It was to the following effect:—

"It is essential that in important questions affecting the administration and safety of Egypt the advice of Her Majesty's Government should be followed, as long as the provisional occupation continues. Ministers and Governors must carry out this advice or forfeit their offices. The appointment of English Ministers would be most objectionable, but it will no doubt be possible to find Egyptians who will execute the

Khedive's orders under English advice. The Cabinet will give you full support."

England for half a century has now ruled the Land of the Pharaohs. The country is at present independent " with reservations ". This status has existed since 28th February, 1922. During the eighty odd months immediately preceding this date Great Britain maintained a protectorate over Egypt. From 1882 until 1914 British suzerainty did not exist in law, but obtained in fact under the style of a provisional occupation. But the Magna Charta of these successive regimes under which Egypt has flourished, and has emerged from poverty to prosperity, has been and is this " personal and confidential " message addressed by Lord Granville to Sir Evelyn Baring.

On communicating the views of the Foreign Office to Chérif Pasha, Baring found, as he had anticipated, a strong determination to reject the policy of withdrawal from Khartoum. Her Majesty's representative was therefore obliged to make use of the instructions contained in Lord Granville's confidential telegram. " The result," as the author of *Modern Egypt* laconically expresses it, was " that on 7th January Chérif Pasha tendered his resignation to the Khedive ". That same night the Viceroy sent for the real ruler of Egypt and informed him that " he accepted the resignation of his Ministers, and accepted cordially the policy of abandoning the whole of the Sudan, which, on mature reflection, he believed to be the best in the interests of the country ". On 8th January Baring telegraphed to the Foreign Office that Nubar Pasha had consented to form a Ministry and that " the new Prime Minister entirely concurred in the wisdom of abandoning the Sudan, retaining possession of Suakin ".

Thus the general policy which was to be pursued was definitely settled. Sir Evelyn Baring breathed a sigh of relief. He had before him a despatch sent from Khartoum by Colonel Coetlogon, addressed to the Khedive, reading : " I would strongly urge on Your Highness the great necessity for an immediate order for retreat being given. Were we twice as strong as we are, we could not hold Khartoum against the whole country, which, without a doubt, are one and all against us." It was a great satisfaction to the indefatigable Consul-General to know that the urgency of the decision recommended by him was thus approved, in no uncertain language, by the British military expert who commanded the Khartoum garrison.

## Chapter XVII

# GLADSTONE DRAFTS GORDON

It is as statesman and diplomatist that the name of Evelyn Baring, first Earl of Cromer, is written in letters of gold across the pages of history. But it was as soldier and financier that he first studied the Egyptian problem.

Born in 1841, he entered the Royal Artillery in 1858, and attained the rank of Major before retiring from the army. In 1876 he was appointed British Commissioner of the Egyptian Public Debt. The selection of a comparatively untried major of artillery as the English representative on a Financial Board composed of delegates of all the Great Powers was considered a bold step. Within a short time, however, it was recognized that the Englishman, though keeping himself carefully in the background, was unmistakably the predominant factor on the Commission.

Baring had an outstandingly brilliant mind, and a natural aptitude for finance. Military directness and business acumen thus paved his approach to the Egyptian question, when, in 1883, he became British Diplomatic Agent and Consul-General at Cairo. He understood Egyptian finance through and through. He knew that the Khedive's treasury could not stand the strain of stamping out Mahdiism and pacifying the Sudan until he had had an opportunity of putting the Egyptian fisc in order. And with the singleness of purpose of a soldier, he devoted the full force of his driving power to defining and executing the policy thus worked out by his financial genius.

But no such unerring logic guided English public opinion. Mass psychology is almost invariably swayed either by passion or by sentiment. It is not guided by reason, although it is occasionally led by instinct. The heart, not the mind, exercises a predominant influence over the crowd. England did not reason why. She knew that Hicks had been slain. His memory swayed her. We therefore read in Cromer's *Modern Egypt* that "few measures have formed the subject of more severe criticism than the policy adopted by Mr. Gladstone's Government in 1883–4 in connection with the Sudan. On 12th February, 1884, a vote of censure was moved by Lord Salisbury in the House of Lords and by Sir Stafford Northcote in the House of Commons. It was couched in the following terms: 'That this House is of opinion that the recent lamentable events in the Sudan are due to the vacillating and inconsistent policy pursued by Her Majesty's Government.'"[1]

Lord Salisbury, in speaking to this resolution, said: "We may think it was a right policy to maintain the Sudan, or we may think it was a right policy to abandon it; but we must, whatever opinion we hold, condemn the policy of the Government." Such Parliamentary thunder, however, was drowned in the universal acclaim which welcomed the news that Gordon had triumphantly entered Khartoum. The Gladstone Cabinet had atoned for any sins of omission that might have been charged up against it for the cruel fate of General Hicks by dispatching Chinese Gordon to the Sudan. The magic of Gordon's name won for Mr. Gladstone a substantial majority in the Division Lobby.

If the magnetism of Gordon's personality thus saved the Ministry from a defeat born of indignation at the death of Hicks, the Government had evinced no enthusiasm in sending the man of the hour to

[1] Earl of Cromer, op. cit., vol. i, p. 384.

Khartoum. On the contrary, Baring, who took the rudder of Egyptian affairs in hand when he obtained from Lord Granville those instructions of 20th November, 1883, which contained the momentous words : " If consulted, recommend the abandonment of the Sudan," was opposed to the employment of the former Governor-General. The future Lord Cromer assumed this attitude when Lord Granville asked him on 1st December whether Gordon's services could be utilized. No petty motives actuated the British Consul-General. He was above anything that even savoured of smallness. He consulted Chérif Pasha as to the advisability of enlisting Gordon's support, and as early as 2nd December telegraphed the Foreign Office that :—

" The Egyptian Government is very much averse to employing General Gordon, mainly on the ground that, the movement in the Sudan being religious, the appointment of a Christian to high command would probably alienate the tribes who remain faithful. I think it wise to leave the whole responsibility of the Sudan to them, and not to press them on the subject."

There were other reasons, dictated by statesmanship, which made Baring reluctant to press the nomination upon the unwilling Chérif Pasha. Gordon had not been popular with Egyptian officialdom even when he had Ismail's ear. " The Pashas all hate me,"[1] he wrote on 31st August, 1879, after Tewfik had become Khedive of Egypt. The British diplomat was aware of this. It made him doubly hesitant to overrule a decision which the Egyptian Prime Minister had carefully based upon other grounds. Baring knew that in the Near East the personal equation works miracles, and that the animosity of the Egyptian bureaucracy would have made Gordon's task almost insuperably difficult.

[1] Hill, op. cit., p. 400.

But to the British public Gordon and the Sudan were almost interchangeable terms. His name was bound to be forced to the fore whenever the Black Country was mentioned. The prejudices of Egyptian statesmen and the cold logic of the Foreign Office may have brushed him aside, but as long as the Sudan question remained unsettled and Hicks unavenged, "Chinese Gordon" was foremost in the minds of everybody interested in foreign affairs. *The Times* on New Year's Day, 1884, published a letter from Sir Samuel Baker giving concrete expression to this universal undercurrent of opinion. The great explorer urged that his successor as Governor-General of the Egyptian Equatorial Provinces be sent out as British High Commissioner to the Sudan.

This communication in *The Times* appeared before Chérif Pasha had resigned, and thus before the Egyptian Government had officially decided to abandon the Sudan. The day following the announcement that Nubar Pasha had agreed to form a Ministry pledged to carry out Baring's policy of withdrawal, the *Pall Mall Gazette* of 9th January carried a lengthy interview with General Gordon. Its every word is pregnant with meaning. It rings like an alarum bell. It is illuminating, combative, and constructive. It begins with a question.

"So you would abandon the Sudan?" asks the man who had ruled that land. "But the Eastern Sudan is indispensable to Egypt. It will cost you far more to retain your hold upon Egypt proper, if you abandon your hold on the Eastern Sudan to the Mahdi or to the Turks, than it would to retain your hold upon the Eastern Sudan by the aid of such material as exists in the provinces. . . . The danger to be feared is not that the Mahdi will march through to Wadi Halfa. The danger is altogether of a different nature. It arises from the influence which the spectacle of a conquering Muhammedan power established close to your frontier will exercise upon the population you govern." [1]

It is not difficult to follow the thoughts which ran through Gordon's mind as he thus gave his tongue full rein. He was not thinking of the Sudan as a whole, or even of the Eastern Sudan. He was looking at the entire problem solely from the point of view of England's Egyptian commitments. He knew that Britain was in Egypt, on a temporary mission, it is true, but with a mandate to put Egyptian finances in order, and with a moral obligation to maintain the rule of law in that country. He therefore felt that the British nation was entitled to know that if the Sudan were evacuated this abandonment would react with immediate and stunning force upon Egypt.

Having driven home this point, the interview discussed the practical mechanics of evacuation. Lord Morley, in his *Life of Gladstone*, describes Gordon as " the creature, almost the sport of impulse ". We see, however, from the emphasis laid upon the physical difficulties of withdrawal that the man thus assailed was a block of hard commonsense. He was willing to jump, but he insisted upon knowing where he was going to land.

" There is another aspect of the question," he urged. " You have 6,000 men in Khartoum. What are you going to do with them ? You have garrisons in Darfur, in Bahr Gazelle, and Gondokoro. Are they to be sacrificed ? Their only offence is their loyalty to their sovereign. For their fidelity are you going to abandon them to their fate ? You say that they are to retire upon Wady Halfa. How will you move your 6,000 men from Khartoum, to say nothing of other places—and all the Europeans in that city through the desert to Wady Halfa ? Where are you going to get the camels to take them away ? If they

[1] H. W. Gordon, op. cit., p. 297.

are to escape with their lives, the garrison will not be allowed to leave with a coat on their backs. They will be plundered to the skin, and even then their lives may not be spared.

"Whatever you may decide about evacuation," he continued, "you cannot evacuate, because your army cannot be moved. You must either surrender absolutely to the Mahdi or defend Khartoum at all hazards. The latter is the only course which ought to be entertained." [1]

There was nothing hesitant about such language. It was attuned to a note of imperative finality. It was the outspoken expression of a brave man who was greatly moved, and whose eyes were bloodshot with righteous anger. And the dramatic emphasis of this interview was underscored by the *Pall Mall Gazette's* vigorous editorial which accompanied it. W. T. Stead's trenchant pen fairly burned into the columns of that paper this clarion appeal :—

"We cannot send a regiment to Khartoum, but we can send a man who on more than one occasion has proved himself more valuable in similar circumstances than an entire army. Why not send Chinese Gordon with full powers to Khartoum, to assume absolute control of the territory, to treat with the Mahdi, to relieve the garrisons, and to do what he can to save what can be saved from the wreck in the Sudan?" [2]

The dominant note of Stead's editorial blast was, therefore, that Gordon was worth more to England than an army and that he should be sent to the Sudan "with full powers to assume absolute control". The next day the great morning dailies took up the refrain. They carried copious extracts from the *Pall Mall* interview, in which, again to quote that journal's leading article, Gordon "not only impeaches directly the policy of evacuating the Sudan, but absolutely

[1] Archer, op. cit., vol. iii, p. 11.

[2] Allen, op. cit., p. 217.

denies the possibility unless we are willing to admit that when we say evacuation we mean massacre".

These Press comments, and the intervention of Queen Victoria, built a fire under the Foreign Secretary. Accordingly, on 10th January, he sent the following telegram to Baring:—

"Would General Charles Gordon or Sir Charles Wilson be of assistance under altered conditions in Egypt?"

The answer came back as straight as a shot: "I have consulted Nubar and I do not think that the services of General Gordon or Sir Charles Wilson can be utilized at present."[1]

But when the public conscience is aroused it is all-engulfing in its power. The *Morning Advertiser* of 12th January gave voice to this surging wave of popular feeling when it proclaimed that—

"It is not too much to say that all England has been looking for the employment of General Gordon in the present crisis in Egypt."

When this universal demand that the Ministry send "Gordon with full powers to Khartoum, to assume absolute control of the territory" was beginning to develop irresistible momentum, he was in Brussels. As early as 25th October he had accepted an offer from King Leopold to go to the Congo in the spring. He had gone to Belgium to arrange certain details necessitated by this assignment. His letter resigning his commission in the British Army had been mailed from Southampton on 7th January, almost immediately upon his return to England. It thus came to pass that when the *Pall Mall* article, before referred to, appeared on 9th January, Gordon felt that he was unalterably committed to go to the Belgian Congo. In fact, when his old friend, Sir Andrew Clarke, called attention to the public outcry, the soldier-explorer wrote:—

[1] *Life of Sir Andrew Clarke*, p. 264, quoted in Allen, op. cit., p. 218.

"The deed was done on the 7th January resigning my Commission; so I cannot help it. I also promised the King, and I cannot break my word.

"Things are too mixed in the Sudan and Egypt for me to think of it; and you know this well enough. As to Tewfik, I could never serve under him: for he would never forgive my letter; so there is an end to that."[1]

The poet, however, has said that:—

> "The best laid schemes o' mice and men
> Gang aft agley,
> And leave us naught but grief and pain
> For promised joy."

Gordon had set his heart on going to the Congo because he felt that that region was then the strategic point where the slave trade could best be dealt a mortal blow. The Sudan did not appeal to him as offering quite so admirable a vantage point in this warfare upon the enemies of civilization. But when, on 13th January, a telegram came to him from Lord Wolseley requesting the former Governor-General of the Sudan to call at the War Office, the courteous message received a reply asking for an appointment on Tuesday the 15th at 3 p.m. This answer was momentous in its consequences.

When these telegrams, ostensibly bearing upon Gordon's resignation of his commission in the Army, were exchanged, Mr. Gladstone was at Hawarden. Lord Granville had had his ear to the ground and knew that the nation wanted Gordon to go to the Sudan. The Foreign Secretary thought that it would be good politics and prudent statesmanship to yield to this pressure. Therefore, on 14th January, he sounded the Prime Minister regarding the advisability of "putting a little pressure on Baring" to make that

[1] Ibid., p. 264, quoted in Allen, op. cit., p. 219.

strong-minded and resourceful diplomat agree to the dispatch of Gordon if that officer said " he believed " he could by his personal influence excite the tribes to escort the Khartoum garrison and inhabitants to Suakin ".

Mr. Gladstone gave his blessing to Lord Granville's suggestion. The Foreign Secretary then sent his chief a copy of the telegram putting " a little pressure on Baring ". To this the Prime Minister replied on 16th January :—

" I can find no fault with your telegram to Baring *re* Chinese Gordon, and the main point that strikes me is this : While his opinion on the Sudan may be of great value, must we not be very careful in any instructions we give, that he does not shift the centre of gravity as to political and military responsibility for that country ? In brief, if he reports what should be done, he should not be the judge *who* should do it, nor ought he to commit us on that point by advice officially given. It would be extremely difficult after sending him to reject such advice, and it should therefore, I think, be made clear that he is not our agent for the purpose of advising on that point." [1]

Mr. Gladstone's massive head was the seat of a great brain, but of a single-track mind. Of retentive memory, wide reading, and alert scholarship, he was self-centred and, as Disraeli put it, " inebriated with his own verbosity." He was a man, as W. E. Forster once said in the House of Commons when discussing the Sudan question, who " can persuade most people of most things, and, above all, he can persuade himself of almost anything ". Impeccably and fearlessly honest, he had that degree of conceit which is so often begotten by a clear conscience. He was an extremely busy statesman, and, when he wrote this reply of 16th January to Lord Granville, he was seventy-five

[1] *The Life of William Ewart Gladstone*, by John Morley ; London, Macmillan and Company, Limited, vol. ii, p. 390.

years of age. He felt that he was the bright resplendent star of his Government and that his colleagues were but satellites. What, therefore, remained indelibly impressed upon his thoughts from first to last, in all matters bearing upon Gordon's mission to the Sudan, was this letter of 16th January. It was the Ark of the Covenant wherein, to his mind, was to be found the touchstone for all questions bearing upon Gordon and the Sudan.

While all this is but too true, Mr. Gladstone naturally allowed the details of putting this "little pressure on Baring" to be left to his Foreign Office. Lord Granville, gratified at the receipt of Mr. Gladstone's telegram approving of the wisdom of sounding Gordon, hastened to advise the War Office of this new orientation of policy. When, therefore, the latter called upon Lord Wolseley to keep his appointment, the Adjutant-General pitched the interview upon the crisis in the Sudan and brought out that the Government were thinking of asking for Gordon's assistance in dealing with the problem. "Would you be prepared to go to Suakin to inquire into the conditions of affairs in the Sudan?" was the categorical question submitted to the Royal Engineer.

He gave the obvious answer. It was that he was ready to go out and study the lay of the land, if requested by the Government to do so. And before he and Wolseley separated Gordon drew up a memorandum tracing the general objects of his proposed mission. It is couched in these words:—

"(1) To proceed to Suakin and report on the military situation of the Sudan and return. Under Baring for orders, and to send through him letters, etc., under flying seal.

"(2) Government not indebted beyond passage money and £3 per diem travelling expenses.

"(3) Notify public.

"(4) Nubar and Baring to be notified so as to give all assistance.

"(5) Admiral Hewett to give me an account of £500 to be accounted for.

"(6) Letters to Brussels saying that leave is given me to go to Congo after my mission to Suakin.

"(7) I understand H.M.G. only wish me to report and are in no way bound to me.

"(8) Telegraph Egypt to Government to send Ibrahim Bey to meet me Suez with a writer to attend on me." [1]

This memorandum is essentially sketchy. It is obvious that it was not drawn by a skilled draftsman. But it meant a great deal to the British Cabinet of the day. The Government had heard the rumbling sound of discontent at their inaction following on the slaughter of General Hicks and his army. They needed the prestige of Gordon's intervention to save them from Parliamentary ire. They had feared that he would refuse to be called away from the Congo, for they knew that his heart was bent upon exterminating the slave trade and that he looked upon the Belgian African Empire as the great cesspool of moral infection. As soon, therefore, as Lord Wolsley obtained this memorandum it was sent to Downing Street.

It differed quite materially from what Lord Granville had outlined to Mr. Gladstone, and from what the latter had approved. It was at variance with the tenor of the letter written by the Prime Minister to his Foreign Secretary, in which he had elaborated the instructions which should be sent to Baring. But Lord Wolseley could not have known all these details. He did his duty as a soldier in submitting Gordon's memorandum to his Minister, and the Secretary of State for War, Lord Hartington, did the proper thing in passing it on, without delay, to Lord Granville.

It appears from what Lord Morley has written

[1] Allen, op. cit., p 221.

that the memorandum interested the Foreign Office. At all events we read in the *Life of William Ewart Gladstone* :—

"Two days later, on 18th January, Lord Hartington (then Secretary of State for War), Lord Granville, Lord Northbrooke, and Sir Charles Dilke, met at the War Office in Pall Mall. The summons was sudden. Lord Wolseley brought Gordon and left him in the anteroom. After a conversation with the Ministers, he came out and said to Gordon : 'Government are determined to evacuate the Sudan, for they will not guarantee the future Government. Will you go and do it ?' *I said* : '*Yes.*' *He said* : 'Go in.' *I went in and saw them. They said* : 'Did Wolseley tell you your orders ?' *I said* : 'Yes.' I said : 'You will not guarantee future Government of the Sudan, and you wish me to go up and evacuate now ?' They said : 'Yes,' *and it was over and I left at* 8 *p.m. for Calais.*"

From a footnote appended by Lord Morley to this recital we learn that the words put into italics were used by Gordon and were copied by the author of *Gladstone* from Gordon's *Letters to Barnes*.[1]

Lord Wolseley and the Duke of Cambridge accompanied Gordon when he left that night for Calais. The Adjutant-General carried the departing man's bag and His Royal Highness held open the carriage-door. But, when the four statesmen who had sent him on his journey met the next day, one of them said : "We were proud of ourselves yesterday—are you sure we did not commit a gigantic folly ?" Politically they had not made a mistake, for they had apprised the Prime Minister of the substance of what had taken place. "He had agreed at once on receiving the news and telegraphed assent the same night." And four days later : "The whole Cabinet met, Mr. Gladstone among them, and the decision was approved. There

[1] Morley, op. cit., vol. ii, p. 390.

was hardly a choice, for by that time Gordon was at Brindisi."[1]

In the light of subsequent events, it is easy to appear omniscient and to reconstruct what really happened on 18th January, 1884. A momentous decision had been taken. All parties concerned were in absolute good faith. Each one of them construed it from his own point of view. None of them appreciated the potentialities of their resolution. They were not temporizing or seeking expedients. They merely misjudged the situation. They miscalculated what the French call the *impondérables* of the case. They forgot that England is a democracy, that Crown and Nation wanted Gordon sent to the Sudan, and that no amount of " blue book " material would be able to wipe out the fact that Gordon's personality and not his official mandate defined his mission.

And the man himself, as he entered the carriage-door, held open for him by the Duke of Cambridge, probably had not whipped his own ideas into shape. One dominant principle guided him. It was his sense of duty. He had consecrated his life to an implacable war on the slave trade. Nothing had ever caused him to swerve from that purpose. He had written into his War Office memorandum a clause which read : " (6) Letters to Brussels saying that leave is given me to go to Congo after my mission to Suakin." He had done this because he intended to make it clear that the Sudan assignment was but temporary, and that the Congo was his eventual goal.

The Sudan itself was not a magnet which drew him to the East. He wrote to Lord Granville on 22nd January that " the Sudan ever was and ever would be a useless possession, and that he thought the Queen's Ministers fully justified in recommending evacuation, inasmuch as the sacrifice necessary towards securing good government would be too onerous to admit of

[1] Ibid., p. 391.

such an attempt ".[1] But he did not mean by this letter to give the lie to his *Pall Mall Gazette* interview of 9th January. Gordon was not a weather-vane whose angle of vision changed with the wind. On the contrary, he was a hard-headed Scotsman. He approved of evacuation as an objective, but condemned it for the practical reason that evacuation meant massacre unless he was able to devise ways and means " to save what can be saved ".

It should not be forgotten that Gordon had agreed " to proceed to Suakin and report on the military situation of the Sudan and return ". When he wrote this letter of 22nd January he sought to stress the point that the Sudan meant nothing to him and that he was in favour of its abandonment provided " evacuation does not mean massacre ". Notwithstanding the " many variations of mood " which Lord Morley attributes to the man whom Gladstone drafted " to proceed to Suakin ", Gordon had enough Highland blood in his veins to know that every member of the British Cabinet had read his *Pall Mall* interview and that the Government had retained his services with full knowledge that he was prepared to die to defend every sentiment and every thought expressed in it. He therefore assumed that Lord Granville understood the idea which the letter intended to convey. It was " I am going out with an open mind as to the modalities of keeping evacuation and massacre from being synonymous terms. I shall report to you upon my return."

But if the four Cabinet Ministers felt on 19th January that they had made a mistake the previous day in dispatching a soldier of Gordon's temperament on a piece of business needing vigilant sanity and self-possession, and if the agent selected by them had an open mind rather than a preconceived plan of campaign, Sir Evelyn Baring was quick to

[1] Ibid., p. 387.

grasp the trend of events. He had always persistently maintained that whoever went to the Sudan would "undertake a service of great difficulty and danger". Never afraid to accept responsibilities, he asked that Gordon be instructed to proceed to Cairo before going to Suakin. The Foreign Office assented, and thereby unwittingly completely changed the orientation of the policy which had grown out of the original interview between Gordon and the four Cabinet Ministers.

## Chapter XVIII

# GORDON'S INSTRUCTIONS

The Government were in such a precipitate hurry to get Gordon off to the Sudan that his official instructions do not appear to have been read by him until his ship was ploughing through the Mediterranean. He had them in his pocket when he left London. They are dated 18th January. It appears, nevertheless, that they had reached him as he was leaving for the railway station. They read :—

" Her Majesty's Government are desirous that you should proceed at once to Suakin to report to them on the military situation in the Sudan, and on the measures which it may be advisable to take for the security of the Egyptian garrisons still holding positions in that country, and for the safety of the European population in Khartoum.

" You are also desired to consider and report upon the best mode of effecting the evacuation of the interior of the Sudan, and upon the manner in which the safety and good administration by the Egyptian Government of the ports on the seacoast can best be secured.

" In connection with the subject, you should pay especial consideration to the question of the steps that may usefully be taken to counteract the stimulus which it is feared may possibly be given to the slave-trade by the present insurrectionary movement and by the withdrawal of the Egyptian authority from the interior.

" You will be under the instructions of Her Majesty's Agent and Consul-General at Cairo, through whom your reports to Her Majesty's Government should be sent, under flying seal.

" You will consider yourself authorized and

instructed to perform such other duties as the Egyptian Government may desire to entrust to you and as may be communicated to you by Sir Evelyn Baring. You will be accompanied by Colonel Stewart, who will assist you in the duties thus confided to you.

"On your arrival in Egypt, you will at once communicate with Sir Evelyn Baring, who will arrange to meet you, and will settle with you whether you should proceed direct to Suakin or should go yourself or despatch Colonel Stewart to Khartoum via the Nile."[1]

Gordon carefully weighed every word of these instructions. By the time he had reached Port Said he had put his reflections into the form of a memorandum. It is made up of seven quite lengthy numbered paragraphs. Colonel Stewart added his observations. The last remarks of the latter officer may well be cited. They read :—

"(5) As it is impossible for Her Majesty's Government to foresee all the eventualities that may arise during the evacuation, it seems to me as the more judicious course to rely on the discretion of General Gordon and his knowledge of the country.

"(6) I, of course, understand that General Gordon is going to the Sudan with full powers to make all arrangements as to its evacuation and that he is in no way to be interfered with by the Cairo ministers."[2]

We shall resort to the very incorrect practice of not quoting Gordon's memorandum. Mr. Gladstone's official biographer has given an accurate synopsis of its contents. This excerpt will be cited. It is not only true to the facts, but it has the added advantage of giving the reaction of Lord Morley to that important document. The distinguished historian said :—

"On his voyage from Brindisi Gordon had prepared

[1] Archer, op. cit., vol. iii, p. 54 (one alteration has been made in the Archer text. The word Egypt has been changed to Suakin upon the authority of Allen's *Gordon and the Sudan*, p. 231).

[2] Ibid., vol. iii, p. 53.

a memorandum for Sir E. Baring in which he set out his opinion that the Sudan had better be restored to the different petty Sultans in existence before the Egyptian conquest and an attempt should be made to form them into some sort of confederation. The petty rulers might be left to accept the Mahdi for their sovereign or not just as they pleased. But in the same document he emphasized the policy of abandonment. 'I understand,' he says, 'that H.M.'s Government have come to the irrevocable decision not to incur the very onerous duty of granting to the people of the Sudan a just future government.' Left to their independence the Sultans would doubtless fight among themselves. As for the future good government, it was evident that this 'we could not secure without an inordinate expenditure of men and money. The Sudan is a useless possession, ever was so, and ever will be so. No one who has ever lived in the Sudan can escape the reflection : What a useless possession is this land'. Therefore—so he winds up—'I think H.M.'s Government are fully justified in recommending the evacuation, inasmuch as the sacrifices necessary towards securing a good government would be far too onerous to admit of any such attempt being made. H.M.'s Government will now leave them as God has placed them.' "[1]

Lord Morley tears this memorandum to pieces. He holds that in view of what Gordon there wrote it is pure sophistry to contend that Gordon's policy was evacuation not abandonment. And, growing insistent, the biographer adds : "To say that the Sudanese should be left in the state in which God has placed them to fight it out among themselves, if so minded, is as good a definition of abandonment as can be invented."

It is a facile thing for a Liberal to become a doctrinaire and for a Radical to worship at the shrine

[1] Morley, op. cit., vol. ii, p. 393.

of dialectics. Men of that school are temperamentally predisposed to burn incense at the altar of metaphysics. Lord Morley was so convinced an idealist, so pronounced a pacifist, and so logical a reasoner that he resigned from the British Cabinet in 1914 when Germany drove England into war. And it was from this same Kantian conception of " pure reason " that he has analysed Gordon's words. He forgot the personal equation. He overlooked the soldier's background. He brushed aside the man's *Pall Mall* interview which, when all is said and done, forced the Gladstone Ministry to send Gordon to the Sudan. He also lost sight of the Granville instructions.

The memorandum, in a word, should be read not as an isolated piece of historical literature, but as a living document inseparably linked with Gordon's personality and supplementing his *Pall Mall* pronouncement, as well as the text of Lord Granville's instructions. So interpreted, it is obvious that Gordon envisaged not abandonment but evacuation. The crux of his paper is not what he added about " leaving them as God has placed them ". The pulsating reality is found in the two opening paragraphs. They read :—

" (1) I understand that Her Majesty's Government have come to the irrevocable decision not to incur the very onerous duty of securing to the people of the Sudan a just future government. That as a consequence Her Majesty's Government have determined to restore to these peoples their independence, and will no longer suffer the Egyptian Government to interfere with their affairs.

" (2) For this purpose Her Majesty's Government have decided to send me to the Sudan to arrange for the evacuation of these countries, and the safe removal of the Egyptian employees and troops." [1]

It is, accordingly, obvious that all this reference to allowing the Sudanese to stew in their own juice

[1] Archer, op. cit., vol. iii, p. 51.

referred to what would probably happen after evacuation. Gordon understood perfectly that he had no mandate to arrange for the future government of the Sudan. What was incumbent upon him was (1) to evacuate that country and (2) "to pay especial attention to the question of the steps that may usefully be taken to counteract the stimulus which," to continue to quote Lord Granville, "it is feared may possibly be given to the slave trade by the present insurrectionary movement."

In order to safeguard this evacuation and to devise ways and means for preventing the expansion of the slave trade, Gordon had to turn over Khartoum to somebody. He knew that he could not walk out of that capital with the Egyptian employees and troops unless somebody with authority took over from him who had the energy, the power, and the willingness to prevent evacuation and massacre from becoming synonymous. Even if he had been prepared to forget all about the slave trade, he had to ensure his line of retreat, or, in leaving Khartoum, he would have been merely courting death for those whose safety was committed to his care.

Lord Granville as well as Gordon looked upon the necessity of taking means to counteract the spread of the slave trade as part of the soldier's mission. Gordon's life-work warrants the assumption that he had given great weight to the Foreign Secretary's words on that score. The latter meant them. He was a Liberal statesman, and Nonconformists, the backbone of the anti-slavery movement from the days when William Wilberforce became converted to Evangelical Christianity, were, in 1884, predominantly Liberals. The Gladstone Cabinet was not averse to capitalizing Gordon's popularity. It welcomed the opportunity of strengthening itself with its Nonconformist wing by keeping anti-slavery in the foreground.

The memorandum, written on shipboard, which

plays such an important part in the controversy revolving around Gordon, was sent to Lord Granville. It was an official document upon which the Foreign Secretary was entitled to pass judgment. At all events, its author was justified in assuming that it was Lord Granville's interpretation of the memorandum which would be the decisive factor. It appears, however, that in respect of things Egyptian the Foreign Secretary allowed himself to be largely effaced by his Cairo Consul-General—except in matters bearing upon stamping out the slave trade. In all subjects that related to the war on slavery the Minister was adamant and enforced his authority. In regard, nevertheless, to current Egyptian problems he almost always accepted the advice of Sir Evelyn Baring.

In other words, before London had agreed to send Gordon to Suakin, the forceful soldier who had become a diplomatist and who ruled Egypt had been consulted. At first reluctant to impose Gordon upon the Egyptians who were opposed to such a nomination, Baring finally consented. It appears, however, that official and private telegrams were exchanged between him and Lord Granville, before Sir Evelyn gave the nomination his imprimatur.

Dr. Allen, in his masterly *Gordon and the Sudan*, demonstrates that, through a crossing of the telegrams thus exchanged between London and Cairo, and through the bracketing together of two divergent proposals in one, Baring was justified in assuming that an executive and not an advisory officer was being sent out to him. It would carry us somewhat far afield to go into the evidence upon which Dr. Allen's proof is based. Suffice it to say that even if Sir Evelyn Baring were justified in inferring that Gordon had instructions which were mandatory and which left him no discretionary latitude, it was the Foreign Office's interpretation of the soldier's orders which should be taken as the pivotal criterion.

Baring, like Gordon, was an agent. It is the point of view of the principal which predominates. And Lord Granville, as a Liberal statesman, had his eye fixed on the dual goal : evacuation without massacre and the curtailment of the slave trade. His emissary, Gordon, knew this. The fact that Sir Evelyn Baring may have seen matters from a different angle supports that statesman's good faith, but does not change the salient factor that both Granville and Gordon were in accord. Baring's deductions cannot validly be set off against the contemporaneous construction of his Foreign Minister.

While the peer and the knight were so busily exchanging personal and official messages that their telegrams became crossed and bracketed together, Gordon was still in England. The Granville instructions, as has already been said, were written on 13th January. They were therefore drawn up after the Foreign Secretary and the Consul-General had finished their rapid-fire reciprocal telegraphic bombardment. So essentially personal were Lord Granville's orders that they were written out in his own hand and appear to have been drafted by him and not to have been revised by his permanent staff. But while Gordon was tossing about on the sea, Baring again used the cables. He asked that Gordon be directed to proceed to Cairo before going to Suakin. A telegram, accordingly, awaited the soldier at Port Said, which read : " Baring gives strong reasons why you should go to Cairo, in which we hope you will concur."

Gordon did not hesitate. He went to Cairo. Once there all the personal touch that Lord Granville had given to his 18th January instructions became blurred. Baring was the active man on the spot whose sub-conscious mind became dominated by the conviction that he, and not the Foreign Secretary, was tracing Gordon's line of conduct.

And yet, before reaching Marseilles on his way to the East, Gordon had already put into black and white a concrete plan of action. He did not contemplate carrying it into effect on his own responsibility. It dealt with fundamentals. Accordingly, he mailed his proposals to the Foreign Office so as to have London's sanction for them. His first suggestion was that the Khedive should issue a proclamation that Egypt had decided to grant independence to the various Sultans of the Sudan and that Gordon was going to Khartoum as the representative of the Khedive and of the British Government to arrange "for the evacuation of the country and the withdrawal of the troops". His second proposal was that he, Gordon, should give out an appeal to the tribes in arms near Suakin couched in these words :—

"I, Gordon Pasha, hope to be with you in 14 days, and as I am authorized by the Khedive and the British Government to visit you with a view to arranging as to your future government, I trust you will allow the beleaguered garrison to retire on Suakin, thus avoiding useless loss and misery to your co-religionists." [1]

These draft proclamations reached the Foreign Office on 21st January. Their contents were cabled to Baring. He replied, on 23rd January : "All Gordon's suggestions are excellent and harmonize with the lines on which we have already been working." But while the great Proconsul telegraphed in this strain the P. & O. steamer was carrying from Cairo to London a personal letter written by him to Lord Granville, and dated 21st January, in which the Foreign Secretary was informed that—

"It is all well that Gordon should be under my orders, but a man who habitually consults the Prophet Isaiah when he is in difficulty is not apt to obey the orders of any man." [2]

[1] Allen, op. cit., p. 237.
[2] Earl of Cromer, op. cit., vol. i, p. 448 (note).

This means that when Sir Evelyn Baring sent his official message of 23rd January, approving of Gordon's policy, as defined in the two proclamations drafted on the P.L.M. train, Her Majesty's Consul-General knew perfectly well that the terms of the soldier's mandate were but of secondary import. The Gladstone Ministry needed Gordon's name to protect it from the storm of discontent set in motion by the death of General Hicks. Gordon's reputation was his power of attorney. And the Prophet Isaiah whom he consulted when in difficulty was just the kind of directing power that the Nonconformist Liberals preferred to the impersonal, soulless, colourless terms of official instructions.

Accordingly, we should resolutely look the facts in the face. It is merely a matter of academic interest and of historical pedantry to seek for the terms of Gordon's mandate in Blue Books and musty archives. There is no statue of Sir Christopher Wren in Saint Paul's Cathedral. The visitor is told : "If you seek his monument, look around you." Taking his cue from this, the heroic Briton who met his death at Khartoum might well have said to Gladstone, Granville, and Baring : "My instructions are written across the pages of my life of accomplishment." He would have been accepted on these conditions. The Ministry would not have dared to reject them. Yet he agreed to receive orders. Sir Evelyn Baring was convinced that Gordon was temperamentally incapable of following instructions. And yet, though dominated by this obsession, the Maker of Modern Egypt backed himself against the Prophet Isaiah and gave orders to Gordon. The sequel will show how faithfully the soldier endeavoured to execute them.

## Chapter XIX

# AT CAIRO

It was only because Gordon and Baring were gentlemen that they failed to have an acrimonious discussion when they met at the British Consultate General at Cairo. They had nothing in common except that they sprang from the same social stratum and had both of them begun life as soldiers. This similarity of origin accentuated their basic dislike for one another. It gave each a more exaggerated idea of the barrier that separated them than would have been the case had they not come out of the same mould. Baring looked upon Gordon as a subaltern who had become a religious fanatic. The latter beheld in the former an officer who had forsaken the sincerity of the barracks for the duplicity of a Chancellery.

The two men were temperamentally the antipodes of one another. Each got on the other's nerves. And, if the truth must be told, each held the other in abiding contempt. When Baring wrote that " a man who habitually consults the Prophet Isaiah when he is in difficulty is not apt to obey the orders of any man ", he meant to say that Gordon was a consummate idiot, and should be allowed to die in a gutter unwept, unhonoured, and unsung. And Gordon paid back Baring in the same coin when he wrote : " I must say I hate our diplomatists. I think with few exceptions, they are humbugs ; and I expect they know it." Gordon's journals show that Sir Evelyn Baring was not looked upon as being one of these rare exceptions.

But since the sons of English gentlemen learn, even in the nursery, how to control their nerves, the two antagonists did not fly at one another's throat. On the contrary, they subordinated their ill-will to the necessities of the hour and collaborated in apparent amity. So harmoniously did they work together that Baring wrote privately on 28th January to Lord Granville : " It is impossible not to be charmed by the simplicity and honesty of Gordon's character."

This same letter, nevertheless, shows the working of its writer's subconscious mind, for it went on to say :—

" My only fear is that he is terribly flighty and changes his opinions very rapidly. I am glad that Stewart, who impressed me favourably, is going with him, but I do not think Gordon much likes it himself. He said to me : ' They sent him (Stewart) with me as my wet-nurse.' "[1]

And in this atmosphere where the future Lord Cromer received the impression that " impulsive flightiness was, in fact, the main defect of General Gordon's character which rendered him (in Baring's opinion) unfit to carry out a work which required a cool head and steady hand ",[1] Her Majesty's Diplomatic Agent on 26th January gave the man whom he did not trust instructions couched substantially in these terms :—

" It is believed that the number of the Europeans at Khartoum is very small, but it has been estimated by the local authorities that some 10,000 to 15,000 people will wish to move northwards from Khartoum only when the Egyptian garrison is withdrawn. These people are native Christians, Egyptian employees, their wives and children, etc. The Government of His Highness the Khedive are earnestly solicitous that no effort should be spared to ensure the retreat both of these people and of the Egyptian garrison without loss of life. . . .

" You will bear in mind that the main end to be

[1] Earl of Cromer, op. cit., vol. i, p. 433.

pursued is the evacuation of the Sudan. . . . You think that it should take a few months to carry it out with safety. You are further of opinion that 'the restoration of the country should be made to the different petty Sultans who existed at the time of Muhammad Ali's conquest, and whose families still exist, and that an effort should be made to form a confederation of those Sultans'. In this view the Egyptian Government entirely concurs.

"It will, of course, be fully understood that the Egyptian troops are not to be kept in the Sudan merely with a view to consolidating the power of the new rulers of the country. But the Egyptian Government have the fullest confidence in your judgment, your knowledge of the country, and your comprehension of the general line of policy to be pursued. You are, therefore, given full discretionary power to retain the troops for such reasonable period as you may think necessary, in order that the abandonment of the country may be accomplished with the least possible risk to life and property." [1]

The Foreign Office took cognizance of these instructions, and wrote to Baring that :—

"Her Majesty's Government, bearing in mind the exigencies of the occasion, concurred in these instructions, which virtually altered General Gordon's mission from one of advice to that of executing, or at least directing, the evacuation, not only of Khartoum, but of the whole Sudan, and they were willing that General Gordon should receive the very extended powers conferred upon him by the Khedive to enable him to effect this very difficult task." [2]

At the time when the Foreign Secretary thus permitted his Cairo Consul-General to direct the Sudan policy of the British Government, both Lord Granville and Sir Evelyn Baring thought that they read the inner workings of Gordon's mind. They looked upon

[1] Ibid., vol. i, p. 444. [2] Ibid., vol. i, p. 447.

him as an irresponsible visionary who could not keep step, who changed his mind overnight, and to whom instructions meant nothing. They were mistaken. But it is their point of view, not the real facts, which must be weighed in considering the orders issued on 26th January by Baring and subsequently approved of by Lord Granville. And, we repeat, this Granville-Baring interpretation implied but one thing. It is that the Foreign Office, yielding to the exigencies of the hour and the insistence of public opinion in England, made of Charles George Gordon's personality his sole and only mandate for the conduct of his mission to the Sudan.

Gordon did not remain idle during the days when Baring was holding the conferences with Nubar Pasha, Sir Evelyn Wood, and Colonel Stewart which guided the British Diplomatic Agent in drawing up his instructions to the soldier who was about to proceed to Khartoum. On the contrary, determined (1) that evacuation should not mean massacre, and (2) that the abandonment of the Sudan should not give an impetus to the slave trade, he got into immediate touch with Zobeir Pasha and sought to win that redoubtable leader to his cause.

It will be recalled that in June, 1878, the latter's son, Suleiman, had raised a revolt in the Bahr el Ghazal province, and had killed 200 of the Egyptian regular troops. Gessi, the Italian, was sent against the rebel and put down the revolt. Suleiman was executed. His father's property in the Sudan was confiscated. Zobeir Pasha, however, had other assets, having amassed great wealth in slave-hunting. When Gordon reached Cairo in 1884 the old slaver was living in the Egyptian capital and growing fat on a luscious pension. He was detained there, but his liberty of action in Cairo was not hampered. He was a power in the land. He hated Gordon with his whole soul, for he held him responsible for his son's death.

While Gordon, with that singleness of purpose so often characteristic of religious zealots, was working to enlist Zobeir under his banner, precisely because he knew that the Black Pasha was "the greatest slave-hunter who ever existed", Lord Granville and Sir Evelyn Baring construed this championship of the old brigand as proof of Gordon's inconstancy of character. The Foreign Secretary wrote to his Consul-General : "I own your letters about Gordon rather alarm me. His changes about Zobeir are difficult to understand." Gordon, however, knew what he wanted and submitted to Baring on the morning of 26th January a written memorandum in which, after sketching the history of the events which had led up to Zobeir's expulsion from the Sudan, he went on to say :—

"Zobeir without doubt was the greatest slave-hunter who ever existed. Zobeir is the most able man in the Sudan ; he is a capital general and has been wounded several times. Zobeir has a capacity for Government far beyond any man in the Sudan. All the followers of the Mahdi would, I believe, leave the Mahdi on Zobeir's approach, for the Mahdi's chiefs are ex-chiefs of Zobeir. Personally, I have a great admiration for Zobeir, for he is a man and is infinitely superior to those poor fellows who have been Governors of the Sudan. But I question in my mind, 'Will Zobeir ever forgive me the death of his son ?' and that question has regulated my action respecting him, for I have been told he bears me the greatest malice, and one cannot wonder at it, for he is a father. I would even now risk taking Zobeir, and would willingly bear the responsibility of doing so, convinced as I am that Zobeir's approach ends the Mahdi."

There is practical common sense in this memorandum. It shows that Gordon was a realist who strove for results. He knew Zobeir's shortcomings. He recognized the personal animosity that the old chief felt towards him. He sought to enlist the slave-hunter's support, because the ability, the courage, and the very villainy of the embittered Pasha were what were needed to assure the evacuation of the Sudan and the control of the slave trade. "Honesty is the best policy." Gordon had made up his mind that Zobeir would act upon this principle and reduce slave-running to a minimum.

In order to establish amicable relations between Gordon and Zobeir an interview was arranged between them. Sir Evelyn Baring, Nubar Pasha, Sir Evelyn Wood, Colonel Stewart, Colonel Watson, and Giegler Pasha were present, with an interpreter and a stenographer. Lord Cromer's book says that:—

"The scene was dramatic and interesting. Both General Gordon and Zobeir Pasha were labouring under great excitement and spoke with vehemence. Zobeir Pasha did not deny that his son had rebelled against the Egyptian Government, but he denied his own complicity in the rebellion."

The interview was devoid of practical results. Whoever counselled that the two men should meet with so many witnesses present showed bad psychology. Such an array of officialdom was bound to put Zobeir Pasha on his guard. The stenographer's pencil was a challenge to him. At all events, Gordon and the slave-runner reviewed the past, and the talk ended on a better note than had accompanied its earlier moments. The upshot, however, was that the Cairo mouthpiece of the Foreign Office positively refused to allow Zobeir Pasha to accompany Gordon. "And so it came about," as Dr. Allen puts it in his *Gordon and the Sudan*, "that the first request which Gordon made, in response to Baring's promise of co-operation and support, was refused."

This refusal to do what the soldier wanted may, perhaps, have played a decisive part in the eventual death of Gordon. Like St. Augustine, St. Benedict,

St. Dominic, and all the founders of the great Roman Catholic clerical orders which have survived the march of the ages, Gordon, though a religious zealot, was a born organizer. He was a nineteenth-century crusader, and war on slavery was his shibboleth. Khartoum did not fall until January, 1885. Had the advice of the practical idealist been heeded, one of the saddest chapters in the history of the English-speaking peoples might never have been written.

With consistent tenacity of purpose and undeviating singleness of conception, he had worked out a plan of campaign based upon using Zobeir and his cohorts to fight the Mahdi and slavery. He held to his political strategy as long as there was a hope that Baring and the Foreign Office might recall their veto. When Downing Street unequivocally announced that it would not recede, Gordon yielded to the inevitable. But the delays which had intervened were so long drawn out that the road to safety was closed before the imprisoned hero learned that Zobeir was anathema to Gladstone.

Baring can hardly be blamed for taking the stand that he did. It is all very well, in the light of the developments that followed, to criticize him. Enormous responsibilities were put upon him. He made but one radical mistake. Most strong-minded men would have fallen into the same error. He did not know that so-called visionaries are very often, in respect of their goal in life, extremely practical, methodical, matter-of-fact beings. Unaware of this, he heeded the advice of men whom he took to be competent observers. Subsequent events permit us to doubt the soundness of the decision arrived at by such a pillar of wisdom. But Baring did his duty as he saw it. His point of view is certainly defensible. At all events, he is entitled to state his own case. He does so in these words :—

"In the first place, the employment of Zobeir

Pasha would be sure to raise an outcry in England. I should not have minded this if I could have felt certain that his employment was desirable. But was it desirable? I was not, at that moment, prepared to take the responsibility of answering this question in the affirmative. The weight of authority was decidedly against sending him to the Sudan. My wish was to follow Gordon's lead, but he himself hesitated as to what course to pursue. It was impossible to say how far this impulsive man was animated, not so much by a consideration of the political necessities of the case, as by a chivalrous feeling that possibly, in former times, he might have done some injustice to Zobeir Pasha and that he wished to atone for such injustice by giving his old adversary an opportunity of retrieving his position."

The dominant note of this statement is crystallized in Baring's reference to Gordon as "this impulsive man", who might have been prone to allow quixotic considerations to sweep him off his feet. And, in summing up, the great Proconsul added :—

"The argument, however, which convinced me that, for the time being at all events, it was undesirable to employ Zobeir Pasha was that forty-eight hours before I received General Gordon's memorandum proposing that Zobeir Pasha should accompany him to the Sudan, I had received through Lord Granville a proposal also emanating from Gordon that Zobeir Pasha should be deported to Cyprus. . . . It might eventually be desirable to employ Zobeir Pasha, but it was necessary to give General Gordon more time to think over the matter before taking action." [1]

The incriminatory letter upon which the author of *Modern Egypt* thus largely pitches his defence was written while Gordon was on his way to Egypt. It was addressed to Lord Granville, and stated that the writer "considers it most important that Zobeir

[1] Ibid., vol. i, p. 458.

Pasha should be well watched by a European to prevent his sending emissaries to the Sudan ". It suggested, to make assurance double sure, that the advisability of deporting the Pasha to Cyprus should be considered.

These words, interpreted in the light of a better knowledge of Gordon's mentality, emphasize the canniness of his mysticism. They show that, in matters bearing upon his mission, he was circumspect, prudent, and worldly-wise. He believed in taking time by the forelock. The Foreign Secretary advised Baring that " there is no legal power to detain Zobeir in Cyprus ". The Pasha was, therefore, not deported, but the secret police were put on his track. All this happened before Gordon had reached Cairo.

When the latter surveyed the lay of the land in Egypt, he saw that Zobeir was still at Cairo, more powerful than ever, and the police shadows worse than useless. That shrewdness which so often guides the visionary prompted him to argue along these lines : " I cannot get Zobeir out of the country : as long as he remains here, he is a menace to the Sudan ; I must make use of him by convincing him that honesty is the best policy."

It was not any " mystic feeling ", as inferred by Baring, but what the vernacular calls " horse sense ", that guided Gordon's act. He had not changed his gears. They were always in the forward notch. He had merely adjusted them to altered conditions because the Foreign Office had looked up the law instead of envisaging the facts. Lawyers are often incorrigible nuisances.

It has already been said that the upshot of the matter of employing Zobeir was that Baring considered it " necessary to give General Gordon more time to think over the matter before taking action ". On the night of 26th January, that officer and Colonel Stewart left Cairo on the ill-fated expedition from which they were destined never to return. With that constancy of purpose characteristic of him, Gordon kept hammering away at Baring and urging the necessity of sending Zobeir Pasha to the Sudan clothed in the robes of office. Yielding to the driving power of the man whom he considered impulsive, the Consul-General finally took up the refrain and urged London to recede and approve the Black Pasha's nomination.

Lord Granville was adamant, but perhaps without the ring of finality in his refusal. He was afraid of the Nonconformists and of the orthodox Gladstone, both of whom looked upon Zobeir as the incarnation of the slave trade, and yet had neither the vision nor the imagination to see that there was method in Gordon's madness. Knowing that Baring was pleading his cause, and that the diplomat was hopeful of winning over the Foreign Office, the Governor-General cherished the illusion that Downing Street would see the light.

It did not. When Gordon learned the truth the door of egress from the Sudan had already been blocked. Had a brutal, irrevocable, and decisive "No" met Baring's reluctant but sincere espousal of Gordon's plea the resourceful soldier would have taken another tack. But the Fates had already decreed that across the ruins of Khartoum "too late" should be written in letters of blood. Against their fiat there is no appeal. But an appeal does lie against the charge of inconstancy and inconsistency brought against Gordon in respect of Zobeir. The proof is self-evident that the idealist who reasoned like a realist stuck to his guns, that it was Baring who vacillated, and Gladstone and Granville who took weeks to put driving power into their veto of Baring's eleventh-hour conversion to Gordon's espousal of the slave-trader.

## Chapter XX

# *EN ROUTE* TO KHARTOUM

While Gordon was hurrying to Khartoum—and not to Suakin as Lord Granville had originally planned—a force of 3,715 Egyptians, under the command of General Valentine Baker, was marching to the relief of Sinkat and Tokar, two Egyptian garrisons on the Red Sea Coast. Though commanded by an Englishman, who had several British officers with him, the expedition was under the orders of the Khedive. Neither Gordon nor London was responsible for the enterprise. Osman Digna, a Sudanese chieftain, attacked this army at El Teb on 2nd February. The Egyptians were routed, 2,375 of their number being killed in the battle. Among the dead were three English officers, Captain Forrestier-Walker and Lieutenants Carroll Smith and Watkins, not to speak of the wounded or of the other Europeans who lost their lives.[1]

Baker's crushing defeat threatened not only the safety of the two Egyptian garrisons of Sinkat and Tokar, but also that of Suakin. British mastery of the seas made it possible to leave the defence of the latter place to English bluejackets. But such measures were beside the issue. The victory won by the Mahdi's lieutenant, at the very time when the Gladstone Ministry was endeavouring to capitalize Gordon's personality, caused the Sudan question to enter on a new phase. It added enormously to the difficulties with which the Governor-General was called upon to contend. He had to deal with a population fanned by

[1] *The Egyptian Campaigns*, 1882 *to* 1885, by Chas. Royle; London, Hurst and Blackett, 1886, vol. ii, p. 116.

religious exaltation and now encouraged by the notion that its tribesmen were invincible. That moral ascendancy which was Gordon's outstanding advantage was undermined by General Valentine Baker's misadventure.

Parliament was in session when the tragic news reached London. Articles appeared in journals that were usually friendly to the Government hinting that the wickedness of conniving at a massacre of Egyptians would be as great as that of condoning Bulgarian atrocities. On 11th February *The Times* published a bitter message from its correspondent at Cairo, stating that a high English official had recently exclaimed: "I am ashamed to call myself an Englishman." [1]

The Government were in a difficult position. Mr. Gladstone ordered his Foreign Secretary to communicate with Gordon and to inquire whether the news "affected his judgment as to going to Khartoum" and whether he had anything to suggest as to the two garrisons.[1] The message was sent on 7th February. It did not reach Gordon until 11th February. He replied: "I must say it would reflect great discredit on our name to recall me after having seen these people. Also I firmly believe, in spite of all, that God will bless our efforts."

This reference to Divine help was probably the very type of official reply that best suited the Liberal leader's militant Christianity. But be that as it may, the great orator wrote out, in his own hand, on 11th January, instructions to Gordon which may or may not have been a reply to the soldier's cable. They ran as follows:

"It has been suggested by a military authority that to assist the policy of withdrawal, a British force should be sent to Suakin sufficient to operate, if necessary, in its vicinity. Would such a step injure or assist your mission?"

[1] Allen, op. cit., pp. 264 and 265.

The following afternoon Gordon's reply was received in London. It reads like a leaf out of Marshal Lyautey's successful administration of Morocco. It ran thus :—

" As to sending forces to Suakin to assist withdrawal, I would care more for rumours of such an intervention than for forces. What would have greatest effect would be rumour of British intervention." [1]

There is deep insight in this reply. Gordon knew the Sudan. He wanted to put the fear of God into the breasts of the rebels. He was afraid, however, that the fate of Khartoum would be decided before the help envisaged by the Prime Minister was available. Always shrewd and far-seeing in matters affecting his mission, he jumped at the opportunity of having a well-defined rumour started in the hope that it would cause Osman Digna to hesitate about marching on Khartoum.

Not only did this defeat of General Valentine Baker cause the veteran British Prime Minister to write, with his own hand, the message sent to Gordon on 11th February, but it also affected the Governor-General's line of conduct. He had left Cairo impressed with the idea that the formidable force under his compatriot would be able to relieve Sinkat and Tokar. Such a result would have cast a damper upon the military enthusiasm of the Mahdi and prevented the rebels from rushing troops to the Nile Valley. Gordon had such confidence in British leadership that his mind refused to admit the possibility that General Baker would be routed.

When he reached Asswan on his journey southwards he was buoyed up by the hope that the prospective relief of the two Egyptian garrisons would facilitate the pacification of the Sudan. His optimism was reflected in his telegram to Baring. It received its first shock when the official news of the holocaust at El Teb reached him at Berber on 11th February.

[1] Ibid., p. 266.

He knew what it meant. The following entry in Colonel Stewart's journal, dated 12th February, shows how the information reacted upon Gordon :—

" I was called up at 5 a.m. by General Gordon," wrote the second-in-command, " who, having pondered deeply all night, had come to the decision of opening the Pandora Box and openly proclaiming the divorce of the Sudan from Egypt, and the forming of local militias, and the appointment of Sudan officials in every important post."

Continuing in the same strain, Colonel Stewart wrote on 13th February :—

" At 2 p.m. Hussein Pasha Khalifa and the leading men of the province assembled in secret conclave, and General Gordon, after a speech, showed them the secret firman. This document caused the most profound astonishment, but in so far as one could judge from what they said, nothing could exceed their delight."[1] In a letter to Baring of the same day, Colonel Stewart characterized the revelation of the secret firman as " Gordon's leap in the dark ". Sir Reginald Wingate, one of the great architects of the present day Anglo-Egyptian Sudan, alludes to " the fatal proclamation which gave the Sudan away ". And Lord Cromer's masterly book not only criticizes Gordon for showing the firman to the Berber notables, but asserts that his " main defect was that he was constantly forming strong opinions on imperfectly known facts."

All these attacks overlook the fact that Gordon was suddenly brought face to face with a dire catastrophe. His proposals made after 12th February were in direct contradiction with the tenor of his previous dispatches to Cairo. It is true that there was something dramatically sudden about the confidential communication made to the Berber *sheikhs*. It was, however, the receipt of that cablegram from the

[1] Earl of Cromer, op. cit., vol. i, p. 468.

Foreign Office, confirming the news of General Baker's rout, which brought about this complete reversal of policy and this momentous announcement.

Gordon had enormous responsibilities. That he did not act after immature reflection is shown by Colonel Stewart's reference to his chief having " pondered deeply all night ". The truth is that the Governor-General knew his people. He saw the tide of Mahdiism swollen by the Baker defeat. He sought to stem that current by appealing to the sordid interests of the Sudanese leaders. He held out before their eyes the glamour of political patronage as a bait to keep them from going over to the False Prophet. His decision was not taken impulsively. It was reached quickly, but not hurriedly ; rapidly, but not precipitately.

Having been compelled by circumstances over which he had no control to change his plan of campaign, Gordon not only acted with the promptness of a born leader of men, but carried out his new tactics with unswerving constancy. In that night of mature deliberation which followed the news of General Baker's defeat, the practical idealist resolved to make the self-interest of the Sudanese the pivotal point of his political strategy. His appeal to their lust for office was followed by an argument addressed to their purse.

Colonel Stewart's journal describes how his Commanding Officer drove home his decision when they were still at Berber. The *sheikhs* were delighted at the thought of getting luscious governmental plums. The landowners wanted to know what their share of the delicacies would be. " A deputation of Notables came to inquire whether the Treaty, which had been printed and published by General Gordon in November, 1877, by which all slaves would be freed in 1889, was in his present programme. General Gordon, knowing the futility of saying ' Yes ', replied 'No', and published a Proclamation to this effect. It is probable that this Proclamation interested and pleased the people more than anything else."[1]

In order better to appreciate the difficulty with which Gordon was thus called upon to cope on the very morrow of the Baker disaster, it may not be amiss to recall that in 1877, as we have said above,[2] a Convention was signed, between the British and Egyptian Governments, having for its object the abolition of the slave trade and of domestic slavery in the dominions of the Khedive. The Treaty was not to come into operation in the Sudan until the end of 1888. It was the Nemesis of this impending complete readjustment of the economic life of the Black Country which caused the Berber spokesmen to put to Gordon this most pertinent question. He could not refuse to answer. His Proclamation was his official reply.

London did not hear of this Berber Proclamation. It learned, however, of a similar ukase which Gordon published the day after his arrival at Khartoum. The latter order caused great excitement in England. We read in *Modern Egypt* :—

"That a man who had heretofore been considered a champion of the anti-slavery cause should immediately on his arrival at Khartoum sanction slavery, and thus run counter to the traditions of his previous career, seemed, indeed, astonishing. The special supporters of the anti-slavery movement were up in arms. Party managers, moreover, were not likely to let slip such a good opportunity for attacking the Government. On 18th February Sir Stafford Northcote, speaking in the House of Commons, asked, amid 'loud cheers' of his supporters, whether General Gordon's powers extended to the issue of such a Proclamation."[3]

[1] Ibid., p. 471. [2] See page 112, Chapter xi. [3] Cromer, op. cit., p. 462.

Lord Cromer's book stoutly defends Gordon for having issued this Proclamation, and says that the soldier "probably reasoned thus : 'As I cannot stop slavery, there is no harm in my saying so and in acting accordingly.' A section of British public opinion, on the other hand, reasoned somewhat as follows : 'We know that you cannot stop slavery, but you had better hide the unpleasant fact from the eyes of the world.'" But while Cromer thus warmly espoused Gordon's action in fearlessly recalling the old anti-slavery regulations, he did not bring out the fact that the Governor-General had suffered no change of heart. He was as much an anti-slavery man in 1884 as he had been in 1877. He was as much an idealist in the latter year as he had been in the earlier. The truth is that Baring really thought that the 1884 Proclamation "ran counter to the traditions of Gordon's previous career". It did not. It confirmed them.

Gordon always believed that even if the 1877 ukase could be temporarily carried out, it would bring disastrous results. He consistently distinguished between the holding of domestic slaves, which was a custom of the country not to be soon eradicated, and the hunting or stealing of natives for the purpose of selling them into slavery. Against the depopulation of villages, the seizing of men, women, and children and their deportation across the desert and in slave dhows on the Nile he was as firmly set as ever. As far as the retention of slaves was concerned, what he held was that the owners of slaves should not be compelled to forfeit their "property" unless the British or the Egyptian Government were prepared to put troops into the Sudan to carry out the terms of the 1877 firman. Neither the moulders of English public opinion nor Lord Cromer had taken the trouble to read Gordon's writings. Had they done so, they would have been struck not only by the abiding common sense that peered through his religious exaltation, but also by his unfaltering consistency in things which he considered essential.

Yet Dr. George Birkbeck Hill's *Colonel Gordon in Central Africa* had been published three years before the English nation and Press thus misinterpreted the traditional attitude of Gordon towards slavery. This old work is based entirely upon the explorer's letters and official documents. It thus affords an opportunity of testing the charge of inconsistency levelled against him.

As early as April, 1877, and therefore before the Anti-Slavery Convention came into effect, Gordon wrote :—

" I have no easy task before me, but (D.V.) I have solved the difficulty. My scheme is not yet matured or approved. You have little idea of the great difficulty and the many questions involved in it, viz. in domestic slavery. First, I have to disband some 6,000 Turks and *Bashi-Bazouks*, who are the frontier guards, and who must be replaced, for they let the caravans pass. . . . Second, consider the effect of harsh measures among an essentially Mussulman population carried out brusquely by a Nazarene—measures which touch the pocket of everyone. Who that had not the Almighty with him would dare to do that? I, who am now on the spot, am able to judge how impotent he [the Khedive] at Cairo is to stop the slave-trade. I can do it with God's help. . . . I hope I have solved the slave-question by recommending to H.M. Consul-General, Mr. Vivian, the following scheme : 1st, By enforcing the law which compels runaway slaves to return to their masters except when cruelly treated. 2nd, By requiring masters to register their slaves prior to 1st January, 1878. 3rd, By not enforcing law No. 1, if not so registered. 4th, By stopping all registration of slaves after 1st January, 1878. By this I prevent, after 1st January, 1878, any new slaves being considered as property, which they are rightly considered to be until either the masters are compensated or a term of years has elapsed, we here being in the same state now as the West Indian colonies were at the passage of the Abolition of Slavery Act." [1]

Gordon's own words thus make it clear that he had undergone no change of heart, and that the English nation as well as the Cabinet and Press should not have thrown up their hands in holy horror when they read the Khartoum proclamation rescinding the 1877 Anti-Slavery Proclamation. Wendell Phillips, Harriet Beecher Stowe, and Lloyd Garrison, to speak of American Abolitionists only, refused to admit that men and women were or could be property. Their minds stood aghast at the idea of " human chattels ". Looking back at the matter across the span of years, we can readily sympathize with such a point of view. It was, however, not Gordon's. He appears to have found nothing " shocking " in slaves " being considered as property ". He was, in a word, a conservative anti-slavery advocate, because in him the idealist was dominated by the realist. This was as true in 1877 as it had been in 1884.

Dr. Hill's book, published, we repeat, in 1881, shows that long before Gordon went to the Sudan on his last fateful mission the British Press had assailed him for his attitude towards slavery.

A few months later, smarting under the lash of criticism given wide publicity by the London Press, Gordon wrote on 1st September, 1877 :—

" Now understand me. If it suits me I will buy slaves. I will let captured slaves go down to Egypt and not molest them, and I will do what I like and what God in his mercy may direct me to do about domestic slaves ; but I will break the neck of slave-raids even if it costs me my life. I will buy slaves

[1] Hill, op. cit., p. 225.

for my army; for this purpose I will make soldiers against their will to enable me to fight raids. I will do this in the light of day and defy you and your resolutions."[1]

Citations of this type could be multiplied. They show that, as has already been pointed out in these pages, Gordon looked upon domestic slavery as something that: "God has allowed to go on for so many years, (that) born in the people it needs more than an expedition to eradicate it; open out the country and it will fall of itself." This was his shibboleth when he first left England for Central Africa on 28th January, 1874. He adhered to the same battle-cry throughout the succeeding years. It is folly to accuse him of vacillation when his principles in regard to domestic slavery, as opposed to the slave-trade, were thus publicly proclaimed. If Cabinet, nation, and Press preferred to forget, in 1884, what they knew in 1877, it is unfair to Gordon to accuse him of inconsistency because their memories played them false.

Almost from the very beginning, Gordon recognized the fact that slavery was an economic and not a moral issue. He foresaw that tinkering with domestic slavery would cause a revolution in the Valley of the Nile. What he sought to do in 1884 was, therefore, by his attitude towards domestic slavery to repair, as far as possible, the evils of the economic unrest of which Mahdiism was but an excrescence. Here is the very language used by him on 20th April, 1879:—

"If the liberation of slaves takes place in 1884 in Egypt proper and the present system of Government goes on, there cannot fail to be a revolt of the whole country; but our Government will go on sleeping till it comes, and then have to act *à l'improviste*. If you had read the account of the tremendous debates which took place in 1833 on the liberation of the West

[1] Ibid., p. 280.

Indian slaves, even on the payment of £20,000,000, you would have some idea how the owners of slaves (even Christians) hold on to their property. . . . Seven-eighths of the population of the Sudan are slaves, and the loss of revenue will be more than two-thirds if it is carried out. Truly the Egyptian problem is a thorny one if you look beyond your nose." [1]

All this means that Gordon saw that an economic revolution had created the unrest which the Mahdi had capitalized. The False Prophet had sought to gain by the social anarchy brought about by scrapping a fundamental institution of the Sudan. Gordon did his utmost to take the props from under his adversary by meeting the economic issue thus presented. He did so by endeavouring to put into effect in 1884 the principles which he had so vigorously defended in 1877. He countenanced domestic slavery in order "to break the neck of slave-raids". In a word, he was consistent.

And he felt most keenly the attacks levelled against him when he thus stuck to his guns. There he was, almost alone, in the cauldron of an economic revolution which had been brought to boiling-point by the fire of religious fanaticism. He sought to quench the flames by removing the embers of industrial unrest. He alone of all available Britons understood the Sudan. Even Baring, just installed in Cairo, was abysmally ignorant of the Black Country. It cut Gordon to the quick that, vested with responsibility and surrounded by seething discontent, he was not accorded by the English nation that absolute confidence to which his record of past achievements entitled him. He wrote at Khartoum on 19th September, 1884, when already besieged :—

"To-day is the Muslim Sabbath, and there is no office work. . . . This has given me time to think over the outburst of indignation *in re* the slave circular.

[1] Ibid., p. 351.

We did not see the papers, so can only guess what they said, but expect that this diabolical fact caused upraised hands in horror, 'was the world coming to an end?' What complete rubbish! Was it not openly announced that the Sudan was going to be abandoned and consequently that the Sudanese were to be allowed to follow their own devices (which are decidedly slave-hunting inclined)? What possible influence could my saying that the feeble Treaty of 1877 was going to be enforced have on people who were going to be abandoned? The sole and only object of my mission was to get out the garrisons and refugees without loss of life. And in saying what I did I merely told the people a platitude." [1]

[1] *The Journals of Major-General C. G. Gordon, C.B., at Khartum*, introduction and notes by A. Egmont Hake; London, Kegan Paul, Trench & Co., 1885, p. 54.

## Chapter XXI

# ARRIVAL AT KHARTOUM

Gordon did not tarry at Berber. He had consolidated his position at that point by appealing to the interests of the local inhabitants and by assuring them against injustice. He knew, however, that Khartoum dominated the Sudan. He was, therefore, in a hurry to get there in order to arrest the strong current in the Mahdi's favour which had been intensified by General Baker's defeat.

Gordon left Berber on his way south on 14th February. The news of his slavery proclamation had preceded him to Shendy. It won him the support of the notables of that place. They regarded him as their champion and assembled with their followers to give him a hearty welcome. Their acclamations meant that the seed planted at Berber was already bearing fruit. It was with high hopes that Gordon entered Khartoum on 18th February.

His arrival was the signal for a tremendous demonstration of good will. Enthusiastic crowds came forward to kiss his hands and to salute him as the saviour of their country. Their economic life had been shattered by the menace of the doom of domestic slavery. Muhammad Ahmad, the Mahdi, was the son of a Dongolese carpenter and not in the good graces of the leading spirits of Khartoum. They felt no ardent zeal for the religious fanaticism of the uncompromizing partizan who was not of their little group. What they had wanted was to be assured that Khartoum would be relieved from the overhanging pall of the abolition of slavery. They read in Gordon's Berber Proclamation a guarantee of the end of hard times and a harbinger of prosperous days. In a word, they welcomed in the person of the Briton the advance agent of prosperity.

He caught the spirit of the welcoming crowds. He exploited their cordial dislike of Egyptians and Turks by appealing to the Arabs and Blacks who made up the great mass of the native population. He said to them :—

" I come without soldiers, God on my side, to redress the evils of the Sudan. I will not fight with any weapons but justice. There shall be no more *Bashi-Bazouks*." [1]

Suiting the action to the word, Gordon summoned the Khartoum officials to appear before him. Peremptory instructions were given them to cancel all arrears of taxation. The Government records of these old debts were publicly burnt in front of the Palace. When the bonfire was blazing, *kourbashes* and whips were thrown into the flames. The Governor-General and his suite then made their way to the jail. Two hundred wretches loaded with chains were confined there. They were of all ages. Among them were boys and old men, some of whom had never been tried. Others had been acquitted, but had been forgotten and had not been released. Some of the prisoners were, no doubt, hardened criminals ; but the doors were thrown open and everybody was liberated.

The applause of debtors and prisoners, however, was not what Gordon needed to buttress his position. He required the whole-hearted support of the great landowners, the wealthy burghers, and the prosperous merchants. To gain their backing he issued without delay a new Slavery Proclamation, which read :—

" To all the inhabitants :

" Your tranquillity is the object of our hope. And as I know that you are sorrowful on account of the slavery which existed among you, and the stringent

[1] Archer, op. cit., vol. iii, p. 97.

orders on the part of the Government for the abolition of it and the punishment of those who deal in slaves, and the assurances given by the Government for its abolition, seizing upon and punishing those concerned in the trade ; according to Imperial decrees, and the firmans forwarded to you—all this is known to you. But henceforth nobody will interfere with you in the matter, but everyone for himself may take a man into his service henceforth. No one will interfere with him, and he can do as he pleases in the matter, without interference on the part of anybody ; and we have accordingly given this order. My compassion for you."[1]

There is something exotic about the English of this Proclamation. It appears to be a translation of a translation. The original version was in English. It was put into Arabic and issued in that language and has now been reconverted into English. But all these changes have not taken the vital spark out of the text. It shows that Gordon gave the people of Khartoum his word that he would not interfere with domestic slavery. That was what they wanted more than anything else. His promise worked like magic. Frank Power, British Consul and correspondent of *The Times* at Khartoum, was so encouraged by the change thus brought about, that the very next day, 19th February, he telegraphed to Sir Evelyn Baring : "Everything is now safe here for troops and Europeans. He (Gordon) is giving the people more than they expected from the Mahdi."[2]

But while Gordon was using practical common sense to deal with a dangerous situation and applying economic remedies to an economic evil, the British Parliament was debating with torrential eloquence a subject of which most of the orators were blissfully

[1] *The Egyptian Campaigns* 1882–5 *and the Events that led up to them*, by Charles Royle ; London, Hurst and Blackett, 1886, vol. ii, p. 129.

[2] Earl of Cromer, op. cit., vol. i, p. 475.

ignorant. It thus came about that on the very day when the trained journalist and improvized Consul was spending some four shillings a word to tell his readers and the British Consul-General that Gordon was bringing order out of chaos because that officer was " giving the people more than they expected from the Mahdi ", Lord Hartington was proclaiming from the Government benches :—

" I contend that we are not responsible for the rescue or relief of the garrisons either in the Western or the Southern or the Eastern Sudan." [1]

This categorical statement by a responsible Minister of Her Majesty's Government voiced the sentiments of the Gladstone Cabinet. It was an official utterance. It is no doubt on permanent record in *Hansard*. It was given due publicity in the London Press. It did not, however, reach Gordon's ears. He believed on 19th February, as he had when he left England, that the Government still regarded themselves as responsible for the relief of the garrisons of the whole of the Sudan. He thought that the national honour was involved in carrying out the work of rescue. And on 23rd September, 1884, he noted in his journal :—

" As for '*evacuation*' it is one thing ; as for '*ratting out*' it is another. I am quite of advice as to No. 1 (as we have not the decision to keep the country), but I will be no party to No. 2 (this '*rat*' business), 1st, because it is *dishonourable* ; and 2nd because it is not *possible* (which will have more weight)." [2]

As late as 26th January, the Khedive wrote to Gordon that :—

" You are aware that the object of your arrival here and of your mission to the Sudan is to carry into execution the evacuation of those territories, and to withdraw our troops, civil officials, and such of the

[1] Allen, op. cit., p. 271.

[2] *Journals of Major-General C. G. Gordon at Khartum*, p. 80.

inhabitants, together with their belongings, as may wish to leave for Egypt." [1]

This letter appears to have reached Gordon at Berber. He was justified in assuming that it had received Baring's blessing, for the Governor-General had every reason to believe that Tewfik Pasha would not have dared to write in such terms without first consulting the British Diplomatic Agent. At all events, when the Khartoum embargo on anti-slavery activities was announced Gordon felt that he was carrying out a policy which concurred with the views of the London Foreign Office's accredited mouthpiece. He therefore went full steam ahead, encouraged by the Khedivial message and by what he took to be Baring's sanction of it.

But the fact that, at the very moment when Gordon was thus emboldened to carry out his economic relief measure, the Cabinet was proclaiming in Parliament that England was " not responsible for the rescue or relief of the garrisons ", means that Gordon and Gladstone at one and the same time set sail in opposite directions. Neither was aware of what the other had done. Thousands of miles separated them. The soldier went to his grave without knowing that on 19th February the statesman had turned an intellectual somersault. The Prime Minister did not know that when he performed his feat of mental acrobatics, his emissary had declared that domestic slavery was no longer taboo in the Sudan. Had Gordon been able to read *The Times* as he sipped his morning tea on 20th February, he would no doubt have made a well-directed effort towards meeting the emergency created by the Government's gymnastic agility. Had Gladstone been temperamentally able to grasp that his appointee could not find out in Khartoum what was going on in London, he would unquestionably have taken steps to keep the Governor-General posted. But the Fates

[1] Ibid., p. 30.

willed that Gordon was to pull away at one oar and Gladstone at another without any co-ordination of effort, though with equal sincerity of purpose and strength of will.

An inscrutable Providence thus decreed that Gordon should follow up his Khartoum slavery pronouncement by a second telegram of the same date, 18th February. His critics harp upon his idiosyncrasies and dwell tediously upon his volatility. They refuse to see that in the few things which he deemed essential he was tenacity personified, and the embodiment of practical common sense. In other words, as soon as he had issued his Berber Proclamation of 12th February and had followed it up by his Khartoum ukase of 18th February, he set to work to give effect to both these decrees. He saw that his words would be mere froth unless a strong hand were to take over the reins of government. He was prepared to evacuate the Sudan, but, to use his own words, he was against "ratting out". His constructive mind, therefore, on this same day, 18th February, drew up for Sir Evelyn Baring the following additional telegram :—

"I have stated that to withdraw without being able to place a successor in my seat would be the signal for general anarchy throughout the country, which, though all Egyptian element was withdrawn, would be a misfortune, and inhuman. Also I have stated even if I placed a man in my seat unsupported by any government, the same anarchy would ensue. Her Majesty's Government could, I think, without responsibility in money or men, give the commission to my successor on certain terms which I will detail hereafter."

And after thus showing why creative statesmanship required that something should be done to prevent evacuation from being but the precursor of anarchy, Gordon added :—

"I would select and give a commission to some man,

and promise him the moral support of Her Majesty's Government and nothing more. . . . As for the man, Her Majesty's Government should select one above all others, namely Zobeir. He alone has the ability to rule the Sudan, and would be universally accepted by the Sudan. He should be made K.C.M.G. and given presents." [1]

It is obvious that this suggestion ran counter to the 19th February point of view of the Gladstone Cabinet. It is also clear that the British Ministry and not Gordon was charged with the responsibility of defining the policy of Her Majesty's Government. It is likewise manifest that it was the duty of the latter to carry out instructions, to obey, and not to argue. But when he forwarded his dispatch of 18th February, no mental telepathy could have told him what Lord Hartington was going to announce on 19th February. And, we repeat, Gordon never at any time learned of the categorical language used by the British Government on the latter date. On the contrary, Gordon won over Sir Evelyn Baring to advocate the Zobeir appointment and did not know until the door of egress from Khartoum had been hermetically sealed that Baring's espousal of the slave-trader's nomination had met with a final and peremptory veto.

Lord Cromer took a great deal of trouble to show why he had supported, in February, Gordon's recommendation of Zobeir after having blackballed it in January. The author of *Modern Egypt* seems to have recognized, with that loyalty characteristic of him, that it was he, not the Governor-General, who went to the mat with Gladstone in support of the old slaver. This is what the diplomatist wrote :—

"I thought that General Gordon, when at Cairo, had made his proposal to utilize Zobeir Pasha's services without sufficient deliberation. When, however, I found that, after an interval of three weeks,

[1] Earl of Cromer, op. cit., vol. i, p. 483.

and after having had an opportunity of judging of the situation at Khartoum, General Gordon still thought that Zobeir's services could be utilized, it appeared to me safe that he was expressing something of the nature of a matured opinion, and that he was not, as so frequently happened, dashing off an ill-considered proposal on the spur of the moment." [1]

There was nothing half-hearted about Baring's advocacy of Zobeir. The Consul-General made Gordon's cause his own. It will be recalled that the latter did not communicate direct with the Foreign Office. It may not be out of place to repeat, at least in part, the terms of his original instructions. They read :—

"Colonel Gordon will be under the orders of Her Majesty's Minister at Cairo and will report through him to Her Majesty's Government and perform such other duties as may be entrusted to him by the Egyptian Government through Sir Evelyn Baring."

This means that until Her Majesty's Diplomatic Agent at Cairo had advised Gordon that Zobeir would not or could not be appointed to the Khartoum post, the personality of the Governor-General was effaced. His orders came from Cairo. Baring was his immediate superior, the lightning-rod which insulated him from the thunderbolts of Downing Street. It follows, therefore, that even if Gordon had known of the Hartington pronouncement of 19th February—and he did not—the man on the spot was not to blame for adhering to his 18th February policy as long as his chief failed to tell him that it was vetoed by London and had to be abandoned. This information was only conveyed to Gordon when the Mahdi had already completely encircled Khartoum and when, without Zobeir's aid, escape was impossible. It reached the Briton "too late" to be of any avail.

The inference should not be drawn that Baring

[1] Ibid., p. 484.

should have advised Gordon more promptly of the Government's decision. The truth is that he passed on the information to his subordinate as soon as he had become convinced that the Cabinet was adamant in its refusal to accept Zobeir. Baring was a redoubtable fighter. Convinced by Gordon's tenacity and arguments that the old slaver was the only man with enough prestige to hold the country together and to bring into line the *sheikhs* and people who were anxious to be loyal but who were afraid of the Mahdi. the resourceful diplomatist kept on hammering at the Foreign Office in the hope of causing it to see the light.

And one is reluctant to criticize the British Government for refusing to give in to Baring. Whether the Ministry did or did not vacillate, tergiversate, and wobble previous to applauding Lord Hartington's categorical statement of 19th February is largely beside the issue. The truth is that the Cabinet was sharply divided in regard to the advisability of appointing Zobeir. Three of the Commons' members inclined to favour his nomination, but were agreed that Parliament would refuse to sanction his choice. Mr. Gladstone was prevented by his physician from attending the two meetings of the Cabinet where the subject was discussed. One of the Ministers went to see him in his bed. They conferred for two hours. Upon joining his colleagues the emissary reported, with some ironic amusement, that the Prime Minister "considered it very likely that they could not bring Parliament to swallow Zobeir, but believed that he himself could".[1] And his health nailed him to his bed. It was, therefore, the tyranny of irresponsible public opinion which really overruled Baring.

It would be pushing things too far to blame Mr. Gladstone for yielding to Parliamentary pressure when we are forced to admit that any attempt by his

[1] Morley, op. cit., vol. ii, p. 399.

Government, in his absence, to override the popular will would, in all probability, not have been successful. Gordon was, it is true, a name to conjure with. Zobeir's reputation, on the other hand, was such a challenge to the Anti-Slavery Society that ignorance of the true facts would, it is to be feared, have wiped out even the influence of that fearless champion of the black race.

True, Gordon had finally persuaded Baring that he was right in insisting upon the appointment of Zobeir to the Khartoum post. The great diplomat had been able, by throwing his personality into the scales, to convince certain members of the British Government to sacrifice prejudice to common sense. But with the Prime Minister immobilized by illness, there was nobody who could have told this same truth to the British Parliament. Time or the eloquence of a Gladstone could have driven home the message from Khartoum. But so insistent was some strange fatality that "too late" should be engraved on Gordon's heart, that it decreed that the Grand Old Man should be ill when every instant counted.

## Chapter XXII

# FIRST DAYS AT KHARTOUM

It was not until 11th March that the Gladstone Ministry put its definitive veto upon the appointment of Zobeir. Its decision was communicated to Baring in a message couched in these words : " Her Majesty's Government have carefully considered your telegram of the 9th inst. with regard to the future government of Khartoum and the Sudan, but they do not consider that the arguments against the employment of Zobeir Pasha have been satisfactorily answered. They are prepared to agree to any other Muhammedan assistance, as well as to the supply of any reasonable sum of money which General Gordon may consider necessary in order to carry out successfully the objects of his mission." [1]

The date of this telegram should be underscored. It is of primary importance that it be remembered. The contents of the message did not reach Gordon. The telegraph line was cut near Halfayah while the fateful words were being flashed across the Mediterranean. This break isolated Khartoum.

The gist of these undelivered instructions was that London tabooed the Zobeir appointment, but that it did not reject, in principle, Gordon's proposal in regard to turning over his mandate to a successor. A second telegram from Lord Granville, addressed to Baring and dated 12th March, leaves no doubt on this score. It read :—

" Her Majesty's Government desire to learn whether General Gordon's proposal as to his eventual successor

[1] Earl of Cromer, op. cit., vol. i, p. 520.

refers to the whole of the Sudan, and if not to what districts of it." [1]

These two telegrams, neither of which reached its eventual goal,[2] require no comment. They show that the Government, after proclaiming on 19th February that "we are not responsible for the relief of the garrisons", agreed on 11th March "not to force General Gordon's hand prematurely, to extend his appointment," and to "supply any reasonable sum of money which he may consider necessary in order to carry out successfully the objects of his mission". This decision to trust the man on the spot implicitly in all things, except the designation of Zobeir, was made with full knowledge of Gordon's actions since reaching not only Cairo but Khartoum. And yet we read in *Modern Egypt* :—

"Before General Gordon had been long at Khartoum, his combative spirit completely got the better of him. As a soldier, he could not brook the idea of retiring before the Mahdi. Moreover, as a civilized European, he winced at the idea that a country in which some germs of civilization had been sown should relapse into barbarism. . . . He wished, therefore, to 'smash up' the Mahdi, and perhaps it was natural that he should do so." [3] "The truth is that General Gordon was above all things a soldier, a very bellicose soldier. His fighting instincts were too strong to admit of his working heartily in the interests of peace." [4]

The argument developed under this head by Lord Cromer is that Gordon, the religious fanatic, was a truculent soldier who, to use a popular expression, "carried a chip on his shoulder" while waiting for the Foreign Office to reach a decision in

[1] Earl of Cromer, op. cit., vol. i, p. 520.
[2] Allen, op. cit., p. 304; and Earl of Cromer, op. cit., vol. i, p. 521.
[3] Earl of Cromer, op. cit., vol. i, p. 493.
[4] Ibid., p. 562.

regard to the employment of Zobeir. A dispatch sent by Gordon to Baring, dated 26th February, is largely relied upon to prove this assertion. This message in part reads :—

"If Egypt is to be quiet, the Mahdi must be 'smashed up'. The Mahdi is most unpopular and with care and time could be smashed. Remember that once Khartoum belongs to the Mahdi the task will be more difficult ; yet you will, for safety of Egypt, execute it. If you decide on smashing Mahdi, then send up another £100,000 and send up 200 Indian troops to Wadi Halfa." [1]

This dispatch does not prove that Gordon was a sword-rattling, bellicose, quarrelsome fanatic who was bent on making trouble. The message was sent in reply to a telegram from Baring inquiring whether any other name could be substituted for that of Zobeir. The Governor-General sought to show why this could not be done by stressing the point that "the Mahdi's agents are active in all directions" and that the situation was so serious that its repercussion extended to Egypt. He knew that the diplomatist was not interested in the Sudan. But he was aware of the fact that the welfare of Egypt meant everything to Baring. It was in order to get the latter to see the immediate connection between Cairo and Khartoum that Gordon said "if Egypt is to be quiet, the Mahdi must be smashed up". In a word, he resorted to an argument *ad hominem* to drive home his idea. He revelled in using strong words like "ratting out" and "smashing up" when he sought to emphasize a point.

Here is an extract from a letter written by Gordon to Sir Evelyn Baring. It is dated Khartoum, 30th July. He was then besieged, and his nerves might well have been on edge. His language, however, was as follows :—

[1] Ibid., p. 487.

"You may rely on this, that if there was any possible way of avoiding the wretched fighting I should adopt it, for the whole war is hateful to me. . . . I have great trust that God will bring us out triumphantly and with no great loss on either side."[1] A passage in one of Gordon's journals is even more to the point. He there used these extraordinary words: "We have, thank God, succeeded in taking Arabs and killing the Arab Commander-in-Chief. (R.I.P.)."[2] How many examples are there in history of a soldier thus leading in prayer for the repose of the soul of an enemy?

But when all is said and done, this discussion is beside the issue. The Foreign Office knew of Gordon's temperamental idiosyncrasies when it called upon him after the defeat of General Hicks. It had before it his "smashing up" dispatch of 26th February, when it offered to put up additional money to hold Khartoum. It knew all about what *Modern Egypt* calls "his constant and somewhat contradictory telegrams" when it gave him its confidence and extended "his appointment for any reasonable period which may be necessary to enable him to carry out the objects of the mission with which he has been entrusted."

The truth is that Gordon, while most emphatic in regard to the necessity of appointing Zobeir, set to work without delay to evacuate the European and civilian Egyptian population of Khartoum. But as early as 1st March he plainly saw that it was impossible to get the Cairo employees out of the Sudan without help from the Government. He felt that military exigencies required that pressure be exerted both from Berber and Wadi Halfa in order to keep open the avenue of egress. His idea was that unless a display of force were made the Mahdi would continue to make irresistible headway. But while he had decided

[1] H. W. Gordon, op. cit., p. 352.
[2] Archer, op. cit., vol. iii, p. 165.

opinions as to what London should do, he never forgot that he was a soldier and that it was his duty to obey orders. "I shall do my best to carry out my instructions," he wrote on 1st March, "but I feel a conviction that I shall be caught in Khartoum." [1]

And on the same day that he thus made obedience his watchword he wrote to his sister :—

"We are all right here at present, and I have hope, but certainly things are not in a good way ; humanly speaking, Baker's defeat at Suakin has been a great disaster, and now it has its effect up here. 'It is nothing to our Lord to help with many or with few,' and I now take my worries more quietly than before, for all things are ruled by Him for His glory and it is rebellion to murmur against His will." [2]

While thus clearly seeing the menace of being entrapped in Khartoum, he was still encouraged by Baring's assurance, forwarded on 1st March, that the question of Zobeir is "still under discussion and not finally settled".[3] Gordon, therefore, felt that he could write to his sister on 5th March :—

"We are getting on all right, thank God, and I sincerely hope we may have no more bloodshed. I owe all to God and nothing to myself, for, humanly speaking, I have done very foolish things. However, if I am humbled the better for me." [4]

Gordon was justified in feeling most hopeful of the future, when he thus wrote to his dear one at home. General Valentine Baker's defeat at El Teb had been avenged on the same field by Major-General Sir Gerald Graham. This victory was won on 29th February. The success came at a most auspicious moment. It followed the distressing news that Tokar had capitulated, and took place when the fateful words "too late" resounded from one end of England

[1] Ibid., vol. iii, p. 121.
[2] *Letters of General C. G. Gordon to his Sister*, p. 380.
[3] Allen, op. cit., p. 292.
[4] *Letters of General C. G. Gordon to his Sister*, p. 381.

to the other. There was something so dramatic about Sir Gerald Graham's onslaught that it soon wiped out the past and gave Britain renewed confidence in the eventual success of Gordon's mission.

The battle showed, not for the first time in history, that a small body of well-disciplined British troops could defeat a horde of courageous savages. But no important strategic objective was attained. Osman Digna received a severe blow. His power in the Sudan, nevertheless, was by no means broken. That chieftain's own view on the subject may be gathered from a letter written by him at the time and found some years afterwards at Tokar. "The English," he said, "did not stay long. God struck fear into their hearts, and they went back the next morning, staying only one night at the *Mamuriah*, and they started back in their steamer." [1]

It was, perhaps, largely religious fanaticism and oriental conceit which enabled Osman Digna to belittle, in this manner, the severe setback which he had received from the British. But, be the reason what it may, the revolution did not collapse when the Dervishes were defeated at El Teb. On the contrary, within less than two weeks, on 11th March, that is to say on the very day when Lord Granville cabled Baring that Zobeir could not and would not be appointed, Gordon wrote his sister :—

"This may be the last letter I send you, for the tribes have risen between this and Berber and they will try and cut our *route*. We have lots of food for five or six months. They will not fight us directly, but will starve us out. . . . I am indeed glad of the prayers offered for me. Our Lord's promise is not for the fulfilment of earthly wishes ; therefore, if things come to ruin here He is still faithful and is carrying out His great work of divine wisdom. What I have

[1] *Modern Egypt*, by the Earl of Cromer, vol. i, p. 414.

to do is to submit my will to His own, however bitter may be the events which happen to me." [1]

While thus writing with the ardent faith of a mystic, the matter-of-fact realist in Gordon caused him to put into practice the maxim of the Puritan : " Put your trust in God and keep your powder dry." He had not heard that Lord Granville had definitely rejected Zobeir's name. All that he knew was that the slaver's nomination was still in abeyance, that the Mahdi's power was so firmly entrenched that it had successfully resisted the news of Osman Digna's defeat, and that it behoved him, Gordon, to protect Khartoum and to defend himself. He did so with military promptness.

Although no doubt placing great confidence in his sister's prayers, Gordon also looked for relief to the strong arm of the British Government. Several days before the rebels had cut his telegraphic communications he had been advised by Baring that a Proclamation had been issued by Admiral Hewett and General Graham calling upon the Dervishes to submit. Mere words meant nothing to his practical mind. He knew the Near East too well to attach any importance to such wasted energy. But when he was informed by Cairo that on 7th March Lord Granville had telegraphed to Baring that :—

" Her Majesty's Government have approved the recommendation of Admiral Hewett and General Graham to land a force at Suakin to give effect to their Proclamation calling upon the rebel chiefs to come in . . . and will march on Osman's camp to disperse force if the Proclamation is ineffectual," [2] he viewed the whole horizon from a different aspect. He construed this decision to march British bluejackets and soldiers against Osman Digna as implying that the Cabinet had seen the error of its ways and had receded from its 19th February decision that " we are not responsible for the rescue or relief of the garrisons

[1] Ibid., p. 381. [2] Earl of Cromer, op. cit., vol. i, p. 415.

in the Western, or the Southern, or the Eastern Sudan ". He looked for immediate relief for Khartoum from this complete reversal of policy.

The joint naval-military Proclamation produced no effect. Gordon knew that it would not. He counted solely on the coercive measures referred to in the telegram of 7th March. It was not until 13th March, or until after Gordon's telegraphic communications had been cut, that General Graham's force advanced on Tamai, a few miles from Suakin. A Mahdist army of 12,000 was assembled there. On the following morning an engagement ensued. After an obstinate fight 2,000 Dervishes were killed; the remainder fled to the hills. In this action, the British loss was 13 officers and 208 men killed and wounded.

On 15th March Osman Digna's camp was burned and the victorious British force returned to Suakin. On the 17th Sir Gerald Graham telegraphed to the War Office :—

" The present position of affairs is that two heavy blows have been dealt at the rebels and followers of the Mahdi, who are profoundly discouraged. They say, however, that the English troops can do no more and must re-embark and leave the country to them." [1]

Sir Gerald Graham was a gallant soldier but a poor psychologist. His dispatch contains an obvious contradiction. It is folly to say, in one and the same breath, that " the followers of the Mahdi are profoundly discouraged " and then to add " they say that the English troops can do no more and must re-embark and leave the country ". The science of war does not consist in killing men or in dispersing armies. It resides in annihilating the morale of the enemy and in making him bite the dust. This the victor of Tamai failed to do. And, strange to say, the latter part of his dispatch shows that he knew that he had not succeeded.

[1] Earl of Cromer, op. cit., vol. i, p. 415.

Gordon obviously did not receive word of the British Pyrrhic victory. He assumed that Lord Granville's decision that Admiral Hewett and General Graham "will march on Osman's camp to disperse force if the Proclamation is ineffectual", foreshadowed not a mere military success, but the complete pulverization of the very soul of the revolt. He awaited this result with that patient resignation characteristic of the devout Christian who knew that his sister was praying and his army and navy fighting for him. What was his surprise to find, on the evening of 13th March, about 3,000 rebels, horse and foot, drawn up under arms, with banners waving, on the right bank of the Nile opposite the palace at Khartoum. This demonstration meant to Gordon's mind that something had gone astray in the Eastern Sudan. He did not know that General Graham was then marching on Tamai and that the morrow would witness a British victory. All that he could fathom was that six days had passed since Lord Granville's change of front and that the rebel offensive in the neighbourhood of Khartoum was continuing to grow in intensity.

And while Gordon was seeking to penetrate the hidden mystery of the Dervish activity in the face of the British offensive against Osman Digna, night threw her mantle over the enemy's camp. The darkness was soon pierced by their camp fires. A few hours before dawn there was a heavy sound of rifle-fire and the flashes of the guns of the insurgents could be seen from the roof of the palace. The firing continued until daybreak, when about 6,000 rebels returned from the direction of the river and drew up in four ranks each nearly two miles long. Later in the day they commenced making huts and putting up tents amidst a great beating of drums.[1]

The firing was discovered to have been an attack on a party of 300 of Gordon's black soldiers who had

[1] Archer, op. cit., vol. iii, p. 133.

been sent down the river for firewood, and by some unaccountable negligence of the officers had been left there. They were cut off by the advance of the Arabs and attempted to get back to Khartoum at night by means of boats. They were seen by the rebels, who opened fire on them, killing several. Eight of the boats were captured. In consequence of some further carelessness the steamers that should have gone to their rescue did not get under headway for several hours. All this meant that the besiegers had tasted blood and felt the thrill of success before Osman Digna's defeat at Tamai. And there was Gordon, walled in at Khartoum, with not a single British trooper to aid him and Stewart in their plight. Inaction meant feeding the courage of his assailants. He could not wait indefinitely for news of General Graham's expected victory. It was imperative that he assume the offensive. He was confronted by the possibility of internal dissensions if he adopted a policy of passive resistance.

Accordingly, on the morning of 16th March, Gordon determined to attack the enemy forces which were massed at Halfayah, not far from Khartoum. He assailed them from three sides, from the capital, from the beleaguered garrison, and from armed steamers. The rebels had entrenched themselves along the river bank, being thus able to fire with impunity on passing steamers. It was necessary to dislodge them. Gordon's troops numbered about 2,000, made up in large part of Egyptian regulars. In order to be able to survey the field he and Frank Power—*The Times* correspondent—stationed themselves on the roof of the Palace. As the Khartoum troops drew near the rebels, the latter began to disappear behind the sandhills. This retreat continued for an hour. " Our line," wrote the journalist, " still advanced and the artillery fired two shells at the retiring rebels. Our horsemen having entered the woods at the foot of the sandhills, we saw, to our astonishment, the five principal officers of our force, who had been riding a little ahead, dash back, breaking through their own ranks."

"At that moment," continued Power, "the rebel cavalry shot out at full gallop from behind the sandhills. Their appearance was the signal for a disgraceful *sauve qui peut* on the part of our men, who broke up and dashed back without firing a shot. The sixty horsemen, who were only armed with lances and swords, dashed about cutting down the flying men. I saw one Arab lancer kill seven Egyptians in as many minutes. He then jumped off his horse to secure a rifle and ammunition, when a mounted *Bashi-Bazouk* officer cut him down. The rebel infantry now appeared, and rushed about in all directions, hacking at the men disabled by the cavalry charge. The slaughter continued for nearly two miles, our men not stopping to fire a shot." [1]

The moral effect of this rout was heartrending in its consequences. Not only did it teach Gordon that he could not depend upon his Egyptian troops, but it told the neighbouring tribesmen that Muhammad Ahmad was irresistible. It also meant that whatever had been or might be the result of Sir Gerald Graham's attack upon Osman Digna—news of which had not yet percolated through to Khartoum—its lesson would be more than neutralized by the Alleluias of joy which had greeted the flight of the Egyptian forces. Gordon, therefore, had the conviction thrust home to him that not only was he isolated, but that unless British troops spanned the desert and routed the assembled Dervishes his fate was sealed. He feared that help would come "too late". Yet so great was his moral ascendancy over everybody who came into personal contact with him that even though he was in a cauldron of Muhammadan unrest, he not only

[1] Ibid., p. 136.

maintained his hold upon the loyalty of the inhabitants of the capital, but appears to have had no fear of internal disloyalty. He was also able to induce messengers to risk their lives by creeping through the enemy's lines and communicating dispatches to the outside world. Unfortunately for him, however, he rarely received the replies which were addressed to him.

## Chapter XXIII

# THE BERBER EXPEDITION

The refusal to employ Zobeir, coupled with the siege of Khartoum, brought the Sudan question into a new phase. It became evident, even to the most casual observer, that without assistance Gordon could not stem the tide which had set in against him. Egyptian troops were obviously unequal to the task. This meant that British forces were required. But the work carved out for them was not merely the evacuation of beleaguered Egyptian garrisons. Upon them devolved the responsibility of rescuing Gordon and Stewart.

Sir Gerald Graham did his utmost to save the situation. Though he made the blunder of telegraphing to the War Office on 17th March that "the rebels and followers of the Mahdi are profoundly discouraged", only two days before thus underestimating the fanatical zeal of the enemy, he had cabled to Lord Hartington, the Minister of War, that both Admiral Hewett and he were of opinion that "an advance to Sinkat would now have a great effect and ratify the late victories". A copy of this message was sent to Baring. His active mind at once caught its significance. He lost no time in telegraphing to Lord Granville warmly supporting General Graham's proposal. His dispatch added :—

"It has now become of the utmost importance not only to open the Berber-Suakin route, but to come to terms with the tribes between Berber and Khartoum. If we fail in the latter point, the question will very likely arise of sending an expeditionary force to bring away Gordon. I do not think that he is in any immediate danger. He has provisions for six months." [1]

On the following day, 16th March, Lord Granville replied : " Graham's movement on Sinkat has been approved, but we cannot authorize the advance of any troops in the direction of Berber until we are informed of the military conditions and are satisfied that it is necessary for Gordon's safety. Our present information is that it would not be safe to send a small body of cavalry as proposed and that it would be impossible to send a large force." [2]

The substance of this answer was that the Foreign Office, which knew that Gordon was besieged and that the wires were cut between Khartoum and Cairo, expressed its approval of a military diversion near the coast of the Red Sea, but refused to sanction the advance of troops in the direction of Berber until satisfied that it was necessary for Gordon's safety. In adopting this attitude Lord Granville appears to have overlooked the fact that Berber was a position of extreme importance and that it was the key to the policy of evacuation. It was through Berber that the retiring garrisons and civilians would have to pass to make their way back to Egypt. On reaching Berber they could then proceed northward by either of two routes—one by the Nile to Abu Hamed and thence across the desert to Korosko or by desert to Suakin.

One of the last despatches sent by Gordon to Baring had stressed the importance of a British expedition to Berber. The Consul-General replied without delay :—

" So far as I know there is no intention on the part of the Government of sending an English force to Berber." [3] It is therefore obvious that the Foreign Office, when refusing, at all events for the moment,

[1] Earl of Cromer, op. cit., vol. i, p. 537.
[2] Ibid., p. 527.
[3] Allen, op. cit., p. 306.

to send British soldiers to Berber, took this decision with full knowledge that Gordon, the specialist in Sudan affairs, considered such an expedition essential to the success of his mission.

But Baring kept on hammering at Downing Street. He was not the man to be called off by bureaucrats or politicians. On 21st March he telegraphed to Lord Granville :—

"It appears to me undesirable to debar General Graham from attacking Osman Digna, if he thinks it necessary to do so in order to open up the road to Berber." This message provoked a reply asking the Consul-General's opinion whether it would be desirable to :—

"Dispatch a portion of the Egyptian army to garrison Wadi Halfa in order to lend moral support to General Gordon at Khartoum," and whether some British officers "with some knowledge of Arabic and experience in dealing with natives might not advantageously be sent to Berber, there to await instructions from Gordon ".[1]

It need not be repeated that at the time when the Foreign Office sent to its accredited Cairo representative this most extraordinary telegram Gordon was not only penned in at Khartoum but unable to communicate with the outside world except by fortuitous messages passed through the besieger's lines. Baring knew that Downing Street was aware of this. He did not labour the point, therefore, that Gordon was a prisoner, but hastened to send to Berber Major Kitchener—subsequently known as Lord Kitchener of Khartoum—and Major Rundle. By the time they reached Asswan it was found imprudent for them to proceed any further. The road was blocked. Baring accordingly on 21st March sent a long dispatch to his chief in which he said :—

"General Gordon is evidently expecting help

[1] Earl of Cromer, op. cit., vol. i, p. 539.

from Suakin, and he has ordered messengers to be sent along the road from Berber to ascertain whether any English force is advancing. Under present circumstances I think that an effort should be made to help General Gordon from Suakin, if it is at all a possible military operation."

The very next day, 25th March, came back the answer :—

" Having regard to the dangers of the climate of the Sudan at this time of the year, as well as the extraordinary risk from a military point of view, Her Majesty's Government do not think it justifiable to send a British expedition to Berber, and they wish you to communicate this decision to General Gordon, in order that he may adopt measures in accordance therewith. Her Majesty's Government desire to leave full discretion to General Gordon to remain in Khartoum, if he thinks it necessary, or to retire by the southern or any other route which might be found available." [1]

A second cable confirmed that which we have just transcribed. It added : " The Government have no intention of sending British troops to Berber."

Lord Cromer confesses in his oft-quoted book that when he received these two telegrams he found it difficult to preserve the " diplomatic calm which formed the subject of General Gordon's sarcasms ". He grit his teeth and sent to Lord Granville a reply which the Foreign Secretary called " a heavy cannon-ball ". It read, in part :—

" I cannot say whether it will be possible for me to communicate your Lordship's message to Gordon, but in any case I cannot reconcile myself to making the attempt to forward such a message without again addressing your Lordship. Let me earnestly beg Her Majesty's Government to place themselves in the position of Gordon and Stewart. . . . No one

[1] Ibid., p. 542.

regrets more than I do the necessity of sending British or Indian troops to the Sudan, but, having sent Gordon to Khartoum, it appears to me that it is our bounden duty, both as a matter of humanity and policy, not to abandon him." [1]

The Ministry which had so often changed its policy was adamant. It refused to modify its instructions of 25th March. But, unable to remain inflexible, it recalled on 29th March the War Office orders of 16th March approving of General Graham's movement on Sinkat. British troops were thus directed to leave Suakin as soon as they were relieved by Egyptian troops from Cairo. This retirement, of course, gave Osman Digna and Muhammad Ahmad and all the Dervish leaders an opportunity to proclaim that God had struck fear into the hearts of the English and that they had abandoned Gordon to his fate. The result was that the British victories of 29th February and 14th March were sterile of results, and that Gordon's position was made doubly dangerous, both by the inflexibility and by the vacillation of the Ministry of the day.

Queen Victoria played a noble part in this sad story. She was alarmed by Baring's "heavy cannon-ball" despatch. She at once telegraphed to Lord Hartington that :—

"Gordon is in danger. You are bound to try and save him. Surely Indian troops might go from Aden : they could bear the climate. You have incurred great responsibility." [2]

This telegram from the Queen to the Minister for War, coupled with Baring's dispatch to the Foreign Secretary, caused Lord Hartington and Lord Granville to hurry down to Coombe Warren to consult Mr. Gladstone. Her Majesty also got into communication with the Prime Minister and told him

[1] Ibid., p. 544.

[2] Allen, op. cit., p. 312, quoting *Letters of Queen Victoria*, vol. iii, p. 485.

that Sir Evelyn Baring had expressed her feelings. She was indignant that what Gordon "had asked for repeatedly nearly five weeks ago" had been refused. The Liberal leader held his ground, and in concluding a somewhat lengthy reply to his sovereign wrote :—

"Mr. Gladstone humbly joins Your Majesty in the hope that, when adequate intelligence shall have been received from General Gordon, there will be every disposition to support him to the full extent which national interests will permit, and without too nice a computation of risks merely Ministerial." [1]

We read, however, between the lines of Lord Morley's laconic words that Mr. Gladstone had to crack the party whip to force his colleagues to override the Queen's intervention. The Prime Minister appears to have reminded his monarch "of the imperfect knowledge, and he might have said blank ignorance, with which the Government was required on the shortest notice to form conclusions on a remote and more than half-barbarous region".[2] But Queen Victoria would not yield. She no doubt knew that Mr. Gladstone had, on 11th March, become "a strong convert to the plan of sending Zobeir" to Khartoum.[3] She could not understand why "he had changed his mind" and in early April obstinately refused to accede to Gordon's cry for help. She very probably became convinced that the statesman who always spoke to her as if he were addressing the House of Commons, was, like many other old men, as variable as the wind and as stubborn as a mule.

One wonders whether Mr. Gladstone would have held so tenaciously to his April theories, and whether he would not have gone back to his March principles, if Queen Victoria had not, perhaps, indisposed him to do so by interfering with his constitutional prerogatives. All that we know with certainty is that

[1] Allen, op. cit., p. 315.
[2] Morley, op. cit., vol. ii, p. 402.
[3] Ibid., p. 399.

"the Cabinet decided against an immediate expedition, one important member vowing that he would resign if an cxpedition were not sent in autumn, another vowing that he would resign if it were. On 7th April the question of an autumn expedition again came up. Six were favourable, five the other way, including the Prime Minister".[1] One is tempted to infer from Lord Morley's language that Mr. Gladstone again "changed his mind" when called upon to vote. But whether this was so or not, the Ministry vetoed the sending of an expedition. It appears to have yielded to the eloquence poured forth by its chief when still stung by his sovereign's interference.

Although Baring did his utmost to prevent the British Government from taking its tragic decision of 7th April, so obsessed was that forceful and brilliant diplomat with the idea that Gordon's policies were many and very mutable that his *Modern Egypt* infers that the Governor-General was, in a measure, to blame for the action taken by the Cabinet. The great Proconsul quotes a dispatch from Gordon which reached Cairo on 9th April, that is after the momentous veto had already been recorded. It had been delayed in transmission. It reads :—

"I wish I could convey to you my impression of the truly trumpery nature of this revolt, which 500 determined men could put down. Be assured for the present, and for two months, we are as safe as at Cairo. . . . If you could only put your pride in your pocket and get, by good pay, 3,000 Turkish infantry and 1,000 Turkish cavalry the affair, including the crushing of the Mahdi, would be accomplished in four months."[2]

This message does not prove that Gordon did not know his own mind or that he blew hot and cold. It obviously had no effect on the Government's action, because it got through the enemy's lines some time

[1] Ibid., p. 402. [2] Earl of Cromer, op. cit., vol. i, p. 549.

after the six to five vote had sealed the soldier's fate. But all that his words were meant to imply was: "I am not asking that you mobilize the entire British Army to carry out the orderly evacuation of Khartoum. Show your teeth. Send at once 500 red-blooded Englishmen under capable officers, with adequate equipment, and this revolt will melt before their onward march. I know the Sudan. The Mahdi and his followers cannot stand the continuous, unrelenting, constant pressure of 500 Tommies determined to burrow their way through to Khartoum. If you cannot give me 500 Englishmen, send 4,000 Turks, but see that they are well paid. I am not asking you to shed either British or Ottoman blood in vain. It will take a relief corps some little time to reach me. I can hold out for the time necessary for assistance to get to me."

Can it be said that he overestimated the driving power of 500 British soldiers or that he made a mistake in considering them the equal of 4,000 well-paid Turks? What he was endeavouring to hammer into the brain of Downing Street was that Egyptian units were worthless. Lord Granville's instructions to Baring, dated 11th March, it will be recalled, had said: "Her Majesty's Government are prepared to agree to any other Muhammadan assistance (other than Zobeir) as well as the supply of any reasonable sum of money which General Gordon may consider necessary in order to carry out successfully the objects of his mission." When this message finally got through to Khartoum Gordon felt that in proposing an expedition of Turkish troops, financed by British gold, he was falling in with the Foreign Office's wishes. He knew the Sudanese, and was convinced that this combination of Ottoman man-power and English capital could put down the revolt. What proof is there that he was mistaken?

This use of Turks subsidized by London was no

passing whim of Gordon's. The man was not capricious. He had clear-cut ideas in respect of his mission and held to them most tenaciously. It is in Lord Cromer's *Modern Egypt* itself that we read :—

" General Gordon attached great importance to this proposal (to send to the Sudan Turks financed by England). He constantly alluded to the subject in his journals. 'If,' he said, 'the Sudan is given back to Egypt, in a couple of years we would have another Mahdi ; therefore our choice lies between Zobeir and the Turks. Now the time has gone by when Zobeir almost alone would suffice. Therefore, give the country to the Turks.' " Statesmanship, not a sudden fancy, dictated this suggestion. He thought of England's commitments in Egypt and, with the far-seeing prescience of an Ignatius of Loyola, he sought to assure the maintenance of law and order in the Khedive's dominion at the price of having Turkish rule, as opposed to anarchy, in the Sudan.

But while Baring was dominated by the hallucination that Gordon was a visionary who took his orders from the Prophet Isaiah, had no conception of obedience to hierarchical superiors, and was swayed solely by the fleeting impulse of the moment, he fought the Scotsman's battle even after the Cabinet had overridden Queen Victoria and pronounced its 7th April verdict. The diplomatist may have known but little of Egypt when General Hicks left for the Sudan, but his alert brain had mastered many problems since the departure of that gallant officer. Baring was convinced that sooner or later London would have to recede from its refusal to send troops to the Black Country. What worried him was that preparations for the expedition had to be made within the immediate future or else be " too late ". He elaborated this point of view, therefore, in a somewhat lengthy despatch to the Foreign Office, dated 14th April, in which he said :—

"As it appears to me, we are in this dilemma—as a last resource the Government would, I conceive, be obliged to go to the help of General Gordon. All the authorities whom I have consulted say that, if any operations are to be undertaken along the Valley of the Nile, which is by some considered the best route, no time should be lost in making preparations, so as to be ready to move directly the water rises. It may be, and I hope it will be, that General Gordon will be able to extricate himself without any expedition. On the other hand, unless they are undertaken now it may be that, when the necessity for moving arises, so long a delay will ensue as to frustrate the objects of the expedition." [1]

This same advice was sent by mail. Before it had left Cairo Gordon was able to get through the Mahdi's lines a message which, as Mr. Egmont Hake observes, "at once became historical." Its date requires a passing comment. It was sent from Khartoum on 7th April. This tells us that when the Cabinet Ministers were voting to disregard the Queen's appeal and to refuse to send relief to Gordon, he was putting his opinion on record. This is what he said :—

"As far as I can understand, the situation is this: You state your intention of not sending any relief up here to Berber, and you refuse me Zobeir. I consider myself free to act according to circumstances. I shall hold out here as long as I can, and if I can suppress the rebellion I shall do so. If I cannot, I shall retire to the Equator, and leave you the indelible disgrace of abandoning the garrisons of Sennar, Kassala, Berber, and Dongola, with the certainty that you will eventually be forced to smash up the Mahdi under great difficulties if you would retain peace in Egypt." [2]

[1] Ibid., p. 557.

[2] Ibid., p. 555.

The strong expressions employed in this telegram were caught up by political partizans who dwelt with rapturous emphasis on "the indelible disgrace" which the British Government was said to have incurred. Lord Cromer strongly dissents from the view thus so emphatically expressed by Gordon. The diplomatist declares that "he cannot understand how any impartial person can consider that the British Government were responsible for the difficulties which at that time beset the garrisons of Sennar, Kassala, Berber, and Dongola".

No attempt will here be made to ascertain whether Gordon was or was not justified in speaking of "indelible disgrace". All that will be said is that his message which used this language got through to Cairo without delay, whereas his "Khartoum is as safe as Cairo" telegram did not reach Baring until 9th April. This means that both despatches probably travelled to London in the same diplomatic pouch. If their contents were forwarded by wire, the probabilities are that they were decoded more or less at the same moment and were placed on the Foreign Secretary's desk at the same time.

At all events, the "indelible disgrace" challenge made it comparatively easy for Downing Street to interpret the "Khartoum is as safe as Cairo" statement in the light in which it was made. But whether this surmise be correct or not, the fact stands out that London caught the significance of Gordon's bitter criticism. It was in the face of the adverse public opinion which swept from Palace to hovel and from Queen to barmaid, that the Ministry of the day deviated from its recent practice by sticking to its guns for week after week.

## Chapter XXIV

# THE MAHDI'S LETTER

It has already been said, not once but twice, that Lord Cromer looked upon Gordon as "being above all things a soldier, and, moreover, a very bellicose soldier". With that delightful frankness so characteristic of him and so unusual in diplomats, the author of *Modern Egypt* goes on to say that :—

"His (Gordon's) fighting instincts were too strong to admit of his working heartily in the interests of peace. 'The Arabs,' he said, 'must have one good defeat to wipe out Hicks's disasters and *my* defeats. I do not care to wait to see the Mahdi walk in on your heels into Khartoum. One cannot think of that.'"[1]

One of the earlier indictments drawn up against Gordon by Baring was, nevertheless, that the former had contemplated making a friendly call upon the Mahdi in order to discuss the Sudan question with him. It appears that it was reported to the Consul-General that, while on his way from Brindisi to Port Said, Gordon told a fellow-passenger that "it is possible I may go to the Mahdi and not be heard of for two months, for he might keep me as a hostage for Zobeir". Such a foolhardy adventure would have gone a long way towards proving, not that the soldier was a fire-eater, but that he placed, perhaps, undue reliance upon his powers of persuasion. He had left Cairo before Baring heard of this rumour. When it reached the ears of Her Majesty's Diplomatic Agent, he at once telegraphed Gordon :—

"I hope you will give me a positive assurance

[1] Earl of Cromer, op. cit., vol. i, p. 562.

that you will on no account put yourself voluntarily in the power of the Mahdi. The question is not a personal one." In reply the Governor-General answered that "he had no intention of visiting the Mahdi". His brother affirms that no call upon the Mahdi had ever been contemplated.[1]

But while Gordon was neither swept off his feet by a burning desire to "smash up" the Mahdi, nor so credulous as to believe that he could hypnotize that leader into eating out of his hand, his practical mind told him that it was worth while appealing to the self-interest and conceit of Muhammad Ahmad. It thus came to pass that before the news of General Valentine Baker's defeat at El Teb had entirely changed the political and military aspect of the Sudan, Gordon wrote to the Mahdi, while hurrying to Khartoum, offering him the title of "Sultan of Kordofan", sending him robes of honour, and inviting him to come to a friendly settlement and cease all hostilities.

This letter was a clear indication that Gordon came on a mission of peace. It is useless to conjecture what would have been Muhammad Ahmad's reply if General Valentine Baker's colours had not gone down to defeat. But Gordon's conduct should be judged in the light of conditions as they obtained when the missive was written. Looking at the matter from that angle, it is clear that the appeal to the Mahdi's self-aggrandisement and vanity was excellent psychology and statecraft. It so happened, however, that before an answer could be drafted the Dervish leader became impressed with the idea that he was invincible.

"He laughed at Gordon's proposal," wrote a prisoner in the Mahdi's camp, "and thought him (Gordon) a very cunning unbeliever, who was attempting to delude him (the Mahdi) with vain

[1] H. W. Gordon, op. cit., p. 342.

promises merely to gain time. He could not understand how it was that Gordon came to offer him what he already possessed some time ago. The fact that Gordon had brought no troops with him served to further increase his pride." [1]

Muhammad Ahmad's reply reached Gordon on 22nd March, that is to say several days after the siege of Khartoum had already begun. Gordon, in reporting upon it, wrote :—

"The man who took my letter to the Mahdi came back to-day. He says the Mahdi received the letter ; he assembled his counsellors, and discussed the matter for ten days, then wrote an answer and tore it up. He then talked over the matter for ten days more, and wrote another letter which he tore up ; after another three days he wrote an answer and sent it by two of his men, who are now waiting outside of town. The Mahdi's messengers have come in with the letter, which proposes that I should become a Mussulman. . . . The demeanour of the Mahdi's emissaries was exceedingly cheeky." [2]

It is comparatively easy to reconstruct all that transpired at Government House in El Obeid during the three weeks referred to in Gordon's report. When the Scotsman's first letter reached the Mahdi, the Dervish camp feared that General Valentine Baker was about to relieve the Egyptian garrison at Tokar. Muhammad Ahmad, accordingly, assembled his counsellors and marked time. They decided to be guided by circumstances. When the news came through that the British General had been defeated, the Mahdi's reply struck a defiant note. But he knew that Admiral Hewett was at Suakin and that that officer had landed marines. He also heard rumours

[1] *Ten Years' Captivity in the Mahdi's Camp*, 1882–1892, from the original manuscripts of Father Joseph Ohrwalder, by Major F. R. Wingate ; London, Sampson Low, Marston & Co., 1892, p. 98.

[2] Archer, op. cit., vol. iii, p. 145.

of General Sir Gerald Graham and of an English army. He therefore held up his letter, and then made assurance doubly sure by tearing it to shreds.

In due course word reached the Mahdi that, on 29th February, General Graham had defeated Osman Digna at El Teb. A second letter was therefore written, pitched in a most conciliatory key and gratefully accepting the profferred honours. Oriental canniness delayed the sending of this revised note. Before it got away, the battle of Tamai intervened, and the Mahdi did away with the new draft, in order to make it even more effusive and servile.

While he was getting his hyperboles and adultations into proper form, his intelligence service reported that " the English troops can do no more and must re-embark ". The Dervish chief persuaded himself that this rumour meant that Allah was on his side. He was encouraged by the fact that his forces had not disintegrated after the two British victories. So he framed a third letter breathing defiance and after thinking it over for three days got it off. He did not wait any longer, because he did not want to give his counsellors any unnecessary opportunity to attempt to make him change his mind once more.

All this is obviously nothing but conjecture, and may be entirely erroneous. It is, however, incontrovertible that Gordon showed keen discernment in attempting to win over the Mahdi. If the Scotsman did not succeed in getting the support of the Dervish leader, the result may properly be imputed to causes beyond his control.

It is true that his first use of the phrase " the Mahdi must be smashed up " appears in a telegram of 26th February, but there Gordon was addressing to Baring the argument *ad hominem* already discussed. It was not, however, until after Muhammad Ahmad had thrown down the gauntlet and insulted him, the devout Christian, by proposing that he should abandon Him Crucified, that Gordon changed his tactics and relentlessly favoured crushing the Mahdi. In other words, he did not vacillate. He adopted new tactics to meet changed conditions.

By the end of March, Gordon not only had the answer of the Dervish leader to his invitation, but he also knew that London had left him to his own devices. He did not neglect to defend Khartoum and the inhabitants of that city who placed their faith in him. He was no swashbuckling soldier who set out " to smash the Mahdi ". He was a British officer who sought to do his duty. He did it with the thoroughness characteristic of the race from which he sprang. From 22nd March, the day when Muhammad Ahmad's defiant reply reached him, he considered that he was definitely at war with the Mahdi. Within twenty-four hours he sent out two 10 lb. Krupp guns to shell the enemy's position at Halfayah. At the same time, he despatched a steamer up the Blue Nile to attack the forces which were cutting him off from Sennar on the south.[1] And during the latter days of March as well as throughout April and May, there was ceaseless labour at earthworks, wire entanglements, and expeditions for food.

The intention of the Dervishes was evidently to wear out the patience of the garrison by scarcity of food, and by the moral effect of a continuous attack constantly kept up, but never pressed to a decisive point. Time means nothing to Orientals. They were therefore in no hurry to crush the Khartoum garrison. There is a significant entry in the summary of the events of the first six months of the siege which Gordon wrote to Lord Wolseley, that shows how well these tactics succeeded. It read : " The square was always broken."[2]

[1] Allen, op. cit., p. 320.

[2] *Charles George Gordon*, by Colonel Sir William F. Butler ; London, Macmillan and Company, 1889, p. 218.

And yet, because hope springs eternal in the human breast, while Gordon knew that London was averse to sending a force to relieve Khartoum, Frank Power, *The Times* correspondent, managed, on the very morrow of the receipt of the Mahdi's letter, to get a message through to his paper as follows :—

"23rd March.—We are daily expecting the British troops. We cannot bring ourselves to believe that we are abandoned by the British Government." [1]

This appears to be the first time that the word "abandon" crept into the news that came from Khartoum. But if the journalist wrote on a pessimistic note, he also spoke of the hope which kept alive the faith of the besieged. Nature herself brought solace to them. The Nile began to rise. As the river swelled the position of Khartoum became improved. The Arabs had placed their camps of investment at some distance up the Blue and White Nile. When the sandbanks in the streams were covered it became easier for the armed steamers to inflict damage upon the enemy. The waiting game which the Dervishes were obviously playing encouraged Gordon, Stewart, and Power to believe that with the Nile thus coming to their aid British help would relieve Khartoum before the waters subsided. They knew that when the rivers ceased to be navigable their doom would be sealed. This meant everything to them, for, as Lord Wolseley put it, "all the gold of England could not affect the rise and fall of the Nile or the duration of the hot and cold seasons in Egypt."

The last message which Gordon was able to get through to Baring by the Nile route was dated 8th April. It tells of "scarcely a day passing without our inflicting losses on rebels, which losses are quite unnecessary if we are eventually to succumb". And then, with that dogged determination so typical of him in all essentials, he added :—

[1] Allen, op. cit., p. 324.

"I have telegraphed to Baker to make an appeal to British and American millionaires to give me £300,000 to engage 3,000 Turkish troops from the Sultan and send them here. This would settle the Sudan and Mahdi for ever." [1] His tenacity of purpose caused him to chafe at the fickleness of the Cabinet which appeared to adopt a Sudan policy only to change it overnight. He had finally learned that on 11th March, Her Majesty's Government had officially proclaimed that "they are prepared to agree to any other Muhammadan assistance (other than that of Zobeir) as well as to the supply of any reasonable sum of money which Gordon may consider necessary in order to carry out successfully the objects of his mission". He feared that the Gladstone Ministry might, on 8th April, have been unwilling to put up the money tendered on 11th March. He evolved the plan of a private contribution so as to be assured of that form of Muhammadan assistance which was not anathema to Downing Street.

In this same letter he gave a common-sense reason why this Turkish force, subsidized by unofficial funds, was called for so imperatively. He wrote :—

"I do not see the fun of being caught here to walk about the streets for years as a Dervish, with sandalled feet; not that (D.V.) I will ever be taken alive. It would be the climax of meanness, after I had borrowed money from people here, had called on them to sell their grain at a low price, etc., to go and abandon them without using every effort to relieve them, whether these efforts are diplomatically correct or not."

A letter written on 23rd April speaks of the Nile still rising. Another, dated 26th April, tells of bank-notes issued to the amount of £2,500, redeemable in six months, and adds: "We are making decorations for the defence of Khartoum—a crescent and star,

[1] H. W. Gordon, op. cit., p 346.

with words from the Qurân and date, so we count on victory; officers silver, men copper. You will not be asked to pay for them. We are well and strong." Still another letter written the next day says: "Thanks to our mines, I do not fear for this place; but owing to rebels having a steamer on Blue Nile we must guard against a river attack. It renders difficult any relief of Sennar. We are making all preparations and laying down mines in river. I think we shall hold out all right."

The whole of May and June appears to have passed without any more of these letters from Gordon getting through the lines. The only ones in the next month are dated 30th and 31st July. They are addressed to Sir Evelyn Baring. The first gave the encouraging information that "the Arabs are in poor heart, I should say that about 2,000 determined men alone keep them in the field". Towards the end of this same missive Gordon wrote:—

"You say your feeling is to abandon the Sudan, so be it; but before you do that you must take down Egyptian population and this the Arabs do not see. According to all accounts, 5,000 were massacred at Berber; all is for the best. I will conclude in saying we will defend ourselves to the last; that I will not leave Khartoum; that I will try and persuade all Europeans to escape, and that I am still sanguine that, by some means not clear, God will give us an issue."

The postscript to this letter is of outstanding importance. It will be referred to a second time, when an attempt will be made to show that Lord Cromer was mistaken when he inferred that it was largely through Gordon's own fault that he did not get out of Khartoum. Here is the postscript:—

"Reading over your telegram of the 5th of May, 1884, you ask me 'to state cause and intention in staying at Khartoum knowing Government means to abandon Sudan'. And in answer I say I stay at

Khartoum because the Arabs have shut us up, and will not let us out. I also add that even if the road were opened, the people would not let me go, unless I gave them some Government or took them with me, which I could not do. No one would leave more willingly than I would if it were possible." [1]

The letter dated 31st July speaks of hoping "to send an expedition to surprise and recapture Berber". Its concluding words are: "I repeat, I have no wish to retain this country. My sole desire is to restore the prestige of the Government in order to get out the garrisons and to put some ephemeral Government in position in order to get away." [2]

Reports sent by Power to his paper, *The Times*, fill out the more or less sketchy information thus obtainable from Gordon's letters. The journalist got a message through by way of Kassala, Massowah, and Suakin, dated 28th April, which told of General Gordon being "busily engaged laying out mines in front of the works in all directions". "He is issuing rations to the poor. Food is very dear. We have corn and biscuits for about four months. . . . The Blue Nile is slowly rising, and we hope in ten or fifteen days the steamers will be able to smite the rebels hip and thigh. The health of the town is excellent and we three Englishmen here are well and hopeful. There are now around the lines, in addition to all other obstacles, such as crowsfeet, broken glass, wire entanglements and *chevaux de frise*, three lines of land torpedoes or percussion mines. They are enormously powerful and much feared by the Arabs. We have no news whatsoever of the intentions of Her Majesty's Government."

On 30th July Power wrote:—

"We have been now five months closely besieged, and can at best hold out for two months longer. The soldiers and people live in hopes of English relief. . . .

[1] Ibid., p. 355. [2] Ibid., p. 357.

We have no fears of a rising in the town." On 31st July he reported :—

"Since 17th March no day has passed without firing ; yet our losses in all at the very outside are not 700 killed. . . . Since the dispatch which arrived the day before yesterday, all hope of relief by our Government is at an end, so when our provisions, which we have at a stretch for two months, are eaten, we must fall ; nor is there any chance, with the soldiers we have, and the great crowd of women, children, etc., of our being able to cut our way through the Arabs. We have not steamers for all, and it is only from the steamers that we can meet the rebels."[1]

The message from the outside world to which *The Times* correspondent referred when he said "since the dispatch which arrived the day before yesterday all hope of relief by our Government is at an end", appears to be an official note from the Foreign Office which took weeks to get through to Khartoum. It was drafted by Gladstone on 23rd April, and read :—

"Gordon should be informed . . . that he should keep us informed, to the best of his abilities, not only as to immediate, but as to prospective, danger at Khartoum ; that, to be prepared for any such danger, he advise us as to the force necessary in order to secure his removal, its amount, character, route for access to Khartoum, and time of operation ; that we do not propose to supply him with Turkish or other force for purpose of undertaking military expeditions, such being beyond the scope of the commission which he holds and at variance with his pacific policy which was the purpose of his mission to the Sudan ; that if with this knowledge he continues at Khartoum, he should state to us the cause and intention with which he so continues."[2]

[1] Ibid., p. 362. [2] Allen, op. cit., p. 333.

## Chapter XXV

# THE VEIL OF SILENCE

The veil of silence which lay over Khartoum throughout May and June, and was not pierced until 30th July, aroused London to action. A Blue Book, published on 1st May, carried Gordon's reverberating "indelible disgrace" challenge. It begot intense excitement and animated discussions. Attempts were made in the House of Commons to extract from the Government some definite statement as to whether an expedition would be sent to relieve Gordon.

Ministers were in a quandary. They wanted to do their duty. Their patriotism was unassailable. They did not know what was transpiring at Khartoum. They appear to have assumed that the Foreign Office instructions, sent after 11th March, had reached Gordon, because not a few of his messages and those of *The Times* correspondent had passed through the Mahdist barrier and had reached London after that date. They overlooked two salient factors. The first was Gordon's magnetic personality which made men willingly risk their lives to render him a service. The second was far simpler. It was that it was much easier to get a messenger to carry a note from a city under artillery fire to the outer world than it was to find a person who was willing to run the gauntlet of being killed in order to find refuge under shot and shell.

But while Lord Cromer frankly admits that he does not think that Gordon ever received Lord Granville's important instruction of 12th March,[1] and while it is now obvious that the crucial Foreign

[1] Earl of Cromer, op. cit., vol. i, p. 520.

Office message of 8th April did not get to Khartoum until about 30th July, we must, if we wish to be fair to the Gladstone Cabinet, wipe out these two facts. We must seek to look at the problem with the eyes of the Government presided over by the septuagenarian who, once the hope of the stern and unrelenting Tories, died the titular deity of Orthodox Liberalism. Her Majesty's Ministers saw in Gordon a self-willed, recalcitrant, bellicose swashbuckler, who had refused to obey orders and who had purposely set out to inaugurate a policy of aggression which was in absolute contradiction to his original instructions. The lenses of these officials were entirely out of focus. They distorted the reality. That, however, is foreign to the issue. They did their duty as they saw it. We may deplore the mistake into which they fell, but we should not forget their point of view.

Mr. Gladstone was a fighter and did not accept "the indelible disgrace" assault with contrite humility. Speaking in the House of Commons on 12th May to a Vote of Censure, the Parliamentary gladiator publicly inferred that Gordon had deliberately disobeyed orders. As regards "the support and consideration" which had been promised by the Government, the Prime Minister said :—

"To turn the words 'support and consideration' into a licence to conduct open war and bloodshed is as great a licence of interpretation as I have ever heard applied to a public document."

"The Government," he continued, "were reproached with 'indelible disgrace' for abandoning four garrisons. Were these the only garrisons ? How about the six garrisons in other more distant provinces ? Was it not an equal disgrace to abandon them ?" And, with every molecule of his combative blood stirred to anger, the veteran of many a forensic battle turned to the Opposition and, with great emotion, put the blunt question : Had they any alternative policy? Would they say, here and now, that they would send an army to Khartoum? He stood like some avenging god of a past age awaiting a reply. None came. A look of withering scorn illuminated his rugged features. The sonorous notes of his incomparable voice turned into the cutting tones of sarcasm, and he exclaimed: "Look, dumb!"

A pall fell over the House. But his agile mind was too alert to allow the silence to remain unbroken. Quick as a flash he was again on the offensive. His voice resumed its wonted bell-like clarity and he asked: "What did the sending of an army mean?" And, carried away by the auto-intoxication of his oratory, he answered his question. "It meant," he said, "a war of conquest against a people struggling to be free. Yes, they are a people struggling to be free, and rightly struggling to be free."[1]

Looking back at this debate, after the lapse of fifty years, we are forced to admit that if the Mahdi and his cohorts were "a people struggling to be free" when Mr. Gladstone spoke on 12th May, 1884, their cause was just as righteous when the British Government sent Gordon to Africa on 18th January of the same year. But great orators are so often brilliantly inconsistent that the Liberal leader had ample precedent for allowing his enthusiasm to make a mockery of stern realities. The onslaught of his eloquence was, moreover, so all-compelling that before his hearers had grasped the manifest heresy of his words, he was again at the Opposition with fire and tongs. He had been assailed for the terms of the instructions addressed by the Foreign Office to Baring on 23rd April, which were forwarded to Gordon on 5th May and which the latter did not receive until 30th July—that is to say until weeks after the Parliamentary discussion in which Mr. Gladstone's talents had shone forth so resplendently.

[1] Allen, op. cit., p. 338.

The great orator, not knowing that Gordon had not received these instructions, made it clear :—

"That in that telegram we have entered into a solemn covenant with General Gordon, and have assured him that, upon any reasonable assurance of danger—and reasonable evidence, I suppose, is what it is our duty to look for—we should endeavour to use the resources of this country for his protection. That covenant was printed in the papers just submitted to Parliament. We thus make a covenanted Parliament and a covenanted nation. I am not aware how we can go any further." [1] A majority of twenty-eight votes confirmed this covenant, and thus signified its confidence in the Ministry.

The House of Commons was, no doubt, influenced by Mr. Gladstone's declaration that "there is no military danger at the moment besetting Khartoum". It is true that the siege of that place had begun on 11th March, but the Prime Minister was in good faith when he made his erroneous statement. He cannot be pilloried for having acted upon what he considered reliable information. Nevertheless, one cannot but be struck by the fact that the Foreign Office amended the covenant so solemnly made by Parliament and nation.

On 17th May Lord Granville sent to Cairo the instructions which follow. Baring was then on leave. They were addressed to his second-in-command. They read :—

"Having regard to the time which has elapsed, Her Majesty's Government desire to add to their communication of the 23rd April as follows : 'As the original plan for the evacuation of the Sudan has been dropped, and as aggressive operations cannot be undertaken with the countenance of Her Majesty's Government, General Gordon is enjoined to consider and either to report upon, or, if feasible, to adopt, at the first proper moment, measures for his own

[1] Allen, op. cit., p. 338.

removal and for that of the Egyptians at Khartoum who have suffered for him or who have served him faithfully, including their wives and children, by whatever route he may consider best, having especial regard to his own safety and that of the other British subjects.

" 'With regard to the Egyptians above referred to, General Gordon is authorized to make full use of money rewards or promises at his discretion. For example, he is at liberty to assign to Egyptian soldiers at Khartoum sums for themselves and for persons brought with them per head, contingent on their arrival at Korosko or whatever point he may consider a place of safety.' "[1]

It took the original 23rd April instructions approximately 98 days to reach Khartoum. One infers from Gordon's journals that the amended version of 17th May did not get to him until after a delay of some four months. They appealed to that sense of sarcasm which even his Christian spirit could not suppress. He wrote under date of 17th September :—

" Egerton's telegram carefully written in cypher (and equally carefully without date, but which we ascribe to June), respecting the contracts to be entered into with the Bedwin tribes to escort us down ('and be sure to look after yourself') might have been as well written in Arabic, it would have produced hilarity with the Mahdi. . . .

" The pomp of Egerton's telegram, informing me that 'Her Majesty's Government would (really !) pay on delivery so much a head for all refugees *delivered* on Egyptian frontier, and would (*positively*, it is incredible) *reward* those with whom I might contract with to escort me down."

" It was too generous for one to believe ! Egerton's chivalrous nature must have got the better of his

[1] *The Journals of Major-General C. G. Gordon at Khartum*, p. 39.

diplomatic training when he wrote it ! . . . I hope he will get promoted, and will not be blamed for his overstraining his instructions." [1]

It is manifest that Gordon attacked the wrong man. All that Mr. Egerton did was to forward Lord Granville's instructions—and, perhaps, forget to date the covering message. But, however ludicrous it may have appeared to the man hemmed in at Khartoum to receive such a Foreign Office note, Mr. Gladstone's hallucination, that all that Gordon had to do to get out of Khartoum was to curb his own bellicose tendencies and give *bakshish*, shows the absolute sincerity with which London officialdom clung to the idea that the Governor-General of the Sudan may have been surrounded, but that he was perfectly safe and the absolute master of his own movements. Even when Berber fell on 26th May, and when, by the end of June, all doubt on that score was eliminated, the resiliency of Mr. Gladstone's optimism was such that, when Lord Hartington raised the question of sending relief to Gordon, the Prime Minister offered uncompromising opposition to the proposal. He had already lived beyond the allotted threescore and ten, but he had the buoyant hopefulness of a youth still in his teens. Always persuasive, he had persuaded himself that in spite of the fall of Berber an answer from Khartoum might still come through and bring good tidings.[2]

At length, on 20th July, word came across the sea from Cairo to the effect that the native Governor of Dongola had received a mere line from Gordon, dated 22nd June, saying that Khartoum was still holding out and that the General wished to be informed "of the place where the expedition coming from Cairo is, and the numbers coming". In forwarding this letter the *Mudir* of Dongola requested that he might

[1] *The Journals of Major-General C. G. Gordon at Khartum*, p. 39.
[2] Allen, op. cit., p. 343.

be advised of the nature of the reply which should be sent. Lord Granville answered on 24th July :—

"Her Majesty's Government desire, in the first place, that the messages sent to General Gordon on the 23rd April and the 17th May should be repeated to him, unless you are convinced that he has already received them ; and he should further be informed that these communications will show him the interest taken by Her Majesty's Government in his safety and that Her Majesty's Government continue to be anxious to learn from himself his views and position, so that if danger has arisen or is likely to arise in the manner they have described, they may be in a position to take measures accordingly." [1]

This masterpiece of refrigerating courtesy reached Gordon on 25th November. It was in code. Colonel Stewart had gone away with the official key. The Governor-General was, therefore, saved the unpleasantness of reading these chilling words. They told the same old story. It was that the dominant spirits of the Ministry still held, as late as 20th July, to the idea that the recalcitrant Gordon was insubordinate, would not answer their messages, and was so safe that he could, if he would, find leisure to make up a temperature chart of conditions at Khartoum. The Government wanted diagnosis and prognosis before committing themselves.

One is tempted to wonder whether, through some intuitive faculty, Gordon knew of the importance which London attached, in this undeciphered message, to the Cairo-Khartoum news service, when he wrote in his journal on 24th September :—

"It is the most extraordinary thing, quite incomprehensible, that with only one exception, that of Zobeir's man who came from Cairo (with Egerton's famous dispatch about contracts), not one single messenger has entered this place on the proper

[1] Earl of Cromer, op. cit., vol. i, p. 577.

initiative of outsiders. It has been invariably *my* messengers, who were sent out by me, from Khartoum, who did bring me any news. It would seem as if those outside seemed to think it was my duty to send out and bring in news for myself, and that they had nothing to do with it. Either these officers do not care to spend a " sou " in spies, or else they think it is a matter of supreme indifference whether I know what is going on or not ; I must say when my messengers do come back they bring me scarcely any information of import. . . . Silly, foolish questions are all we ever got from them, and it is not to be wondered at that I am indignant with such unpatriotic conduct, and not inclined to be over civil beyond my duty." [1]

The British public knew nothing of Gordon's note to the *Mudir* of Dongola which had reached London on 20th June. It took Lord Granville four days to draft his reply to it. It is reported in the *Life of Sir Charles Dilke* that the day after the answer left for Cairo there was a Cabinet meeting at which, " for the first time, there was a large majority for a Gordon expedition. The issue was narrowed down to that of sending some sort of British force towards Dongola." The vote was nine for the measure and three against it. Mr. Gladstone headed the minority group. Lord Granville had not recovered from the chilling effect of framing his instructions of 24th July, and said nothing. " By the stoutness of their resistance the three prevailed over the nine." But if Lord Hartington yielded to Mr. Gladstone at the sitting of 25th July, the Minister for War felt a special responsibility in the matter and returned to the charge. He wrote a letter for submission to the Prime Minister in which he said :—

" I gave the assurance in the debate on the Vote of Censure, which certainly had some effect on the decision. I must attach my own meaning to these

[1] *Journals of Major-General C. G. Gordon*, p. 91.

assurances, and no explanation by anyone else can absolve me from what I consider to be their obligation. . . .

"It is a question of personal honour and good faith and I do not see how I can yield upon it."

Mr. Gladstone knew what those words meant. They implied that, if the Cabinet remained obdurate, Lord Hartington would resign. The corollary to this would, most probably, have been the fall of the Government. The Prime Minister yielded. On 5th August the following notice of motion was entered in the House of Commons :—

"That a sum not exceeding £300,000 be granted to Her Majesty, beyond the ordinary grants of Parliament of 1884–1885, to enable Her Majesty to undertake operations for the relief of General Gordon, should they become necessary, and to make certain preparations in respect thereof."

This credit does not appear to have been asked for, because the driving power of the Ministry believed Gordon to be in danger. The Prime Minister appeared, on the contrary, to be obsessed by the idea that the Governor-General was perfectly safe. This is shown by the very text of the resolution submitted to Parliament. The reference to "operations for the relief of General Gordon should they become necessary" indicates that the motion was made because Lord Hartington's stand created a political contingency which demanded action.

So convinced do Mr. Gladstone and Lord Granville appear to have been that Gordon was refractory to discipline and stubbornly refused to keep London posted in regard to conditions at Khartoum, that when, as late as 18th August, Mr. Egerton asked the Foreign Secretary whether the Consulate-General should advise Gordon of the nature of the preparations envisaged by the vote of Parliament, his inquiry received the following answer :—

"Inform General Gordon of the preparations for his relief in case of need; refer him to former messages with directions from Her Majesty's Government to conform to them, and ask the causes of our not having received any reply." [1]

It took over a month for a response to this message to reach London. The reply did not come as an answer to the instructions of 18th August. It bore an earlier date. It took the shape of a postscript of 31st July, which read: "You ask me to state cause and intention in staying at Khartoum knowing Government means to abandon Sudan, and in answer I say I stay at Khartoum because Arabs have shut us up, and will not let us out."

But if we are tempted to criticise Lord Granville and Mr. Gladstone for adhering to the belief that Gordon was deliberately defying Downing Street by not answering instructions sent to him, it should not be forgotten that Lord Cromer, one of the few great constructive statesmen of the nineteenth century, held to equally erroneous opinions. He has written in his *Modern Egypt*:—

(1) "I do not think that it can be held that General Gordon made any serious effort to carry out the main ends of British and Egyptian policy in the Sudan." [2]

(2) "I have no hesitation in saying that General Gordon cannot be considered to have tried to do his duty unless a very strained and mistaken view be taken of what his duty was. He appears to me to have set up for himself a certain standard of duty without any deliberate thought of the means by which his objects were to be accomplished, or of the consequences which would probably ensue to the British Government and the British nation from attempting to accomplish them." [3]

[1] Earl of Cromer, op. cit., vol. i, p. 577.
[2] Ibid., p. 570. [3] Ibid., p. 567.

(3) " The truth is that . . . he tried to force the hand of the Government and to oblige them to send an expedition to the Sudan."[1]

When so clear a thinker, so well-balanced a man, and so pure a patriot as the great Cromer can thus go astray one should be loath to be too severe on party leaders, however inconsistent their conduct may appear to be. On the contrary, the fairest thing to do is to take the accusations which *Modern Egypt* brings against Gordon. They are, in the last analysis, compressed into charge No. 1. It indicts the soldier-explorer for having made no " serious effort to carry out the main ends of British and Egyptian policy in the Sudan ".

What was that policy ? Was it ever fixed, stabilized, and constant ? Was it not, on the contrary, protean in its metamorphosis and volatile in its instability ? Did it not begin by making Suakin the objective of Gordon's mission and a report on the military conditions on the Sudan the end envisaged ? This plan was changed by London before Gordon had reached Port Said. Baring was brought into the foreground and made Gordon's immediate hierarchical chief. The latter became convinced that the co-operation of Zobeir Pasha was essential to the success of his mission. Being a man with well-defined principles and great tenacity of purpose, Gordon spoke out his mind and finally won over Baring to the imperative need of having Zobeir sent to Khartoum.

It was not insubordination on Gordon's part to hold to his convictions regarding the Black Pasha during the weeks when Her Majesty's diplomatic agent at Cairo was urging Lord Granville to agree to Zobeir's appointment. When did the Foreign Office announce for the first time, in peremptory tones, that it would not accept Zobeir ? The answer to this inquiry is the touchstone of the entire question. The

[1] Ibid., p. 570.

decisive reply came in two instructions dated 11th and 12th March. The rebels had cut the wires between Khartoum and Cairo before these messages could be relayed to Gordon. Accordingly, we read in *Modern Egypt* :—

"I repeated Lord Granville's telegrams to General Gordon, instructing him at the same time to hold on to Khartoum until I could communicate further with the British Government. . . . I do not think that General Gordon ever received this message." [1] He did not.

Even if Gordon had received it, did it not tell him to hold on to Khartoum until his hierarchical superior could communicate further with the British Government? Who was the man who here counselled the Governor-General not to abandon Khartoum until a further attempt could be made to induce Downing Street to agree to the nomination of Zobeir? Who was the superior power who thus talked in terms which savour of undue opposition to London? It was Baring.

But this message did not reach Gordon. He was hemmed in at Khartoum from and after 11th March. From that date his capital city was his jail. His own words, written on 31st July, may well be repeated. They are: "The Arabs have shut us up and will not let us out." The whole problem is compressed into these twelve syllables. Their effect goes back to 11th March. In other words, Gordon was caught in a trap before he knew that London would not permit him to turn over his mandate to Zobeir.

[1] Ibid., p. 521.

## Chapter XXVI

# DEMOTED

During those fateful months when Gordon was surrounded by a wall of fire, the experts of the British War Office were studying plans for the relief of Khartoum. Lord Wolseley knew that time governed the entire question. The Valley of the Nile was not a closed book to him. To his mind all hope of reaching the capital of the Sudan before it was " too late " depended upon taking advantage of the high river. Its flood tide served a double purpose. It enabled Gordon to make use of his steamers and it permitted him to profit by the inundations which divided the Mahdi's forces in twain. Lord Wolseley dreaded what would happen when the recession of the waters should circumscribe the field of operation of the boats and also allow the Dervish bands to close in, more tightly than ever, upon Khartoum.

But though it was possible for the army leaders to prepare tentative plans, while Mr. Gladstone and his Cabinet were still obsessed by the idea that the disobedient and changeable Gordon was in no military peril, nothing could be done to give vitality to them until the Government said the word. It is a trite saying that—

" When doctors disagree
Patients then are free."

These words are recalled by the discussions which went on in the War Office while Her Majesty's Ministers were still dominated by their pet theory that Gordon was a " naughty boy " who did not want to move away from the fire. The experts were divided among themselves regarding the manner in which the imperatively necessary relief should be sent. One is tempted to believe that had his professional advisers been able to submit to Lord Hartington a concrete proposal, shortly after the vote in Parliament of 13th May, when the House of Commons applauded Mr. Gladstone's "solemn covenant" speech, the Secretary for War would have applied pressure to the Prime Minister long before 29th July. But the subordinate Cabinet officer could hardly have been expected to take the initiative against his chief, unless he had a plan to propose. It is to be feared that he had not. At all events, we read in Colonel Sir William F. Butler's graphically written *Charles George Gordon* that :—

"And what, it may well be asked, had been the action taken during all those months since the fall of Berber had sealed the last hope of a peaceful evacuation of Khartoum ? Ah ! The answer to that question is, indeed, a sad one. May, June, July, and almost half-way through August before an undecided executive above, and congested clerkships, rival theories, and varying ambitions below, can shape themselves into any fixed plan of action. It is by railway from Suakin to Berber that you must relieve Khartoum, say one set of counsellors. But the route has many mountains, and the passes are three thousand and four thousand feet above sea-level, and for distances of eighty miles there is not a drop of water along the proposed line. . . . It will take two campaigns and two years to complete such a line. No ; the true route of advance is the one which nature points out. The Nile in its long reaches of open water gives easy transport for men and stores, and even in its worst cataract it yields that first necessity of desert warfare—water." [1]

"Thus," continues Sir William Butler, "during the

[1] Butler, op. cit., p. 22.

early summer months of 1884 the strife of routes went on." It had, however, been practically settled before Mr. Gladstone, on 5th August, moved in the House of Commons for the credit necessary to undertake operations for the relief of Gordon. In Dr. Allen's admirable *Gordon and the Sudan* we read that the loss of time brought about by what he styles "the Cairo advocates of the Suakin-Berber route and the London advocates of the Nile",[1] was but a fortnight. So accurate is the scholarship of Dr. Allen that his estimate may be accepted without hesitation. However, it is not easy to suppress the subconscious feeling that if this divergence of view had not persisted for so long, Lord Hartington would have forced Mr. Gladstone to act, at the latest, on the morrow of the fall of Berber. That decisive event occurred, it may not be amiss to repeat, on 26th May, and well before the end of June London had no further doubts in regard to the capitulation.

News of all these discussions appears to have drifted through to Gordon. One of his favourite quotations from Holy Writ was: "Blessed is the man who does not sit in the seat of the scornful."[2] Yet when he heard on 17th September that troops were on the way to relieve Khartoum, he could not restrain his pen from writing: "I have the strongest suspicions that these tales of troops at Dongola and Merowé are all gasworks, and that if you wanted to find Her Majesty's forces you would have to go to Shepheard's Hotel at Cairo."[3]

This sarcastic outburst, while obviously unwarranted in so far as it might be interpreted as reflecting upon the professional zeal of Lord Wolseley and staff, was probably due to the fact that, again to quote Colonel Sir William Butler, during "the strife of routes"—

"Contracts for the railroad between Suakin and

[1] Allen, op. cit., p. 348.
[2] *The Journals of Maj.-Gen. C. G. Gordon*, p. 60. [3] Ibid., p. 38.

Berber were gravely discussed and given out, officers were sent from Egypt to England to ascertain by protracted experiments at Aldershot whether it would be possible to pump condensed water from the Bay of Suakin to the top of the land between that place and Berber, a distance of nearly one hundred miles and some three thousand five hundred feet above the level of the sea. It was found that water could indeed be pumped a considerable distance, but two things were also discovered which also put a stop to further researches into this interesting question—the water came out at the end of the third or fourth mile at a temperature of boiling point, and it was also seen that between condensing and pumping through pipes, water delivered at the height of land between the Red Sea and the Nile would cost per quart about the price of the choicest of brands of celebrated vintages."[1]

Be all this as it may, on 9th September Lord Wolseley arrived at Cairo to take command of the relief expedition. Before he and his staff were able to leave that capital for Wadi Halfa Mr. Gladstone launched a bombshell against Gordon. The Prime Minister acted from the most laudable of motives. He was travelling through Scotland fulminating against the House of Lords and its entrenched authority, when the Dundee morning papers of 18th September published a news item which said that Gordon was "careering up and down the Nile crying for the blood of the Mahdi, and burning towns and slaying rebels to his heart's content". The information agreed so perfectly with the Premier's conception of the militant and cantankerous Gordon that the vigilant party leader immediately got into touch with the Foreign Office. The result was that on 19th September Lord Granville drew up instructions which were sent to Baring and which

[1] Butler, op. cit., p. 222.

directed (1) that Gordon was to be placed under the orders of Lord Wolseley and (2) that the Khedive was to modify his original decree so that Gordon, instead of being Governor-General of the Sudan, was only to be Governor of a limited area.

On 21st September the Khedive sent Gordon a telegram in Arabic which told him that with the arrival of British troops the situation had considerably changed and that the conduct of negotiations was now in the hands of Colonel Chermside at Suakin and of Major Kitchener at Dongola. " Under the circumstances," continued the Khedive, " it is so far necessary to revise the firman granted to you as to limit your powers as Governor-General of the Sudan to Khartoum, Sennar, and the immediate neighbourhood of Berber.

" You are not, without further instructions, to send steamers on any expeditions up the White Nile for the relief of Bahr El Ghazel and Equatorial garrisons.

" You are to use every endeavour to bring the Sennar garrison back to Khartoum, as I am glad to see by your telegram that you propose.

" I am glad to see from your last telegram that you have abandoned the idea of burning Berber, of which I cannot approve.

" You will receive instructions of the British Government through Sir Evelyn Baring and Lord Wolseley." [1]

It was not until 25th November that the Khedive's message reached Gordon. With it came a Foreign Office telegram, presumably along the same lines. The latter, however, was in code, and could not be deciphered as Colonel Stewart had carried away the key. The outstanding feature of the Viceroy's instructions, as the interpreter explained the Arabic text to Gordon, was that " Baring is coming up with Lord Wolseley ".[2]

Under date of 1st December, Gordon's journal reads :—

[1] Allen, op. cit., p. 351. [2] *Journals of Maj.-Gen. C. G. Gordon*, p. 359.

"Tewfik's telegram to me was to-day more fully explained, and I gather that he says Lord Wolseley and Sir Evelyn Baring are coming up and they will settle the question of the Sudan. I have replied that it may be convenient for him (Tewfik), but it does not meet the case, unless these two officials have a firman from him, giving them authority. Now this the two officials will never have, for it virtually would make them *Tewfik's subordinates.* It is implied in the telegram that I am to arrange with these two officials as to the Sudan. A delightful arrangement for Tewfik, but not so delightful for me." [1]

All this makes one feel that, because the Downing Street instructions came in cipher and the Khedive's in Arabic, Gordon failed to grasp that he had been demoted. The Arabic interpreter may not have been able to decipher the text and put it into intelligible English. Or, again, he may have been able to do so and yet have preferred to keep his chief more or less in the dark and impart the important news to spies of the Mahdi. We cannot tell. We are groping in the dark. But it does seem suspiciously strange that Gordon does not appear to have understood even the gist of the Khedive's message. It was, perhaps, better that he did not. *Kismet* was, in this one particular, kind to him. It would have cut him to the quick had the brutal reality been driven home to him.

No bloodthirstiness had prompted Gordon in contemplating the burning of Berber. He was a soldier and was alive to the strategic importance of that place. When it fell he considered that the safety of Khartoum required that an attempt should be made to dominate Berber. The information upon which the Foreign Soecretary had acted—for it is obvious that Tewfik Pasha's instructions were dictated by Downing Street—seems to have been based upon a letter dated 24th August and addressed by Gordon to the officer

[1] Ibid., p. 371.

commanding the royal naval force at Massawah. It spoke of meditating a raid on Berber in order to let pass to Dongola a convoy which accompanies Colonel Stewart and English and French consuls. It added : " We shall (D.V.) destroy Berber and return to our pirate nest here." [1]

When Gordon wrote to his sailor friend on 24th August, he had no inkling that Parliament had agreed on 5th August to undertake operations for the relief of Khartoum. No doubt on this score is possible, for the letter says : " We are very cross with you all, for since the 29th March we have had not one word from the outer world." To blame a soldier left to his own resources for taking the military measures his safety dictated is certainly pressing captious criticism, but it so happened that Gordon had abandoned all intention of making a raid on Berber before Mr. Gladstone and Lord Granville inspired the Khedive's severe language of 21st September.

It appears that Muhammad Ali Pasha, one of Gordon's " fighting Pashas ", persuaded his chief that before attempting to regain Berber it would be the part of wisdom to crush Sheikh El Obeid, who was then massing troops at El Eilafun, some 25 miles from Khartoum. The task was committed to the faithful Muhammad Ali Pasha. He gained his primary objective, but, endeavouring to press his success too far, fell into an ambush and perished with approximately 1,000 of his men.

This defeat took place on 5th September. It deprived Gordon not only of the most valuable of his native leaders, but also of many of his best soldiers. The blow fell at a most inauspicious moment, for in September the Nile begins to recede at Khartoum. This implied that the Mahdi's forces would soon no longer be cut in two and that Gordon's capital would shortly be invested more closely than ever.

[1] Archer, op. cit., vol. iii, p. 165.

Muhammad Ahmad was quick to grasp the moral significance of his victory. He had his spies in Cairo. He knew, even if the Governor-General did not, that the British Government had finally decided to intervene. He accordingly made capital out of his success and drove home to his followers the message that Allah had thus blessed his banners in order to show that the Lord of Hosts was fighting for Islam. In other words, the psychological effect of the certainty of a relief expedition was counteracted by the death of Muhammad Ali Pasha and of his legion.

But if Gordon had no means of drawing all these collateral deductions from the loss which he had suffered through the death of so many irreplaceable men, he at once saw that this reversal would make it foolhardy on his part to attempt to recapture Berber. With the Nile about to fall and with his fighting units reduced, he was faced with the imperative necessity of doing something, and at once to arouse both Cairo and London from their lethargy. He did not then know that on the very day when Muhammad Ali had perished Lord Wolseley and his staff were ploughing the Mediterranean on their way to Cairo. All that he saw was that the Nile was falling and that no replies had ever been received to his letters to Baring.

He gave the matter mature consideration. His decisions were invariably taken after careful meditation and fervent prayer. He reached the conclusion that Colonel Stewart and Frank Power, the only other Englishmen at Khartoum, could best serve the cause of humanity and of British prestige by leaving for Cairo in order to plead for the inhabitants of Khartoum. The two Britons were loath to depart. They had shared Gordon's peril. They insisted that they be allowed to share his fate. But though Gordon may have had the eyes of a dreamer, and the far-away smile of a mystic, he was in all matters affecting his mission the most practical of men. He foresaw that if Gladstone and Granville and Baring and Egerton had been able to resist his missives, British public opinion would not fail to hearken to the spoken word of Stewart and Power. He knew the value of his trump cards and that the time had come to play them. He fairly forced his two fellow-countrymen to leave him.

Here is the letter which preceded them. Its date is 9th September. It was addressed to the Khedive, Nubar Pasha, and Baring. It was written in cipher. Every word of it has a meaning. Its last two paragraphs will be quoted. They read :—

"How many times have we written, asking for reinforcements, calling your serious attention to the Sudan? No answer at all has come to us as to what has been decided in the matter, and the hearts of men have become weary of this delay. While you are eating, drinking, and resting on good beds, we and those with us, both soldiers and servants, are watching by night and day, endeavouring to quell the movement of this false Mahdi. Of course, you take no interest in suppressing this rebellion, the serious consequences of which are the reverse of victorious for you and the neglect thereof will not do (*sic*).

"In two days' time Colonel Stewart, the Vice-Governor-General, and the two Consuls [1] will start from here to Berber and Dongola. The reason why I have now sent Colonel Stewart is because you have been silent all this while, and have neglected us and lost time without doing any good. If troops were sent, as soon as they reach Berber this rebellion will cease, and the inhabitants will return to their former occupations. It is therefore hoped that you will listen to all that is told you by Stewart and the Consuls.

[1] Frank Power, *The Times* Correspondent, was also British Consular Agent at Khartoum. M. Herbin, the French Consular Agent, also accompanied Colonel Stewart.

Look at it seriously and send troops, as we have asked without delay." [1]

One is tempted to doubt whether an Englishman decoded this letter. The text has something exotic about it. But its meaning is obvious. It is the work of a strong man burning with righteous indignation. As it foretold, Colonel Stewart and the two Consular Agents left on 9th September, aboard the steamer *Abbas*.

It is with regret that we read in *The Life of Gordon* by Demetrius C. Boulger that—

"Colonel Donald Stewart was a personal friend of mine, and a man whose courage in the ordinary sense of the word could not be aspersed, but there cannot be two opinions that he, above all others, should not have left his brother-in-arms alone in Khartoum." [2] No enemy could have planted a knife deeper into a man's ribs than do these words of one who proclaims that Colonel Donald Stewart was his personal friend. But that there were two opinions is best shown by Gordon's own words :—

"The matter was thus. I determined to send the *Abbas* down with an Arab captain. Herbin (the French Consular Agent) asked to be allowed to go. I jumped at his offer. Then Stewart said he would go, if I would exonerate him from deserting me. I said : 'You do not desert me. I, I cannot go ; but if you go you do great service.' . . . I wrote them a letter, couched thus : '*Abbas* is going down ; you say you are willing to go in her if I think you can do so in honour—you can go in honour, for you can do nothing here, and if you go you do me service in telegraphing my views.'" [3]

Gordon and Stewart both wore the Queen's livery.

[1] Royle, op. cit., vol. ii, p. 225.

[2] *The Life of Gordon*, by Demetrius C. Boulger ; London, T. Fisher Unwin, 1896, vol. ii, p. 146.

[3] *Journals of Major-General C. G. Gordon*, p. 280.

They were gentlemen in the noblest acceptation of the term. They knew the precious refinement of the word " honour ". And when Gordon put into black and white that his subordinate could " go in honour ", he thought not of Stewart but of the uniform which clothed his fellow-officer. It was because he felt that the glory of that cloth was not tarnished by the departure of his deputy that he assented. He did so conscious that anything savouring of desertion would have been an indelible stain upon an escutcheon which has been held inviolate across the ages.

Gordon's journal entry of 17th September tells how anxious he was that Stewart and Power should build a fire under Gladstone and Granville through the compelling flame of public opinion. Every moment counted. The Nile was falling. The food supply was running low. Gordon was the only Englishman left in Khartoum. His ears had become accustomed to the musket-fire of the contending forces and to the roar of the artillery. His eyes were pinned to his calendar. He counted the days when his two British emissaries would be able to rouse the righteous anger of England and force a reluctant Ministry to act. " If Stewart gets down," he wrote, " he ought to be in communication with Europe on the 22nd of September and Power's telegrams ought to be in *The Times* 23rd September. It makes me laugh to think of the flutter in the dovecot which will follow. *That beastly Sudan again* ! "[1]

Everything hinged on " if " and " ought ". Gordon knew this. No man could have been more meticulously careful than he was in arranging for Stewart's and Power's trip. No minute detail escaped the ceaseless vigilance of the officer whom Baring calls flighty, inconsistent, and fickle. His concentration upon the task of preparing the *Abbas* for her voyage would have been gall and wormwood to a man who was not

[1] Ibid., p. 39.

tenacity of purpose personified. His own pen can best describe not only what he did but the utter futility of all his unremitting care.

It was on 9th November that he wrote :—

"I cannot get out of my head the *Abbas* catastrophe ; that the *Abbas* (with her 970 bullet-marks on her, her gun, and her parapets which were bullet-proof), could be captured by force seems impossible ; that she ran upon a rock seems unlikely, for she had her sides defended by buffers sunk one foot in water. I also had warned them against ever anchoring by the bank, also to take wood from isolated spots ; in fact, so far as human foresight goes, I did all my possible. . . . You will notice the number of Greeks. They were a bodyguard to prevent any treachery on the part of the crew. Thus the question of treachery was duly weighed by me and guarded against, as far as I could, both on the part of the crew and the part of the inhabitants. . . ."

And, continued Gordon : "I escorted them by steamers past every place where danger could be apprehended, viz. Berber and Shendy. They appear to have been captured near a comparatively thinly populated place below Abu Hamed. I feel somewhat convinced that they were captured by treachery—the Arabs pretending to be friendly and surprising them at night. . . . Stewart was a man who did not chew the cud ; he never thought of danger in perspective ; he was not a bit suspicious (while I am made up of it)." [1]

No higher eulogy could be paid to anyone than that which Gordon wrote for the three men who left Khartoum on the *Abbas* and met their death. His exact words are :—

"Stewart was a brave, just, upright gentleman. Can one say more ? Power was a chivalrous, brave,

[1] Ibid., p. 279. A footnote on p. 281 shows that Gordon's surmise was substantially correct, and all these men were killed.

honest gentleman. Can one say more ?] Herbin I liked very much ; he was a most agreeable and gentlemanly Frenchman, and very sharp." What did Gordon mean by "sharp"? He went on to say that "the diplomats . . . called him *names* in a telegram ; but I found him fairly just, though naturally with a French bias".[1] But when Gordon heard that Stewart, Power, and Herbin had probably lost their lives because they had refused to forswear their faith, no distinctions were drawn between Briton and Gaul. On the contrary, he wrote : "If Stewart, Power, and Herbin died because they would not change their religion they are as much martyrs as Peter or Paul."[2]

[1] Ibid., p. 311. [2] Ibid., p. 285.

## Chapter XXVII

# ALONE

Whatever may have been, in the past, the wear and tear of the siege, the anxiety of the watchful nights, the sickening sense of desertion without, and the possibility of treachery within, Gordon had had the comforting presence, stimulating counsel, and sincere friendship of Stewart and Power to bring sunshine into his life. When the *Abbas* disappeared beyond the horizon he was left without a friend, alone among an almost unbroken mass of ebony faces, cinnamon brows, and Arabs. There were a few struggling Europeans, it is true, but they were sons of climes which had no affinity with England and they had become merged into the local population. He had willingly made this sacrifice as the price of his final appeal to Britain.

In the picture of his daily life, however, which commenced on 10th September, when he first began to keep a Khartoum journal, there are a thousand touches which tell that he was happier and more at rest than he had been since his departure from England. The issue was clear. He was alone and entirely dependent upon his own resources. This brought him closer to his Maker and gave more vitalizing force to his religious fervour. He could more readily commune at all hours with his Saviour and find in the discharge of the humblest duty the keenest sense of spiritual pleasure.

His journals are divided into six books. The first entry bears the date of 10th September; the last that of 14th December. It took the form of a postscript. He had said " Good-bye " and had signed his usual signature " C. G. Gordon ". Then, recalling how he had, across the dreary months, begged, pleaded, and implored for just a word from those who held the fate of the British Empire in their hands, he added : " You send me no information, though you have lots of money. C. G. G."[1]

The journals, taken as a whole, are a complete laying bare of Gordon's soul. There is, as Colonel Sir William Butler so aptly puts it, " no word spoken to the gallery, nor yet a sentence that seems to indicate a thought that it is his last testament he is really writing and how lowly is the estimate of self which he gives us in the midst of the superb heroism ! "[2] The first volume is a complete introduction to the personality of the man. Each succeeding page draws the reader closer to him. So firmly does he grip our heart that we have to guard our intellect, as it were, against the hypnotism of the nobility of his character and the charm of his simplicity.

The introductory lines of the first volume give an interesting instance of Gordon's nobility of soul. His back was against the wall. No man knew it better than he. He had no illusions. He was determined, nevertheless, to have nothing to do with Europeans in the Mahdi's camp. They sought to reach him, apparently desiring to betray their new masters. He based his refusal to have anything to do with the renegades primarily upon religious scruples. " If the Christian faith is a myth," he wrote on the day he began his journals, " then let men throw it off ; but it is mean and dishonourable to do so merely to save one's life, if one believes it is the true faith. What can be more strong than these words : ' He who denies me on earth I will deny in heaven ? ' "

But there was always something so practical about Gordon that he preferred to have a second string to his bow. He felt, as a Christian, withering contempt for

[1] *The Journals of Major-General C. G. Gordon, C.B.*, p. 395.
[2] Butler, op. cit., p. 231.

deliberate apostasy. As a soldier charged with the welfare of his fellow-men, he preferred to look at the matter from another angle. His strong common sense was so often the handmaid of his spirituality that we are not surprised to note that he went on to say :—

"Politically and morally, however, it is better for us not to have anything to do with apostate Europeans in the Arab camp. Treachery never succeeds, and however matters may end it is better to fall with clean hands than to be mixed up with dubious acts and dubious men." And not only did the realist in Gordon thus keep pace with the idealist in him, but the canniness inbred in him, through his Scottish forebears, taught him to capitalize these deeply religious and thoroughly practical principles.

He was surrounded by Muslims. The backing of the Muhammedan *Ulema* was necessary to his safety. So he got into touch with these *sheikhs* and saw to it that they knew that he was not attempting to reconvert men who had adopted the faith of Islam. His journal records this worldly-wise step in these words :—

"May be it is better for us to fall with honour than to gain victory with dishonour ; and in this view the *Ulema* of the town are agreed ; they will have nought to do with the proposals of treachery." [1]

While Gordon had the deepest aversion for Christians who renounced their religion in order to save their lives, he felt the same dislike for Muhammedans who bartered their faith for worldly ends. "There is scarcely one great family of the Sudan," he wrote, "families who can trace their pedigree for five hundred years, who have not accepted Muhammed Ahmad as Mahdi, to save their property, though they laugh at the idea afterwards." Always quick to make a point and to tie it to something utilitarian, he continued :—

"I am using this argument with them in saying :

[1] *Journals of Major-General C. G. Gordon*, p. 5.

'You ask me to become a Muhammedan to save my life, and you yourself acknowledge Muhammad Ahmad as the Mahdi, to save your lives ; why, if we go on this principle we will be adopting every religion whose adherents threaten our existence, for you know and own, when you are safe, that Muhammad Ahmad is *not* the Mahdi.' "[1]

While knowing that he had but to say in the presence of two Muhammedans, "There is no divinity but God and Muhammad is the apostle of God" to be perfectly safe, Gordon was too broadminded a man not to recognize that Muslims are not fanatics. He wrote :—

"I do not believe that fanaticism exists as it used to do in the world, judging from what I have seen in this so-called fanatical land. It is far more a question of property, and is more like Communism under the flag of religion, which seems to excite and to give colour to acts which men would otherwise condemn."

And so anxious was he that Christians should not judge Muhammedans harshly that he added :—

"I am sure it is unknown to the generality of our missionaries in Muslim countries that in the Qurân no imputation of sin is made on our Lord, neither is it hinted that He had need of pardon, and, further, no Muslim can deny that the Father of our Lord was God and that He was incarnated by a miracle. . . . As far as self-sacrifice of the body, they are far above Roman Catholics and consequently of Protestants. . . . The God of the Muslims is *our* God. And they do not believe that Muhammad exercises any mediatorial office for them. They believe they will stand and fall by their own deeds ; in fact, they are as much under the law as the Jews."[2]

It may not be out of place at this point to learn what Gordon himself thought of prayer. Lord Cromer makes light of the influence which the Prophet Isaiah

[1] Ibid., p. 15. [2] Ibid., p. 19.

had over the Governor-General of the Sudan. Gordon said :—

" I cannot think that there are any promises for answers to prayer made for temporal things ; the promises are to hear prayer, and to give strength to bear with quiet what may be the will of God. A vial is poured on earth ; events happen ; one is furious with the British Government for these events ; but, if we were logical, we should be furious with the pourer-out of the vial, and that we shrink from being, for He is the Almighty who pours out the vial." [1]

While there was nothing intolerant about Gordon's militant Christianity, his sense of humour was appealed to by the awkward hours at which Muslims say their prayers, and by "the constrained positions" which they assume for a considerable time when praying. " If these Arabs (one's servants) are not *eating* they are saying their *prayers* ; if not *saying their prayers* they are *sleeping* ; if not sleeping they are sick," is the true picture he draws of life in the Valley of the Nile. And to show the force of this tyranny of the weak, he adds : " Now figure to yourself the position : you cannot do anything with them while in these fortresses *eating*, *saying prayers*, *sleeping*, or *sick*, and they know it. You would be a brute if you did (which I fear I often am) ; you want to send an immediate order, and there is your servant bobbing up and down (praying) and you cannot disturb him. It is a beautiful country for trying experiments with your patience." [2]

It was on 23rd October that Gordon wrote in this strain about his domestic worries. Some three weeks later, when the siege of Khartoum had already lasted more than eight months, so absolute was his self-control that he observed :—

" It is really amusing to find (when one can scarcely call one's life one's own), one's servant, already with one wife (which most men find is enough) coming

[1] Ibid., p. 12. [2] Ibid., p. 223.

and asking for three days' leave to take another. Yet such was the case, a few days ago, with one of my servants." [1]

But though Gordon had a heart of gold and nerves of steel and smiled as bullets whizzed by him, his equanimity was shattered by the approach of a diplomat. It is said of the great Nelson that the proximity of a mouse made him tremble. Gordon's mice were the men of "pink peppermints and protocol". Foreign Office men were his pet aversion. "I must say I do not love diplomatists as a rule . . ." he says of them. "I mean in their official attire, for, personally, the few I know are most agreeable . . . but taking them on their rostrums, with their satellites, from their chiefs down to the smaller fry, no one can imagine a more unsatisfactory lot to have anything to do with." [2]

Gordon's journals give us the key to his irrational dislike for diplomats. They are men whose ability to serve their country depends, in most cases, upon their gregariousness. It is in *tête-à-tête* after-dinner talks, in secluded conversations at pink teas—and sometimes through judicious flirtations—that Foreign Office men get their best political information. Without what the craft calls "contacts" no diplomat can succeed, and without admirable digestive organs "contacts" are impossible. Gordon positively refused to recognize any such conventionalities. He preferred the horrors of the siege of Khartoum to the amenities of a London season. His journals under date of 24th October record that—

"I dwell on the joy of never seeing Great Britain again, with its horrid, wearisome *dinner* parties and miseries. How we can put up with those things passes my imagination ! It is a perfect bondage. At those dinner parties we are all in masks, saying what we do not believe, eating and drinking things we do not want,

[1] Ibid., p. 336. [2] Ibid., p. 42.

and then abusing one another. I would sooner live like a Dervish with the Mahdi than go out to dinner every night in London. I hope, if any English General comes to Khartoum he will not ask me to dinner. Why men cannot be friends without bringing the wretched stomachs in is astounding." [1]

It was not the nerve-racking ordeal of the continuous bombardment that dictated such sentiments. There is not a word in the journals which betrays any flinching of Gordon's self-control. He belaboured the Diplomatic Corps and cried out against dinner parties because both of them had long been anathema to him. When he returned from the Sudan in 1880 London society made an attempt to lionize the man whom the people were calling the " uncrowned king ". But he resolutely refused all invitations to dinner and declined to be made one of the attractions of London social life. With his usual contempt for what the world might say, he made up his mind to be absolutely consistent in his refusals. In fact, he went so far as to decline a " command " to dine with the Prince of Wales. The astonished equerry at once came round to see the soldier in his humble lodgings at Chelsea. Dr. Allen's *Gordon and the Sudan* thus tells what then took place :—

" But you cannot refuse the Prince of Wales," said the equerry.

" Why not ? " replied Gordon. " I refused King John when he invited me to go with him to his hot spring in the mountains, and he might have cut off my head for refusing. I am sure His Royal Highness will not do that."

" Well, then, let me say that you are ill."

" But I am not ill," replied Gordon.

" Give me some reason, then, that I can give the Prince."

[1] Ibid., p. 227.

"Very well, tell him that I always go to bed at nine-thirty."

"Fortunately," continues Dr. Allen, "the late King Edward had a sense of humour. He sent back an invitation to a *tête-à-tête* lunch the following Sunday, which Gordon accepted and greatly enjoyed." [1]

A broader-gauged man than Edward VII never lived. Foreign Office officials were shocked by this attitude on Gordon's part. It is said that some of them criticized the heir to the throne for giving way to the bore. This may perhaps be an exaggeration. The statement may, nevertheless, be hazarded that when Gordon refused the "command" to dine with the Prince of Wales the permanent officials of Downing Street registered him in their minds as an unsafe, dangerous, ill-bred person to whom officialdom could not safely commit a mandate. Who can say that this subterranean hostility did not encourage Lord Granville in his opposition to Gordon?

If it did, and the soldier had known of it, it would have appealed to his unquenchable sense of humour. This happy faculty never deserted him even in the darkest days of the siege. He was then very much irritated with Egerton, Baring's right-hand man, for having expressed a wish "to know *exactly* day, hour, and minute that he (Gordon) expects to be in difficulties as to provisions and ammunitions".

Such a request, dated 30th August, and received when the imprisoned soldier was fighting for his very existence, never knowing what the morrow held in store for him, appealed to his appreciation of the ridiculous. He therefore took pen and paper and wrote:—

"I really think if Egerton was to turn over the 'archives' (a delicious word) of his office, he would see we had been in difficulties for months. It is as

[1] Allen, op. cit., p. 168.

if a man on the bank, having seen his friend in the river already bobbed down two or three times, hails, 'I say, old fellow, let us know when we are to throw the lifebuoy. I knew you have bobbed down two or three times, but it is a pity to throw you the lifebuoy until you are really *in extremis*, and I want to know *exactly*, for I am a man brought up in a school of exactitude, although I did forget (?) to date my June telegram about that Bedwin escort contract.'" [1]

Gordon also had no love for Cabinet ministers. He tells a story about the Mahdi and draws from it a moral which he applies to the Government of the day. "The Greek who came in told the Greek Consul," so runs his tale, "that the Mahdi puts pepper under his nails. . . . Those who come in for pardon, come in on their knees with a halter round their neck. The Mahdi rises, having scratched his eyes, and obtained a copious supply of tears takes off the halter. As the production of tears is generally considered the proof of sincerity, I would recommend the Mahdi's recipe to Cabinet ministers justifying some job. The nails (so say the Greeks) must be long, to contain the pepper." [2]

Such frankness, of which the Gladstone Ministry may, perhaps, have had subconscious knowledge, did not help Gordon's cause when the bureaucrats, also stung by his raillery, pleaded that he should be left severely alone. And even the army did not escape the taunts of the officer. During those critical days at Khartoum, when the net around him was getting tighter and tighter, he went so far as to assail the reasons for which certain Victoria Crosses had recently been granted. "The original idea of the Victoria Cross," he said, "was to give the subaltern officers, non-commissioned officers, and men a decoration which would take the place of the Bath, to ranks below that of Major, which by the statutes of the Bath could not be done; then came the mistake to give the

[1] *Journals of Major-General C. G. Gordon*, p. 74. [2] Ibid., p. 33.

Victoria Cross for deeds of *éclat*, and so it is now. . . . A man defends a post; if he loses it his throat is cut; why give him a Victoria Cross? And if given, why not give it to all who were with him? They equally defended their throats."[1]

When we turn over a few pages of these *Journals* we grasp why the innate modesty of Gordon caused him to object to the emphasis placed upon dramatic—or melodramatic—courage. "I think," he wrote, "if, instead of *Minor Tactics* or books on art of war, our young officers study Plutarch's *Lives* it would be better; there we see men (unsupported by any true belief, pure pagans) making, *as a matter of course*, their lives a sacrifice; but in our days it is the highest merit not to run away. I speak for myself when I say I have been in dire anxiety not for my own skin, but because I hate to be beaten, and I hate to see my schemes fail; but that I have had to undergo a tithe of what any nurse has had to undergo who is attached to a querulous invalid, is absurd, and not to be weighed together. When I emerge all are complimentary; when the invalid dies, the question is, what should be given the nurse for her reward."[2]

In another place Gordon gives the story of his own superhuman courage:—

"During our blockade we have often discussed the question of being frightened, which in the world's view a man should never be. For my part I am always frightened and very much so. I fear the future of all engagements. It is not the fear of death; that is past, thank God; but I fear defeat and its consequences. I do not believe a bit in the calm, unmoved man. I think that it is only that he does not show it outwardly."

Following up in the same strain, he recounted that:—

"In the Crimea it was supposed and considered mean to bob, and one used to try and avoid it.

[1] Ibid., p. 65. [2] Ibid., p. 26.

——used to say, 'It is all well enough for you, but I am a family man,' and he used to bob at every report. For my part I think judicious bobbing is not a fault, for I remember seeing on two occasions shells like this 'O' before my eyes, which certainly, had I not bobbed, would have taken off my head. (And a good riddance, too! F.O. would say.)"[1]

And the man who, as he wrote these lines, was doing as fine a bit of hero-work as any known to history, wrote thus of his achievement :—

"A member of Parliament in one of our last received papers asks: 'Whether officers are not supposed to go where they are ordered?' I quite agree with his view, but it cannot be said I was ordered to go. The subject was too complex for any order. It was 'Will you go and try?' And my answer was 'Only too delighted'. As for all that may be said as to why I did not escape with Stewart, it is simply because the people would not have been such fools as to let me go; so there is an end to these 'great-coats' of self-sacrifice."

Although he was unwilling for anyone to look upon him as a hero, his own deeds belie his words. His accomplishments were those of a hero, whatever he may have affirmed to the contrary. "I toss up in my mind whether, if the place is taken, to blow up the palace and all in it, or with God's help to maintain the faith, and, if necessary, to suffer for it (which is most probable). The blowing up of the palace is the simplest, while the other means long and weary suffering and humiliation of all sorts. I think I shall elect for the last, not from fear of death, but because the former has more or less the taint of suicide."[2]

But Gordon was not a saint. No halo blinded his vision to what went on around him. He could get angry like ordinary mortals, and fume in a manner which would interfere with his canonization. There is

[1] Ibid., p. 376. [2] Ibid., p. 31.

nothing of the tranquil peacefulness of a candidate for beatification in such biting language as—

"The Principal Medical Officers are bores and croakers, and want all sorts of attention. A man is a fool or a physician at forty years of age."[1]

Nor is there any of that resignation which is supposed to be the hall-mark of sanctified lives in such passages as :—

"I altogether *decline* the imputation that the proposed expedition has come to *relieve me*. It has come to SAVE OUR NATIONAL HONOUR *in extricating the garrisons*, *etc.*, *from a position our action in Egypt has placed these garrisons. I was relief expedition No.* 1. *They are relief expedition No.* 2. As for myself I could make good my retreat at any moment if I wished. Now realise what would happen if this *first relief expedition* was to bolt and the steamers fell into the hands of the Mahdi : this *second relief expedition* (for the honour of England engaged in extricating garrisons) would be somewhat hampered. We, the *first* and *second* expeditions, are equally engaged for the honour of England. This is fair logic. *I came up to extricate the garrisons and failed. Earle comes up to extricate garrisons and* (*I hope*) *succeeds. Earle does not come to extricate me.* This extrication of the garrisons was supposed to affect our 'national honour'. If Earle succeeds, the 'national honour' thanks him, and, I hope, rewards him, but it is altogether independent of me who, for failing, incurs its blame. I am not the *rescued lamb*, and I will not be."[2]

[1] Ibid., p. 98. [2] Ibid., p. 93.

## Chapter XXVIII

# THE DASH TO KHARTOUM

On 14th December Gordon wrote to his sister: " This may be the last letter you will receive from me, for we are on our last legs, owing to the delay of the expedition." In a postscript he added: " I am quite happy, thank God, and like Lawrence, I have tried to do my duty."[1]

This letter left Khartoum with his six journals. The note and diaries were handed over to Colonel Sir Charles Wilson, as was also a small piece of paper on which was written " Khartoum all right. Could hold out for years." Signed C. G. Gordon, sealed with his Arabic stamp, and dated 29.12.84.[2] A messenger who had joined the steamers at Nasri Island brought the chit. It was the last document of any kind received from General Gordon. It is believed by those who ought to know that it is one of many that the gallant soldier sent out about the same time in order to deceive the enemy.

The same steamer also carried a letter addressed to one of Gordon's friends, Colonel Watson. It was dated 14th December, and read:—

" I think the game is up, and send Mrs. Watson, yourself, and Graham (Sir Gerald) my adieux. We may expect a catastrophe in the town in or after ten days. This would not have happened (if it does happen) if our people had taken better precautions as to informing us of their movements; but this is spilt milk! Good-bye."[3]

[1] *Letters of General C. G. Gordon to his Sister*, p. 384.
[2] H. W. Gordon, op. cit., p. 379.
[3] H. W. Gordon, op. cit., p. 380.

It took sublime courage to write "spilt milk" under such tragic circumstances. But as early as 13th October Gordon had said :—

"We are a wonderful people ; it was never our Government which made us a great nation ; our Government has been ever the drag on our wheels. It is, of course, on the cards that Khartoum is taken under the nose of the expeditionary force, which will be *just "too late"*.[1] He had, therefore, carefully pondered over the question. His subconscious mind had become reconciled to the inevitable. But there were always in him, as in most men, two natures. There was the realist and there was the idealist. There was the Scot who believed in predestination ; there was the sturdy Briton who is convinced that man carves out his own fortune. There was the pessimist in whose ears the words "too late" were for ever ringing ; and there was the optimist who said : "Try again."

It was the idealist, the Briton and the optimist, who wrote on 13th December :—

"We are going to send down the *Bordene* the day after to-morrow, and with her I shall send the journals. *If some effort is not made before ten days' time*, *the town will fall*. If the Expeditionary Forces have reached the river and met my steamers, one hundred are all that we require, just to show themselves."[2]

The next day his journal closed with this entry :—

"*Now mark this*, if the Expeditionary Force, and I ask for no more than two hundred men, does not come in ten days, *the town may fall* ; and I have done my best for the honour of our country." To this was added the postscript already quoted : "You send me no information, though you have lots of money."[3]

These two extracts from Gordon's diary are almost counterparts of what he had telegraphed to Baring

[1] *Journals of Major-General C. G. Gordon*, p. 191.
[2] Ibid., p. 394. [3] Ibid., p. 395.

on 27th February and 2nd March. In the first of these despatches he stressed the necessity of sending " 200 infantry troops to Wadi Halfa ".[1] In the second he was even more specific, and said :—

" I have no option about staying at Khartoum ; it has passed out of my hands, and as to sending a larger force than 200 I do not think it necessary to Wadi Halfa ; it is not the number, but the prestige which I need. I am sure the revolt will collapse if I can say that I have British troops at my back." [2]

Gordon may have been mistaken both in February and in December in holding that 200 men were all that was necessary. Of course, he meant as an advance guard backed up, in the latter instance, by an advancing column, and in the former, by the prestige of England. But, whether he was or was not correct in his estimate, he certainly showed a consistency and a persistency in adhering to his estimate which should go a long way towards disproving the charge of sending " bewildering and contradictory messages " which *Modern Egypt* repeatedly brings against him.

The figures fixed by Gordon were nothing like those which the War Office deemed necessary for the relief of Khartoum. It was at first arranged that not more than 5,000 men should form the Expedition. This number was raised to 7,000. Lord Wolseley was put in command. Colonels Sir Charles Wilson, Brackenbury, Harrison, Henderson, and Maurice, and Lord Anson were appointed to the force for special service. General Sir Redvers Buller was named Chief of Staff and General Earle was told off to command a brigade.[3] Sir Herbert Stewart was also attached to the contingent.

The primary instructions given to Lord Wolseley were to bring away Gordon and Stewart from Khartoum. That purpose effected, no further offensive

[1] Royle, op. cit., vol. ii, p. 194. [2] Ibid., p. 191.
[3] Ibid., vol. ii, p. 204.

operations were to be undertaken. It appears, nevertheless, that when a safe retreat had been secured for these two officers and the Egyptian troops and officials, Lord Wolseley was also to make arrangements concerning the future government of the Sudan and especially of Khartoum.[1] This seems to have been contemplated on account of the slave trade.

The Nile route having been decided on, preparations on a large scale were begun. The first thing was to obtain boats for the transport up the Nile. For these contracts were at once placed in England. Eight hundred in all were ordered. From their shape they were called whalers. They were 30 feet in length. with a beam of 6 ft. 6 in. and a draught of 2 ft. 6 in, They were manned by a dozen men, two boatmen, and two soldiers, and were fitted with twelve oars and two masts with big sails.

To assist in the navigation of the Nile 380 Canadian boatmen called "*Voyageurs*" were engaged. In addition to the Canadians, 300 Kroomen were obtained from the West Coast of Africa to carry stores around the Cataracts.

Throughout the month of August the dockyards and arsenals of England were in full activity. Every effort was made to get the expedition forward in time to take advantage of the high Nile. During the latter part of August and September, troops and stores were arriving almost daily in Alexandria and were forwarded at once to the front. The whalers were sent by rail and river to Assiut. Thence they were towed to Asswan, some 300 miles further south. There they were carried round the first cataract to Shellal. Once through this obstruction all was clean sailing for 200 miles until Wadi Halfa and the second cataract were reached.

A large number of the whalers had already arrived at Wadi Halfa when Lord Wolseley and his staff

[1] Ibid., p. 205.

left Cairo on 27th September. They got to the second cataract on 5th October. This had temporarily become the base of the British operations, as well as the permanent chief depot of the commissariat and ordnance stores of the expedition. The railway at Wadi Halfa, running for a distance of 33 miles along the east bank of the Nile to Sarras, was utilized for transporting material beyond the second cataract.

Up to Wadi Halfa progress had been quite satisfactory, but great difficulty was experienced in getting the whalers through the second cataract. The boats were found to be not nearly strong enough for the work for which they had been built.[1] The rudders were discovered to be too small to be of use. The Canadian "*voyageurs*" objected to the boats having been provided with keels, which they considered not only useless but in the way.

The difficulties of the ascent were increased by the falling of the Nile, which, instead of running smoothly, rushed in broken water over the shallows and multiplied the number of rapids. It was not until 5th November that this series of difficulties was cleared. Other troubles were encountered in hauling the steamers sent up the river for the conveyance of stores. In fact, the work of navigation is described as having been "most severe, beginning at daylight and only ending when it became too dark for the men to see what they were doing. The crews were frequently breast deep in water."[2]

While the expeditionary force was thus working its way to Khartoum, disquieting rumours with regard to Gordon had reached Cairo. On 3rd November Baring telegraphed to Lord Wolseley asking whether there was any foundation for the reports, then current in Cairo, that Khartoum had been taken and that Gordon was a prisoner. Lord Wolseley replied that he had just received a telegram from Major Kitchener

[1] Ibid., p. 213. [2] Ibid., p. 214.

that a man had arrived at Shendy saying that the Mahdi had come with a strong force to Omdurman, opposite Khartoum, and having summoned Gordon to surrender had met with the defiant reply : " I shall hold on to Khartoum for twelve years ! " The information thus furnished fitted in with that sent to Baring from another source that Gordon had attacked the Mahdi at Omdurman, defeated Muhammad Ahmad, and driven him out of that stronghold.

The result of the wires exchanged between Baring and Lord Wolseley was that both men became very hopeful of being able to relieve Gordon. They had been greatly concerned by the receipt, on 1st November, of a note from Gordon, dated 13th July, which had said : " Khartoum is all right and can hold out for four months." This fixed its fall as likely to happen about the middle of November, and tended to confirm the Cairo news that Khartoum had been taken. The pessimism engendered by this chit and the disquieting rumour, was replaced by the optimism born of the later inquirers. The pendulum had swung too far in one direction. It was destined to go too far in the other.

While Cairo and London were thus divided between despair and hope, notwithstanding every effort to get the troops up the river as rapidly as possible, so many difficulties intervened that the task occupied much longer than had been anticipated. Early in November Lord Wolseley telegraphed to Baring that owing to steamers breaking down, difficult coaling, and the scarcity of native labour, he did not expect to be able to concentrate his forces at Ambukol until the end of the year. Korti, a few miles further up-stream, was subsequently chosen as the assembling point for the relief expedition. The Commander-in-Chief reached there on 16th December.

By Christmas the greater part of the troops had arrived at Korti. The camp there was a refreshing, and even a picturesque, place, laid out in broad avenues. On Christmas night, the whole force, from the General-in-Command downwards, assembled in a vast circle round an open-air stage erected by the Royal Engineers. There were no lack of entertainers. "Excellent music, burlesque orations, comic, sentimental, and patriotic songs, part-songs, and other amusing performances were kept going with much spirit in accordance with a regular programme, to which both officers and men contributed. . . . It was a striking, a creditable, and highly enjoyable performance ; and probably no finer body of troops was ever assembled, though they were hardened by toil, sunburnt, and scarred." [1]

The entertainment was to have been repeated on New Year's night. But no more time could be spared for rest or diversion. Rumours many and conflicting began to pour into the camp. A letter received from Gordon, dated 4th November, brought matters to a crisis. It said :—

"At Metammeh waiting your orders are five steamers with nine guns. We can hold out forty days with ease ; after that it will be difficult. The Mahdi is here about eight miles away. All North side along the Nile is free from Arabs. They are on South and South-west and East of town some way off. They are quiet. I should take the road from Ambukol (Korti) to Metammeh where my steamers wait for you." [2]

The period of delay mentioned in Gordon's letter had already expired when it reached Lord Wolseley. Faced with the perilous situation thus presented, the Commander-in-Chief acted with the promptness of a leader of men. He modified his plan of campaign. Korti lies at the head of a great bend in the Nile extending for several hundred miles. As a military operation, the river route offered many advantages. Had time permitted, Lord Wolseley's whole force

[1] Archer, op. cit., vol. iii, p. 261. [2] Ibid., p. 263.

would have gone that way. But the distance to be traversed required months for its accomplishment. It thus became imperative to adopt some other expedient if Gordon was to be saved. And, just as always happened in connection with Gordon and the Sudan, carefully elaborated plans had to be changed.

But they were modified in this instance, as in all others, not by Gordon himself but by somebody else.

The new arrangements divided the expeditionary force into two columns. One was to proceed across the desert to Metammeh, a distance of 176 miles, and thence to Khartoum by river. The other was to carry out the original plan.

The first, or desert column, was placed under the command of Sir Herbert Stewart. It consisted mainly of men belonging to different sections of the Camel Corps, a company of Royal Engineers, part of the 19th Hussars, and detachments of the Commissariat and Medical Units. The force was accompanied by 2,000 camels for purposes of transport. To Sir Charles Wilson was committed the task of opening up communications with Gordon when once the Nile should be reached at Metammeh. Lord Charles Beresford and a small body of seamen were told off to accompany the force to take possession of any of Gordon's steamers which might be found at that river port.[1]

On 30th December part of Stewart's contingent, consisting of 73 Officers, with 1,032 non-commissioned officers and men started on a march to occupy the wells of Jakdul. On the 31st a messenger who had been sent to General Gordon brought into camp a piece of paper about the size of a postage-stamp, on which was written: "Khartoum all right." It was signed C. G. Gordon, and dated 14th December. The bearer of it had been told to deliver a verbal message. He said: —

"The enemy cannot take us except by starving us

[1] Royle, op. cit., vol. ii, p. 231.

out. Our troops suffer from want of provisions ; the food we still have is little ; some grain and biscuit. We want you to come quickly." [1]

On 5th January Sir Herbert Stewart returned from Jakdul. He had taken the enemy completely by surprise. Three days later he was again on the march. This time Metammeh was his objective. His instructions were to attack and occupy that place and then to return to the wells of Jakdul, whence he was to continue forwarding stores to Metammeh. His force consisted, in round figures, of 120 officers and 1,900 men.

The first eight days of the dash across the desert passed without incident. It became obvious, however, during the morning of 16th January, that the Dervishes were determined to block the access of the column to the Abu Klea wells, which lie at about 23 miles from Metammeh. The attack took place the next day. It began "as Venus rose, that being the signal by which the Arabs generally attacked". The battle waged fast and furious. The strength of the Mahdists is variously estimated at from 8,000 to 14,000. "Their losses," says General Sir Herbert Stewart's official report, "were very heavy ; not less than 800 lay dead on the open ground." [2]

The British death toll included nine officers and 65 non-commissioned officers and men. But the enemy was dispersed and the wells of Abu Klea occupied.

The next afternoon Sir Herbert Stewart left the scene of his victory. After passing the wells of Shobaca, the column moved to the right, as it was the Commanding Officer's intention to turn Metammeh, and attack it from the south. At about 7 a.m. on the 19th, when three or four miles from the river the Arabs showed themselves in considerable force on the

[1] *From Korti to Khartum*, by Col. Sir Charles W. Wilson ; Edinburgh, William Blackwood & Sons, 1886, p. xix.

[2] Royle, op. cit., vol. ii, p. 243.

British left flank, and were obviously endeavouring to intercept the English march to the Nile.

Sir Herbert Stewart at once halted and formed a square round the camels. In the battle which ensued he was severely wounded, and Colonel Sir Charles Wilson took over the command. The Dervishes were repulsed and left 250 of their dead on the field. Those who escaped fled towards Metammeh. The British troops marched to the Nile and bivouacked on its banks.

On 20th January a village on a gravel terrace near the Nile was occupied and placed in a state of defence. The next day, a reconnaissance in force was made of Metammeh. It was found to be well fortified.[1] While this was going on word came to Colonel Wilson that Gordon's steamers had been sighted. They brought news from Khartoum which forced the gallant commanding officer once more to modify the plans which had originally been elaborated.

Gordon's messenger carried a minute note, dated 29th December, which read " Khartoum all right ; can hold out for years." It was written for enemy consumption, for with it were personal notes which told the story that the Mahdi's prisoner expected the town to fall about Christmas Day. This meant that every second counted, and that unless Colonel Wilson were to make an immediate dash for Gordon the rescuing party would inevitably arrive " too late ". But ninety odd miles separated Metammeh from Khartoum. That distance, however, marked the dividing line between safety for a hero and death for a martyr.

Sir Charles Wilson's own pen thus sums up the situation :—

" The position was this. The original plan had failed. It was that Stewart was to occupy Metammeh ; then that Beresford was to man the steamers with his

[1] Ibid., p. 252.

Naval Brigade and take me to Khartoum, and that I was to leave Burnaby in command. Burnaby was dead, Stewart and all the officers of the Naval Brigade killed or dangerously wounded, except Beresford, who was ill and could not walk without assistance. The force had lost more than one-tenth of its number and was encumbered by over 100 wounded. It was absolutely necessary to send a convoy off for provisions as soon as the camels could travel, and the horses of the 19th Hussars were too much done up to reconnoitre any distance from camp. I had every reason to believe that forces of the enemy were advancing against us from the north and south, and I could not leave the small force in its position on the Nile without ascertaining whether it was likely to be attacked. I knew that Omdurman had fallen, and that Gordon had expected Khartoum to be attacked on Christmas Day ; but I also knew that Khartoum was still holding out, and I hoped that the pressure upon the town would be relieved by the large number of men sent down by the Mahdi to meet us, and that news of our victory would have got into Khartoum and have given Gordon and his garrison fresh heart. At any rate, there was nothing to show—and I questioned the commanders of the steamers carefully—that the crisis at Khartoum which had been deferred from the 25th December to the 19th January would be hurried on, or that a delay of a couple of days would make much difference."[1]

Edward Dicey, writing in a comfortable library, completely disagrees with Sir Charles Wilson's conception that the number of men sent down to meet the advancing British force in any way improved Gordon's chances of being saved. The author of *The Story of the Khedivíate* holds to the theory that it is well-nigh certain that the Mahdi could have captured Khartoum whenever he thought fit to make the attack.

[1] Wilson, op. cit., p. 113.

"My one surmise, if I had to offer one," writes Dicey, "would be that, being aware, as he probably was, from his informants in Cairo, that the British expedition was sent with the sole object of rescuing Gordon, he thought it wiser not to precipitate the fall of Khartoum, so that in the event of their attack becoming formidable, he might save the situation by handing over Gordon to the advancing enemy. Our victories at Abu Klea and Metammeh . . . upset the Mahdi's calculations. From that moment the fate of Gordon and Khartoum was decided." [1]

Father Ohrwalder, the Catholic priest, who for ten years remained a prisoner in the Mahdi's camp because he would not forswear his faith, is of a contrary opinion. He was on the spot. From the vantage point of this special knowledge he wrote :—

"The unaccountable delay of the English was the cause of the fall of Khartoum and of the death of Gordon, and the fate of the Sudan. The Mahdi only made up his mind to attack when he heard that they had delayed at Gubat. . . . He could not have attacked earlier than he did. When the first news of his defeat at Abu Klea reached him he wished to raise the siege and retire to Kordofan. If the English had appeared at any time before he delivered the attack he would have raised the siege and have retired." [2]

Whether we agree with Dicey or with Father Ohrwalder, it is obvious that, even if Sir Charles Wilson had forgotten all about Metammeh and had overlooked the physical conditions of his force, he would still have arrived "too late". The time necessary to cover the distance between Metammeh and Khartoum was fatal to success. But military considerations of an imperative order left Colonel Wilson no alternative. It would have been unpardonable for him to have ventured into the

1 Dicey, op. cit., p. 384. 2 Wingate, op. cit., p. 148.

unknown without first having undertaken a reconnaissance down the river before starting for Khartoum. This is what he did.

When word came from the scouts that they could see no trace of an enemy, Wilson started his steamers down the river on the morning of 22nd January. The boats were the *Talahawiyah*, the *Bordene*, and a third vessel. It was dark before the boats got back to their starting-point. "The reconnaissance took much longer than I had expected," recorded Colonel Wilson, "but we had clearly ascertained that nothing was to be feared from the Berber direction." [1]

At daybreak of 23rd January Wilson commenced preparations for the final dash to Khartoum. By that time he knew that Omdurman was in the Mahdi's hands and that he would have to fight his way to Khartoum.[2] "The original plan was for Beresford to man two of the steamers with the Naval Brigade, mount his Gardner gun on one of them and, after overhauling them, take me to Khartoum, with about fifty men of the Sussex Regiment," records Wilson's diary. "This was now impossible; all the naval officers were killed or wounded except Beresford, who was himself unable to walk."[3] Forced with these conditions, the gallant Wilson was forced to content himself with nothing but a handful of Englishmen. The flying squad which undertook the race against death was made up of himself and (1) Captain Gascoigne, of the Yorkshire Hussars, ten non-commissioned officers and men of the Royal Sussex, and one petty officer of the Royal Navy aboard the *Bordene*, and (2) Captain Trafford, ten non-commissioned officers and men of the Royal Sussex, Lieutenant Stuart-Wortley, King's Rifles, and one petty officer of the Royal Navy aboard the

[1] Wilson, op. cit., p. 122. [2] Ibid., p. 125.
[3] Ibid., p. 127.

*Talahawiyah.*[1] A small contingent of natives accompanied Wilson and these twenty-five Englishmen.

When the little company was straining at the leash in its desire to spring forward, the old boats would not budge. Their engines failed to respond. So the hours slipped by and no start was made that day. While the engineers were working away at their task a question of military etiquette was happily solved. It appears that :—

"Lord Wolseley had particularly wished the escort to enter Khartoum in red coats, and red coats had been especially sent out for them, but they had disappeared. . . . A call was made for red coats, and a sufficient number was raised from the Guards and Heavies to clothe all, though some of the tunics of the Life Guardsmen were rather too much for the Sussex. By evening all was ready."[2]

But the steamers were still not able to start until 8 o'clock the next morning. "It was at first a great relief to be quietly seated in a steamer and to be able to think over our future proceedings," we read in Wilson's diaries. "We were going to fight our way up the river and into Khartoum in two steamers of the size of 'penny steamers' on the Thames, which a single well-directed shell would send to the bottom ; with crews and soldiers absolutely without discipline, with twenty English soldiers, with no surgeon and with only one interpreter, the faithful Muhammad Ibrahim, still suffering from a flesh wound."[3]

This figure of twenty English soldiers refers to the ten non-commissioned officers and men of the Royal Sussex who were aboard the *Bordene* and to a like number from the same regiment on the *Talahawiyah.* There were also on the former vessel Captain Gascoigne of the Yorkshire Hussars, and a petty officer of

[1] Royle, op. cit., vol. ii, p. 264.
[2] Wilson, op. cit., p. 128.
[3] Ibid., p. 129.

the Royal Navy. The latter carried Captain Trafford of the Royal Sussex, Lieutenant Stuart-Wortley of the King's Rifles, and a petty officer of thc Royal Navy.[1] This means that the final flying squad that covered the last lap to Khartoum was made up of twenty-six Englishmen, every one of them a hero.

Each of the steamers flew two Egyptian flags, one at the foremast and the other at the stern. Wilson thought of pulling them down, as he disliked fighting under a flag which was not that of his Queen. But as he had no others, and as the boats were still the property of the Khedive, he allowed the Star and Crescent to remain. His orders to the Sussex were not to waste ammunition in single shots or on small groups of men. As the native troops were quite undisciplined, and to attempt to check them would have been hopeless, they were told to fire away at anyone who shot at them.

The days passed without any happening of any importance. When night came the steamers were compelled to stop. They got under way again as soon as light appeared and heralded the arrival of 25th January. All went well until near sunset, when the *Bordene* struck a rock at the head of the last rapids which mark the entrance to a long reach of open water. The *Talahawiyah* got safely through the difficult passage and lay to for the night off Hassan Island. But the *Bordene* could not follow, and remained immobilized all night long, notwithstanding the frantic and persistent efforts of the crew to get her into deep water. It was not until near nightfall of 26th January that their efforts were rewarded. The net result was that little or no progress was made, but that everything was ready for an early departure at dawn on 27th January. That day passed without mishap. During the afternoon a man on the left bank shouted out that Khartoum had fallen and that Gordon was

[1] Royle, op. cit., vol. ii, p. 264.

dead. Nobody believed him, and when night came all hands went to bed in high spirits at the prospect of running the blockade the next day and meeting General Gordon after his long siege.

Off again bright and early, on the morning of the 28th, Khartoum was sighted in the far distance above the trees of Tuti island at nine o'clock. About this time a native called out from the friendly right bank that Khartoum had fallen and that Gordon had been killed two days earlier. But no steady firing from the left or enemy bank lent emphasis to his words. It was not until a place called Tighiaiha was reached that a regular fusilade seemed to confirm the ominous message.

When the steamers neared Halfiyeh Wilson observed that the palm-grove had been burned and the houses wrecked and that there were several large boats lying by the bank. The natives with the relief expedition interpreted the presence of these craft as meaning that Gordon had pressed forward and driven the Mahdi before him. While they were arguing their point a fusilade convinced them of their error. When the smoke died away the large Government House at Khartoum stood out plainly above the trees. No flag was flying. Its absence told the fatal truth. Wilson refused to be convinced. Onward he went, hoping against hope and trusting that even if Khartoum had fallen Tuti Island might still be safe and Gordon have found a refuge there. But shots from that quarter drove away this illusion, and again set in motion the feeling that Khartoum might still be safe even if the Egyptian standard could not be seen. " No sooner did we start upwards," are Sir Charles Wilson's words, " than we got into such a fire as I hope never to pass through again in a 'penny steamer'. Two or more guns opened upon us from Omdurman fort, and three or four from Khartoum or the upper end of Tuti ; the roll of musketry from each side was continuous ; and high above that could be heard the grunting of a Nordenfeldt or a mitrailleuse, and the loud rushing noise of the Krupp shells fired either from Khartoum or from the upper end of Tuti Island." [1]

It was past four o'clock before the steamers were clear of the last guns. For four hours they had been continuously engaged with the enemy batteries. Luckily the Arab gunners were bad shots. But even with such poor workmanship Wilson himself was wounded just above the knee and his field-glass was broken in his hand as he was resting it on the top of the turret.

As soon as darkness came the steamers were made fast to an island. Messengers were sent out dressed in the Mahdi's uniform. Their instructions were to collect information. They reported that Khartoum had fallen during the night of 25th–26th January through treachery, and that Gordon was dead.

Wilson had done his best. He was " too late ".

[1] Wilson, op. cit., p. 173.

## Chapter XXIX

# TOO LATE

The last entry in Gordon's journals bears date 14th December. His own pen, therefore, throws no light on the penultimate phase of one of the saddest chapters in history. Sir Reginald Wingate, whose name is indissolubly connected with the conquest and the regeneration of the Sudan, has attempted to fill in this lacuna. He seeks to reconstruct the story of these tragic hours. He describes the apotheosis of the Christian soldier. He does not let his imagination colour his story. He won his spurs as an intelligence officer. He knows how to marshal facts. He presents five different versions of what occurred on that final fateful day.

The first consecutive narrative given by Wingate is based upon the journal of Bordeini Bey, who is described as " an eminent Khartoum merchant who willingly gave up his large stocks of grain to Gordon for the supply of the garrison ".[1] He was at Khartoum throughout the siege. His version is that of the besieged. Gordon appears to have trusted him and to have received him at the palace on the eve of the tragic morning.

" I found him sitting on a divan," runs his story, " and as I came in he pulled off his tarboush (fez) and flung it from him, saying : 'What more can I say ? I have nothing more to say. The people will no longer believe me. I have told them over and over again that help would be here, but it has never come, and now they must say I tell them lies. If this, my last

[1] *Mahdiism and the Egyptian Sudan*, by Major F. R. Wingate ; London, Macmillan & Company, 1891, p. 163.

promise, fails, I can do nothing more. Go and collect all the people you can on the lines and make a good stand. Now leave me to smoke these cigarettes (there were two full boxes on the table).' "[1]

Gordon was obviously very much depressed when Bordeini left him. All the anxiety that he had undergone had turned the soldier's hair to snowy white. But it was not dread of the inevitable that distressed him. He did not fear to meet his Maker. In fact, so clear was his conscience that he would gladly have welcomed death. But he was an English gentleman, and he hated to face the Muslims who had stood by him and who had taken his word that relief was in sight. He feared that when the Mahdi should burst into Khartoum and put them to the sword these Muhammadans would die convinced that a Christian had lied to them. He therefore refused to accompany Bordeini to the fortifications. The two men separated, never to meet again.

Bordeini went from the palace to the walls of the city. Everywhere he heard men saying : " The Pasha has deceived us. We were fools to believe him. The English are not coming. He has lied to us. We were idiots to trust him." And as these words came to him from every side Gordon's voice kept ringing in the merchant's ear, repeating : " If only a couple of English soldiers of the advancing force could be paraded about the lines of Khartoum, I would not fear the enemy's attack."

" But it was not to be, and heavy despair settled down over all. It was a gloomy day, that last day in Khartoum," continues the narrative; " hundreds lay dead and dying in the streets from starvation, and there were none to bury them. At length the night came, and, as I afterwards learned, Gordon Pasha sat up writing till midnight and then lay down to sleep. He awoke some time between two and three a.m.

[1] Ibid., p. 169.

The wild war-cries of the Arabs were heard close at hand. A large body of rebels had crept in the dark close up to the broken-down parapet and filled-up ditch between the White Nile and the Messalamiah Gate. The soldiers never knew of the enemy's approach until about twenty minutes before they were actually attacked, when the tramp of feet was heard and the alarm sounded ; but they were so tired out and exhausted that it was not until the sentries fired that the rest of the men suddenly started up, surprised to find swarms of Arabs pouring over the ditch and up the parapet yelling and shouting their war-cries. Here they met with little resistance, for most of the soldiers were four or five paces apart, and were too feeble to oppose such a rush. The Arabs were soon within the lines and were thus able to attack the rest of the soldiers from behind." [1]

Gordon appears to have been aroused by the noise of this tumult. He hurried to the roof of the palace " in his sleeping clothes ". It was there that he and Power and Herbin had, day after day, scanned the horizon in search of the steamers which were destined to arrive " too late ".

The two Englishmen and the Frenchman were already dead. The sole survivor of the heroic quartette was all alone in the darkness of that January night. His friends had died, to quote his own words, " as much martyrs as Peter or Paul." He was not a Roman Catholic. He did not believe in the intercession of Saints or Martyrs, but, as his ears detected the sound of the advancing horde, and he knew that his end was near, his subconscious mind evoked the memory of those men who had shared the long hours of vigil with him and who had preceded him to the grave. He determined that in his supreme trial he would prove worthy of their friendship. But ever a realist, his religious exaltation did not cause him to forget

[1] Ibid., p. 170.

that, until summoned into the Church triumphant, he belonged to the Church militant, and that it was his duty to fight.

He fought. He was not a lamb. He summoned his guard to his presence and directed them to train the palace guns upon the advancing rebels. The roof artillery roared. Lower and lower was its angle turned as rank after rank of the Dervishes sprang forward. Making light of death, the Arabs knew not fear. When they had crossed beyond the line of fire Gordon saw that his fate was sealed.

" He left the roof," says Bordeini Bey, " and went to his bedroom, which was close to the divan (or office). There he put on a white uniform, his sword, which he did not draw, and, carrying his revolver in his right hand, stepped out into the passage in front of the entrance to the ' office ' and just at the head of the staircase.

" During this interval," continues the journal, " four men more brave than the rest forced their way into the palace, and, once in, were followed by hundreds of others ; of these latter, the majority rushed up the stairs to the roof, where, after a short resistance, the palace guard, servants, and cavasses were all killed, while the four men, followed by a crowd of others, knowing Gordon's room, rushed towards it. Taha Shahin was the first to encounter Gordon beside the door of the divan, apparently waiting for the Arabs, and standing with a calm and dignified manner, his left hand resting on the hilt of his sword. Shahin dashing forward with the curse ' O cursed one, your time is come ', plunged his spear into the body. Gordon, it is said, made a gesture of scorn with his right hand, and turned his back, where he received another spear wound. The other three men closely following Shahin then rushed in, and, cutting at the prostrate body with their swords, must have killed him in a few seconds. His death occurred just before sunrise. He made no resistance and did not fire a shot from his revolver." [1]

After having recorded these facts, Bordeini Bey indulged in the luxury of surmise. He says that—

"From all I know I am convinced that he never intended to surrender. I should say he must have intended to use his revolver only if he saw it was the intention of the Arabs to take him alive."

Gordon's head was immediately cut off and sent to the Mahdi at Omdurman, while his body was dragged downstairs and left exposed for a time in the garden, where many Arabs came to plunge their spears in it. "I heard," the narrative continues, "that the Mahdi had given orders for Gordon to be spared, but what I have stated was told me by the four men I have mentioned; and I believe that the Mahdi pardoned them for their disobedience of his orders. When I escaped from Omdurman they were still living there among the *Ansars*. I myself saw but little of what happened. . . . I saw Gordon Pasha's head exposed in Omdurman. It was fixed between the branches of a tree, and all who passed by threw stones at it. The first to throw a stone at it was Yussuf Mansur, late *Mamur* of police at El Obeid, whom Gordon Pasha had dismissed for misconduct, and who afterwards commanded the Mahdi's artillery." [2]

The value of all this graphic description is spoiled by the fact that Bordeini Bey frankly admits that "he saw little of what happened". We learn from his own words that he got into favour with the Mahdi by means of his niece, "whom he took as one of his wives." Why the man who had the ear of Muhammad Ahmad desired to escape from Omdurman is not made clear. The Mahdi, however, died within less than a year after the fall of Khartoum. We are tempted to infer that the Khalifa failed to yield to the charms of the merchant's niece, and that this fact may have induced

[1] Ibid., p. 171. [2] Ibid., p. 172.

him to flee. Be that as it may, diaries are often made up for publication. One fears that perhaps this journal may have been written by Bordeini Bey in order to ingratiate himself with the British. In other words, it does not, of itself, carry conviction. Even if sincere, it is but a tissue of hearsay evidence.

The proof of the decapitation of Gordon is supplied by Sir Rudolf Slatin. That man, whom the Governor-General never forgave for having sacrificed the Cross to the Crescent, was a prisoner in the Mahdi's camp when Khartoum fell. He writes :—

"I crawled out of my tent and scanned the camp : a great crowd had collected before the quarters of the Mahdi and Khalifa, which were not far off ; then there was a movement in the direction of my tent, and I could plainly see that they were making towards me. In front marched three black soldiers : one, named Shatta, carried in his hands a bloody cloth in which something was wrapped up, and behind him followed a crowd of people weeping. The slaves approached my tent, and stood before me with insulting gestures ; Shatta undid the cloth and showed me the head of General Gordon. The blood rushed to my head, and my heart seemed to stop beating ; but, with a tremendous effort of self-control I gazed silently at this ghastly spectacle. His blue eyes were half-opened ; the mouth was perfectly natural ; the hair of his head and his short whiskers were almost white."[1]

The second version referred to by Sir Reginald Wingate is that furnished by the members of the relief party. Sir Charles Wilson and his gallant comrades were, however, not in Khartoum. They were therefore not in a position to throw any direct light on what happened in that city. We accordingly pass at once to the testimony of one of the besiegers.

[1] *Fire and Sword in the Sudan*, by Rudolf C. Slatin, translated by Major F. R. Wingate ; London, Edward Arnold, 1896, p. 340.

The Arab who was examined by the British Intelligence Officer was an important emir of the Mahdi's forces.

"The first man to lay siege to Khartoum, was present during most of the preliminary engagement, and took an important part in the assault and capture of Khartoum. On the death of Muhammad Ahmad, some months afterwards, he joined in the dispute regarding the claims to the succession of the Khalifa Abdullah Taashi, and was obliged to fly the land. He escaped and subsequently became a teacher at Al Azhar University, Cairo."[1]

According to this witness the Mahdi was very much upset by the defeat of his troops at the battle of Abu Klea but, nevertheless, had the presence of mind to order that a salute of 101 guns be fired in the hope of convincing Gordon and the besieged that the British had been routed. He argued that if one Englishman, Gordon, had held a whole army at bay for an entire year, the English regiments coming up the river would certainly be able to annihilate the Dervishes. Muhammad Ahmad, accordingly, announced that Abdallah told him in a dream that he should flee to El Obeid. His listeners were apparently much impressed by this announcement and would possibly have yielded to the pressure of the Mahdi, if word had not reached them that the British steamers were moving on Khartoum. This meant, said Muhammad Ahmad, that the Prophet had put the lives of the garrison of Khartoum into his hands and that an attack should be made early the next morning.

It is somewhat difficult to follow the logic of such reasoning. But, be the case as it may, that night, 25th January, the Mahdi crossed over to Omdurman and went to the camp of Wad en Nejumi. The faithful were told, in a fiery speech, to make a bold

[1] *Mahdiism and the Egyptian Sudan*, p. 189.

attack very early the next morning, and that all who fell would go direct to Paradise. Positive instructions were given on no account to kill General Gordon.[1]

At about an hour and a half after midnight the assault began. The orders were to march as silently as possible till close up to the fortifications, and not to attack until the soldiers fired from the lines. The advance was carried out as directed. At last the "ditch was almost reached. When it was seen that it was partly filled up with mud and the parapet broken down, the Arabs did not hesitate, but shouting their war-cries, dashed into the ditch and up the parapet; many fell and were trampled under foot, some shots were fired from the lines, but in a few moments it was all over.

"A small party of Arabs arrived at the palace," continues the story of the emir, "and, rushing in, dashed up the steps leading to Gordon Pasha's room. They found him standing by the door of the office at the top of the staircase, and he asked them who was their leader; but they took no notice of what he said, and one of them rushing up stabbed him with a spear; the others then followed and soon he was killed. His death took place just before sunrise. It was a party of Wad En Nejumi's men who killed Gordon, but Nejumi was not with them at the time. He came up shortly afterwards, and seeing that his men had killed Gordon he was very angry. He ordered the body to be dragged downstairs into the garden, where his head was cut off, wrapped in a handkerchief, and taken to the Mahdi. I saw the head being taken to the Mahdi about an hour and a half after sunrise. Gordon's body lay in the garden all that day, and many Arabs came and stabbed it with their spears; the next day I heard that it was thrown into one of the wells. . . . As far as I know, Gordon was killed by sword and spear wounds only, and I never heard

[1] Ibid., p. 192.

that he made any resistance. He was attacked suddenly by wild men who knew no discipline." [1]

We read in *Mahdiism and the Egyptian Sudan* that this statement was corroborated in almost every detail by numerous Arab prisoners. A note appended to it adds, however, that one arrival from Khartoum says that Gordon was killed on the west bank of the White Nile, just south of Omdurman in revenge for the death of a man whom Gordon had ordered to be shot as a spy. Others stated that Gordon was put to death in revenge for the death of Suleiman Zobeir, son of Zobeir Pasha ; " but," says Sir Reginald Wingate, " the evidence in confirmation of Emir Medawi's statement is overwhelming." [2]

All this is most categorical. A second note on the same page says, nevertheless, that—

" The system adopted in obtaining the statements of those within the town of Khartoum, as well as those besieging it, will, it is hoped, assist the reader in forming an opinion as to the accuracy of the details described. Each statement has been given in the name of one individual only—Bordeini Bey and the Emir Medawi—and the probable criticism that neither of these individuals could have been in a position to describe authoritatively all the events set forth in these several statements is probably a perfect and just one. These two individuals were selected as being admittedly the best informed and most reliable men who have reached Egypt up to the present time. . . . The writer has embodied the numerous narratives of besiegers and besieged into the statements of two individuals only, while the number of persons actually examined cannot have been less than fifty. At the same time, it should be understood that the two individuals in whose names the statements are given are agreed as to the accuracy of each and every detail related."

Besides all this evidence, boiled down into the

[1] Ibid., p. 193. [2] Ibid., p. 194.

two statements already cited, there was a court-martial by which Hassan Bahnassawy Bey, Colonel-Commanding the 5th Regiment, was tried for having treacherously given up his post to the enemy. He was acquitted. Sir Reginald Wingate found the verdict perfectly proper, and remarked :—

"The tale is now complete. Of treachery there was none. Only the cruel river filled the ditch with mud and ebbed away. The race was fairly run. Help was at hand, only one short hundred miles away—but hunger and despair decided the issue." [1]

While we accept without hesitation both the verdict of the court-martial and the opinion of the author of *Mahdiism and the Egyptian Sudan* that there was no treachery, we can hardly admit that these so-called Bordeini Bey and Medawi statements carry conviction as to how Gordon met his death. Neither the mouthpiece of the besieged nor the organ of the besiegers was present when the Governor-General answered the last summons. All that these two witnesses did was to repeat what they had heard. And they did not tell the same story. One tale was dramatic ; the other had nothing theatrical about it.

Father Ohrwalder, who like Slatin was a prisoner in the Mahdi's camp when Khartoum was taken, gives an interesting version of how that capital fell. His tale is that on coming through the open space in the parapet the Dervishes broke up into two parties. One dashed along the walls, overthrowing resistance and slaughtering right and left. The other made for the city. The townspeople, roused from their sleep by the shouts of the Arabs and the din of rifle-shots, poured out of their houses. "Like a pent-up stream suddenly released, 50,000 wild Dervishes with hideous yells rushed upon the 40,000 inhabitants and the 5,000 soldiers. The only cry of the fanatical hordes was '*Kenisa! Saraya!*' (To the Church! To the

[1] Ibid., p. 199.

Palace !) They meant the Austrian Mission Church and Gordon's palace, where they expected to find treasure stored up in the cellars and priests and sisters." [1]

After having told how the mob and the rebels thus took possession of Khartoum, Father Ohrwalder went on to say that—

"The surging mass threw itself on the palace, overflowed into the lovely garden, and burst through the doors in wild search for their prey. As they rushed up the stairs, he came forward towards them and tried to speak to them ; but they could not or would not listen, and the first Arab plunged his huge spear into his body. He fell forward on his face, was dragged down the stairs, many stabbed him with spears and his head was cut off and sent to the Mahdi." [2]

This narrative of the Catholic priest seems to furnish the basis for Winston Churchill's colourful lines in *The River War*. But Father Ohrwalder does not claim to have been present when Gordon was attacked. One must therefore hesitate to accept the interesting story about Gordon's attempt at a parley. It reads too well.

Lord (then Major) Kitchener summed up the situation with keen discernment when he wrote in his official report, dated 18th August, 1885, that—

" It is difficult from the confused accounts to make out exactly how General Gordon was killed. All the evidence tends to prove that it happened at or near the palace, where his body was subsequently seen by several witnesses. . . . It appears that there was one company of black troops in the palace besides General Gordon's cavasses ; some resistance was made when the rebels appeared, but I think this was after General Gordon had left the palace. The only account by a person claiming to be an eye-witness of the scene

[1] *Ten Years' Captivity in the Mahdi's Camp*, p. 137.
[2] Ibid.

of General Gordon's death relates : 'On hearing the noise, I got my master's donkey and went with him to the palace ; we met Gordon Pasha at the outer door of the palace. Muhammad Bey Moustafa, with my master, Ibrahim Bey Rushdi, and about twenty cavasses, then went with Gordon towards the house of the Austrian Consul near the Church, where we met some rebels in an open place near the outer gate of the palace. Gordon Pasha was walking in front leading the party. The rebels fired a volley and Gordon was killed at once ; nine of the cavasses, Ibrahim Bey Rushdi and Muhammad Bey Mustafa were killed. The rest ran away." [1]

The Kitchener report abstains from saying whether this witness was or was not worthy of credence. He may have been merely an ordinary fabricator who sought to give himself importance by standing out as the one and only man who could tell the English that he had seen how the Governor-General met his end. He may, on the other hand, have told a truthful story, unembellished by Oriental embroidery. We do not know. The next paragraph says that—

"A large number of witnesses state Gordon was killed near the gate of the palace, and various accounts have related from hearsay of the exact manner in which he met his death. Several reliable witnesses saw, and recognized, Gordon's body at the gate of the palace; one describes it as being dressed in light clothes."

The contradiction between the version of "the only person claiming to be an eye-witness" on the one hand, and the Bordeini Bey and Medawi statements on the other, is obvious. The Kitchener report speaks of a volley. The Wingate testimony refers to death from swords and spears. The first story fixes the death of Gordon as taking place as he walked

[1] *Life of Lord Kitchener*, by Sir George Arthur ; London, Macmillan & Co., Ltd., 1920, vol. i, p. 121.

" towards the house of the Austrian Consul near the Church ". The second theory is that he met his fate in the interior of the palace. In the one instance the Briton was accompanied by two Beys ; in the other he was alone with his servants and cavasses.

In the absence of any inherent evidence of flagrant improbability in the recital of the eye-witness, we might be tempted to accept his tale were it not for the fact that the preponderance of proof tends to show that Gordon was killed near the gate of the palace. If this be the truth, then the story about Muhammad Bey Moustafa, Ibrahim Bey Rushdi, and Gordon going towards " the house of the Austrian Consul near the Church " is manifestly inaccurate, unless the Church and the Palace were so close to one another that the two statements refer to the same spot. But Kitchener knew the lay of the land and would have brought out this fact had such been the case.

If what the eye-witness said in regard to the scene of the attack upon Gordon be open to question, then we are justified in refusing to accept his word that shot and shell and not sword and spear summoned the defender of Khartoum before the Reader of Hearts.

All that we know with certainty is that, to quote the testimony of all the witnesses and to cite the Kitchener report :—

" The Sudan custom of beheading and exposing the heads of adversaries slain in battle was apparently carried out, as was done by the *Mudir* of Dongola after the battle at Korti. The Bagara savages seem to have had some doubt which was Gordon's body, and great confusion occurred in the Mahdi's camp at Omdurman, where the heads were exposed, as to which was Gordon's head ; some recognizing, others denying the identity of Gordon's head. One apparently reliable witness relates that he saw the rebels cut off Gordon's head at the palace gate after the town was in their hands."

Confronted by this mass of contradictory evidence, we are forced to admit that it is impossible to reconstruct the particulars of the final tragedy. All that we can affirm without hesitation is that Charles George Gordon died as he had lived, a Christian, a gentleman, and a soldier. No death could be more inspiring.

# INDEX

*Printed in Great Britain by Stephen Austin & Sons, Ltd., Hertford.*